'Cult' Rhetoric in the 21st Century

Religion at the Boundaries

Series editors: Suzanne Newcombe and Sarah Harvey

Religion at the Boundaries explores new forms of religion, spirituality and belief that lie outside the mainstream. The series is published in collaboration with Inform (Information Network on Religious Movements), an educational charity founded by Eileen Barker in 1988. The volumes expand Inform's mission of providing accurate and up-to-date research on these movements, exploring the social, legal, and ethical issues which they raise. Authors are drawn from prominent and emerging scholars in the field, but members, ex-members and critics are also given a voice. This approach reflects the variety of stances on these topics, encouraging public engagement and debate. The series will be of interest to students and scholars of religion, social scientists, clergy, civil servants, and those involved in the caring and counselling professions.

'Cult' Rhetoric in the 21st Century

Deconstructing the Study of New Religious Movements

Edited by Aled Thomas and Edward Graham-Hyde

BLOOMSBURY ACADEMIC
LONDON • NEW YORK • OXFORD • NEW DELHI • SYDNEY

BLOOMSBURY ACADEMIC

Bloomsbury Publishing Plc, 50 Bedford Square, London, WC1B 3DP, UK
Bloomsbury Publishing Inc, 1359 Broadway, New York, NY 10018, USA
Bloomsbury Publishing Ireland, 29 Earlsfort Terrace, Dublin 2, D02 AY28, Ireland

BLOOMSBURY, BLOOMSBURY ACADEMIC and the Diana logo are trademarks of
Bloomsbury Publishing Plc

First published in Great Britain 2024
Paperback edition published 2026

Copyright © Aled Thomas, Edward Graham-Hyde and contributors, 2024

Aled Thomas and Edward Graham-Hyde have asserted their rights under the Copyright,
Designs and Patents Act, 1988, to be identified as Editors of this work.

For legal purposes the Acknowledgements on p. xiii constitute an extension
of this copyright page.

Cover design: Elena Durey
Cover image © [M]Dudeck, The Archonomicon Scroll (RV-S9-X03) Communal
Interspecies Worship Pattern X9.

All rights reserved. No part of this publication may be: i) reproduced or transmitted in any form, electronic or mechanical, including photocopying, recording or by means of any information storage or retrieval system without prior permission in writing from the publishers; or ii) used or reproduced in any way for the training, development or operation of artificial intelligence (AI) technologies, including generative AI technologies. The rights holders expressly reserve this publication from the text and data mining exception as per Article 4(3) of the Digital Single Market Directive (EU) 2019/790.

Bloomsbury Publishing Plc does not have any control over, or responsibility for, any third-party websites referred to or in this book. All internet addresses given in this book were correct at the time of going to press. The author and publisher regret any inconvenience caused if addresses have changed or sites have ceased to exist, but can accept no responsibility for any such changes.

A catalogue record for this book is available from the British Library.

A catalog record for this book is available from the Library of Congress.

ISBN: HB: 978-1-3503-3321-5
PB: 978-1-3503-3325-3
ePDF: 978-1-3503-3322-2
eBook: 978-1-3503-3323-9

Series: Religion at the Boundaries

Typeset by Deanta Global Publishing Services, Chennai, India

For product safety related questions contact productsafety@bloomsbury.com.

To find out more about our authors and books visit www.bloomsbury.com and
sign up for our

*For my parents, Janet and Vernon, who have always
encouraged me to pursue my dreams.*
A. T.
*For my wife, Britta, who has sacrificed much so that I might crawl
over the finish line of completing and publishing my research.*
E. G. H

Contents

Notes on contributors — viii
Foreword: Introduction to the *Religion at the Boundaries* series
   Suzanne Newcombe and Sarah Harvey — xi
Acknowledgements — xiii

Part I Approaches to 'cult' rhetoric

1. 'Cult' rhetoric in the twenty-first century: The disconnect between popular discourse and the ivory tower *Aled Thomas and Edward Graham-Hyde* — 3
2. Balancing pragmatism and precision: Inform's approach to cult rhetoric *Suzanne Newcombe and Sarah Harvey* — 21
3. A history of anticult rhetoric *George D. Chryssides* — 40
4. The paradigm shift from sacred to profane *William Sims Bainbridge* — 59
5. The dangerous cult exercise: Popular culture and the ongoing construction of the new religious threat *Douglas E. Cowan* — 79
6. The recognition of cults *Roderick P. Dubrow-Marshall* — 96

Part II Contemporary 'cultic' studies

7. The light of the world: La Luz del Mundo, liminality and NRM studies *Donald A. Westbrook* — 115
8. Cults of conspiracy and the (ongoing) Satanic Panic *Bethan Juliet Oake* — 131
9. 'There is no QAnon': Cult accusations in contemporary American political and online discourse *Susannah Crockford* — 154
10. Playing at religion: Understanding contemporary spiritual experiences in popular culture *Vivian Asimos* — 178
11. Attempting to educate journalists about the role of cult essentialism in the Branch Davidians–federal agents conflict *Catherine Wessinger* — 190

Afterword: Responses and conclusions *W. Michael Ashcraft* — 229

Index — 239

Contributors

W. Michael Ashcraft is Professor of Religion at Truman State University. He earned his PhD in American Religious History from the Religious Studies Department at the University of Virginia. He recently published *A Historical Introduction to the Study of New Religious Movements* (2018), the first book-length study of its kind. His research interests include new or alternative religions that cease to be dynamic but retain beliefs about the future that include the species-wide transformation of humanity.

Vivian Asimos is a freelance academic, co-founder of alt-ac.uk and writer at Incidental Mythology. Her specialism focuses on popular culture as contemporary mythology, spanning everything from cosplay to video games to online storytelling. She has written *Digital Mythology and the Internet's Monster* and is a co-editor of *the Bloomsbury Reader in the Study of Myth*.

William Sims Bainbridge has published 30 academic books and about 300 articles or book chapters in areas such as technological development, social movements and innovative religions. For the past thirty years he has served as a programme director at the National Science Foundation, first in sociology then in human-centered computing.

George D. Chryssides is Honorary Research Fellow at York St John University, UK, and formerly Head of Religious Studies at the University of Wolverhampton. He studied philosophy and theology at the University of Glasgow, and obtained his doctorate at the University of Oxford. He was president of the International Society for the Study of New Religions from 2019 to 2022.

Douglas E. Cowan is Professor of Religious Studies at Renison University College. He is the author of numerous books, including, most recently, *America's Dark Theologian: The Religious Imagination of Stephen King* and *Magic, Monsters, and Make-Believe Heroes: How Religion Shapes Fantasy Culture*. He lives with his wife and their black Lab in Waterloo, Canada.

Susannah Crockford is Lecturer in Anthropology at the University of Exeter, UK. Her monograph *Ripples of the Universe: Spirituality in Sedona, Arizona* was published in 2021.

Roderick P. Dubrow-Marshall is Professor of Psychology and is Co-Programme Leader for the MSc Psychology of Coercive Control, and is Visiting Fellow in the Criminal Justice Hub at the University of Salford, UK. He is a member of the Board of Directors of the International Cultic Studies Association and is Chair of the ICSA Research Committee and Network and Co-Editor of the *International Journal of Coercion, Abuse and Manipulation* (*IJCAM*).

Sarah Harvey has been Research Officer at Inform since 2001 and responds to many of the enquiries that Inform receives, helps maintain the database of religious movements, helps manage Inform commissioned projects and co-authors reports. She has a broad interest in all areas of NRM studies, including pagan religions, new Christian movements, the 'holistic milieu' and millennial movements. She is also interested in intersections with health and healing and her PhD research was on 'natural' pregnancy and birth practices.

Edward Graham-Hyde is Associate Lecturer at the University of Central Lancashire, UK, Treasurer of the Information Network Focus on Religious Movements (Inform) and Senior Researcher with Church Army, UK. He has a PhD in the sociology of religion and is a specialist in conversion and recruitment theory, minority religions, Christian evangelism and empowerment studies. His current research focuses on empowered lived experience as central aspects of conversion, organizational retention and approaches towards Christian evangelism.

Suzanne Newcombe is Honorary Director of Inform (since 2020) and Senior Lecturer in Religious Studies at the Open University, UK. She has worked at Inform in various capacities since 2002, responding to complex enquiries, giving media interviews on print, radio and televisions, updating the database, co-authoring commissioned reports, giving training to government departments and talks to schools. Her particular areas of expertise include movements with origins or inspirations from Asian and Indian traditions and contemporary groups which are interested in prophecy and the end of the world.

Bethan Juliet Oake is a PhD candidate at the University of Leeds, UK, with a focus on moral panic, conspiracy rhetoric and alternative religion. Her current research analyses contemporary 'Satanic moral panic' and its integration within online conspiracy discourses.

Aled Thomas is Teaching Fellow at the University of Leeds, UK. He holds a PhD in the study of religion and is a specialist in minority religions (notably Scientology), the sociology of religion and research methods in the study of religion. He is the author of *Free Zone Scientology: Contesting the Boundaries of a New Religion* (2021).

Catherine Wessinger is Rev. H. James Yamauchi, S.J. Professor of the History of Religions at Loyola University, New Orleans. Since 2003 she has been engaged in oral history research with Branch Davidian survivors and other persons associated with the 1993 Branch Davidians–federal agents conflict at Mount Carmel Center outside Waco, Texas.

Donald A. Westbrook is Lecturer at the School of Information at San Jose State University. He holds a PhD in American religious history from Claremont Graduate University and is the author of *Among the Scientologists: History, Theology, and Praxis* (2019) and *L. Ron Hubbard and Scientology Studies* (2022). He has also taught at UT Austin, UCLA, University of South Florida, Cal State Fullerton and Fuller Seminary.

Foreword

Introduction to the *Religion at the Boundaries* series

Inform (an acronym for Information Network Focus on Religious Movements) was founded as a direct response to the 'Cult Wars' of the 1970s and 1980s. During this period, there was a widespread public mistrust and moral panic focused on the religious choices of a very visible minority of middle-class young people in the Global North. Conscious of the relative scarcity of accurate information about these minority ideological movements, Professor Eileen Barker established Inform to provide accurate and evidence-based information. In the pre-internet age, much of the initial work of Inform was cataloguing and responding to enquires, a kind of analogue-Wikipedia run by employees trained in social science.

Religion at the Boundaries, our new book series with Bloomsbury, expands and continues the founding mission of Inform. It aims to explore new forms of religion, spirituality and belief that lie outside the mainstream. There is just as much demand for accurate and up-to-date information about minority religions today as there was when Inform was founded in 1988. However, the nature of the information required is different. Minority religiosity now encompasses many small groups found within immigrant and diasporic communities around the globe. Ideological exploration and socialization have moved into online social spaces. New social and ideological movements continue to arise in response to global challenges and uncertainties, including wars, epidemics, immigration and the climate crisis. The problem now is not how to find basic information about an obscure movement, but how to sift through vast amounts of data efficiently and effectively.

A key aspect of Inform has always been its network; no one person or organization can hold comprehensive knowledge of thousands of new groups and minority movements. Inform's practice has always been to seek out and network with other experts. The first point of call is usually academic experts who might have done extensive research on the subject. However, Inform's method has always been one of triangulation – seeking to also involve the perspectives of other professionals (e.g. counsellors, legal experts, social workers) as well as the perspectives of current and former members with relevant lived experiences. Each perspective offers unique insights, but also has unique biases. Any individual or organization can make a more informed decision with access to a rich and diverse evidence base where positions and agendas are clear. The Inform book series grows out of this methodological approach of networking and triangulation.

This new series continues Inform's original mission of providing accurate and up-to-date research on new and minority movements, exploring the social, legal and ethical issues which they raise. We hope the series will reflect the variety of stances on contemporary topics, encouraging public engagement and debate. Submissions to the series from prominent and emerging scholars for both researched-based monographs and thematic edited collections which give voice to members, ex-members and critics are warmly encouraged.

Suzanne Newcombe and Sarah Harvey
Director and Senior Research Officer at Inform
Co-editors of the *Religion at the Boundaries* book series

Acknowledgements

Compiling this volume has been a team effort. Our thanks go to Suzanne Newcombe, Sarah Harvey and George D. Chryssides and the wider Inform Management Committee for their invaluable guidance, feedback and support when assembling our proposal.

The staff at Bloomsbury, in particular Lalle Pursglove, Lily McMahon and Emily Wootton, made our experience of compiling our first edited volume extremely positive. We thank them for their continued patience and support throughout the journey as well as their enthusiasm for this volume and the wider series with Inform.

As you will see, the contributions to this volume are very high quality. Suzanne, Sarah, George, Donald, Susannah, Catherine, Douglas, Vivian, Bethan, Bill and Rod have all been a joy to work with. Their professionalism and timely contributions are what make this volume a positive contribution to the field.

We would also like to extend a thank you to our colleagues within our respective institutions. The proverbial 'water cooler' discussions and willingness to share expertise has further ensured the quality of this volume.

Finally, but by no means least, we would like to thank all our family and friends who have stood by us through the 'crunch points' of this journey. Their encouragement has been a continued source of motivation through to the end.

Part I

Approaches to 'cult' rhetoric

1

'Cult' rhetoric in the twenty-first century
The disconnect between popular discourse and the ivory tower

Aled Thomas and Edward Graham-Hyde

Cults: Hybridized approaches

As the study of 'new' or 'minority' religions transitions into the twenty-first century, increasing shifts in the religious and political landscape indicate that it is time for scholars across disciplines to revisit the foundations of the field, while also seeking new directions for its future. Research on new religious movements (NRMs) has been dominated by typologies – whether these are 'cults', 'brainwashing', 'charisma', 'conversion' or processes of secularization (to name but a few). As contemporary scholars in the field, it is difficult to ignore the deployment of this terminology in public life. Through reflecting on our research we began to notice the consistent use of value-laden terms in professional conversations (politicians, journalists, teachers and so forth), often forsaking accuracy in the process. The consequences of popularizing problematic terminology comes at a cost which has real-world impact, a consequence we both witness manifesting itself in the lives of our research participants. However, our continued reflections led to us endeavouring to establish an understanding of the everyday usage of NRM terminology which may move us away from the 'orthodoxy' of the field. So, what was our initial realization? 'Cult' rhetoric, which includes terms like 'brainwashing',[1] had become a pejorative battering ram that could be used against religious groups deemed undesirable by others – which is not a novel realization. However, and perhaps more interestingly, contemporary cultic discourses have a clear connotation in popular vernacular, despite a murky etymological foundation. In other words, the increasing popularity of everyday use of terms like 'cult' or 'brainwashing' (such as the 'Cult of Trump') can illuminate our approaches to public understanding of contemporary issues such as religion and politics.

This continuing prevalence of cult discourses in popular vernacular requires a shift in thinking for scholars of minority religions. Regardless of scholarly hesitation surrounding the term, it is undeniable that the use of the term cult is deeply rooted within popular vernacular, appearing in popular culture entertainment, news stories, journalist exposés and (more recently) within hybrids of political, religious and conspiracy narratives (Graham-Hyde 2023). While use of the term is continuously used to delegitimize minority religions, it is important to note its wider uses, which points to more nuanced applications of the term from the moral panics surrounding new and minority religions in the 1970s.

From a critical perspective, it is clear that the term 'cult' is unhelpful as a scholarly category, particularly due to its highly subjective nature. As Benjamin E. Zeller notes, '[l]abelling any group with which one disagrees and considers deviant as a cult may be a common occurrence, but it is not scholarship' (2022: 31). However, while the term lacks scholarly rigour, an analysis of the term 'cult' in everyday life can greatly enhance scholarly inquiry. For example, in a quantitative analysis of American newspapers during the 1990s, Philip Deslippe (2023) outlines the complexities of how the term 'cult' was used across a variety of contexts. These, he notes, range from 'positive cults' (such as cult films and television) to 'negative cults' (such as cults of personality and cult analogies). These complexities create a term that is not possible to define in clear binaries. Accordingly, he urges scholars to understand the term as more than simply a pejorative. Moreover, as Susannah Crockford demonstrates using the example of QAnon in Chapter 9 of this volume, using the term 'cult' can be empowering for ex-members who have experienced harmful or traumatic experiences.

To explore these ideas further, we conducted a survey in 2021 that sought to understand how 'cult' rhetoric is used in popular vernacular. With over 2,000 responses, the data began to highlight that there is a clear theme in how the terms are viewed which would not surprise even the least experienced researcher. What surprised us, however, was the amount of responses connecting the terms to a range of social discourses such as education, media, politics, health and research ethics; building upon the expected religious and conspiracy theory discourses in which we are accustomed. Indeed, 'cult' discourse has transcended the boundaries of religion, becoming an increasingly popular term in wider social discourse, with a variety of usage – both positive and negative (Deslippe 2023).

The survey enabled us to gain a quantitative snapshot of respondent perception while simultaneously collecting qualitative data as to how respondents defined the terms and in what contexts they would apply their use.[2] We collected a quantitative snapshot of whether respondents had come across the terms 'cult', 'brainwashing', 'new religious movement' and 'minority religion', combined with a quantitative snapshot of how they perceived and used the terms in everyday situations.

The data revealed that the terms 'cult' and 'brainwashing' were commonly used terms that were negatively perceived. Terms such as 'new religious movement' and 'minority religion' were more likely to be considered neutral but less likely to be in common usage (see Figures 1.1 and 1.2).

Again, this is not surprising to anyone that researches minority religion. The findings from this survey support the findings of Paul Olson (2006), who had previously demonstrated that the term 'cult' was perceived more negatively than

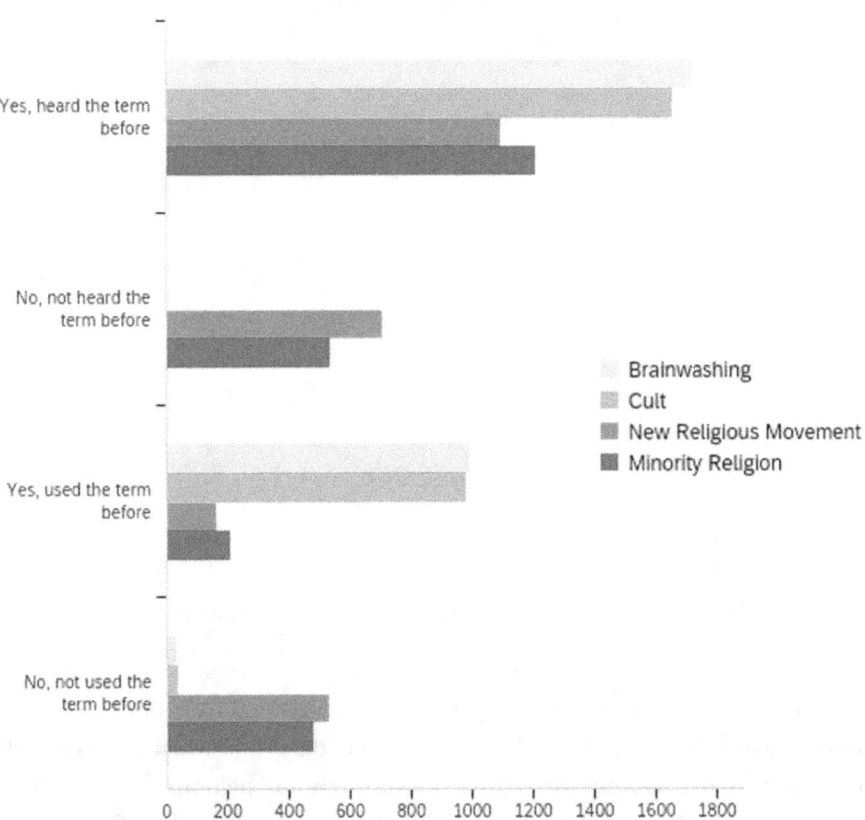

Figure 1.1 Have you heard of and used the following terms before this survey?

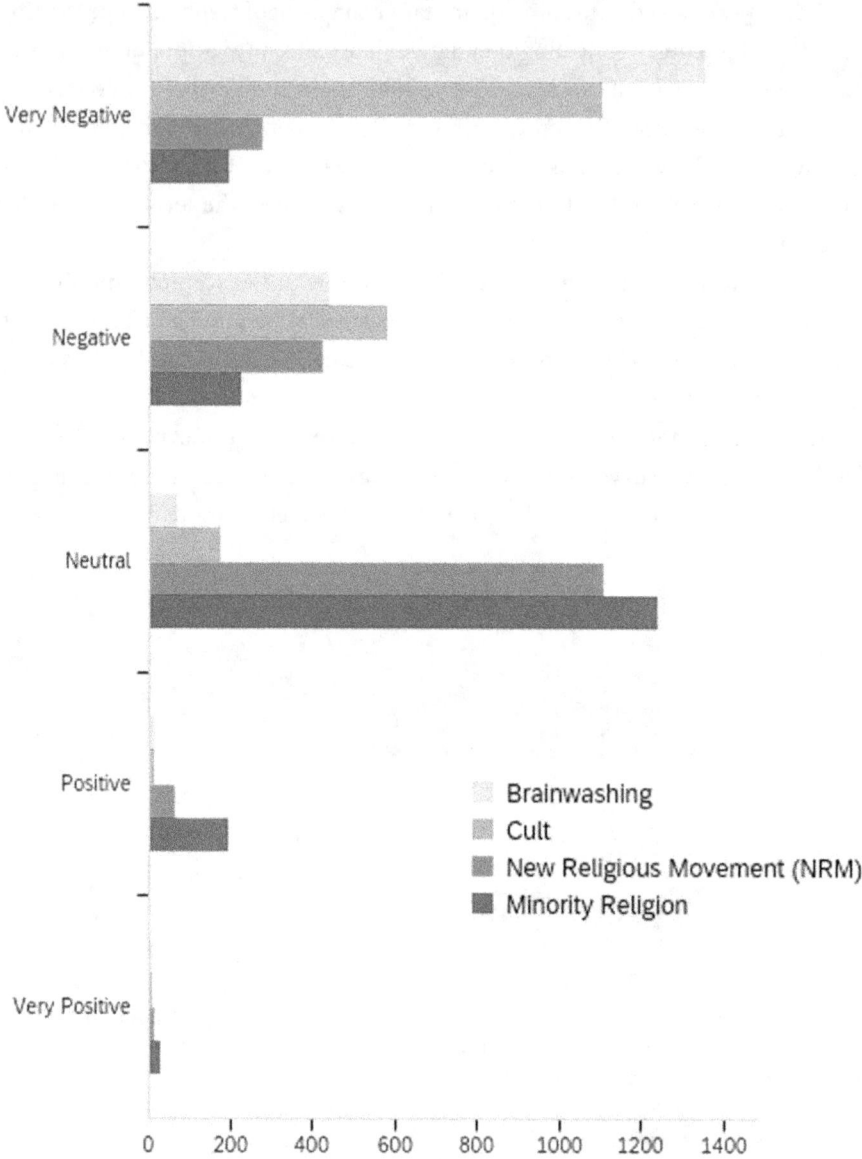

Figure 1.2 How would you personally perceive the following terms?

the terms 'new religious movement' or 'new Christian church'. Prior to Olson's research, Jeffery Pfeifer (1992) had also demonstrated that when the term 'cult' had been applied to a minority group so too were the pejorative assumptions, such as brainwashing, that exist within popular vernacular. Our survey provides contemporary evidence that further supports the scholarly rationale of using 'minority religion' when referring to any group that might be popularly perceived as a 'cult' or previously labelled as a 'new religious movement' within scholarly research.³ If we seek to construct an critical overview of lived religion then avoiding value-laden terminology, unless otherwise justified, is certainly a firm foundation for academic contribution.

In addition to the quantitative snapshot, the survey attempted to capture qualitative data by asking respondents to define the terms 'brainwashing', 'cult', 'new religious movement' and 'minority religion'. While emerging themes and in-depth comparisons between definitions is beyond the remits of this chapter, some of the following examples provide insight into how everyday people apply the terms.

One respondent defined 'cult' as 'a dangerously devoted group of religious people' and defined brainwashing as 'the act of convincing someone not to think for themselves'. However, the same respondent simply defined 'new religion movement' as a 'new religion' and 'minority religion' as 'a less common religion'. Another respondent chose to define 'cult' as 'a dangerous religious group' and 'brainwashing' as 'taking over someone's thoughts and brain'. Unlike the first respondent, 'new religious movement' was defined as 'literally the same as a Cult [sic]'. On first glance, one would be forgiven for thinking that this respondent had not given much consideration for nuance. However, this respondent reflected on how they would define 'minority religion':

> I would consider these differentiated from NRM or Cults [sic], however this term may be used to describe these groups. I'd call a long standing belief system that did not have much awareness in society a minority-religion.

There were many instances of clear nuance and reflection from the responses given. Of course, not all responses necessarily abided by the pejorative use of terminology in popular vernacular. There were responses that detailed the problematic terms with a clear awareness of the literature discussing issues with 'cult'.

The survey results are rich and diverse, and a full analysis will be published in due course; however, these initial snapshots have been helpful in framing our conversations; we suspect they will be helpful to others.

The responses were enlightening but so too were the comments made on the social media posts advertising the survey.⁴ Within the comments on the survey adverts, terminology was being used in virtual spaces to 'other' the opinion or position of individuals that oppose a popular but non-mainstream view. In this case, the view that Covid-19 was dangerous and that government intervention was necessary. Certainly, there was a significant 'anti-establishment' positioning of many of the social media comments made in connection to the survey. Perhaps the most significant finding from the comments alone was the way in which 'cult' rhetoric was being utilized in discourse about Covid-19 (Graham-Hyde 2023).

During Covid-19, the rejection of social distancing, lockdowns and other methods used by governments has formed part of the overall discourse of Covid denialism. J. Hunter Priniski and Keith J. Holyoak (2022) demonstrated that, in the United States, Covid-19 scepticism was initially driven by the preexisting distrust in Democratic politicians and medical science professionals but that 'auxiliary beliefs' became entrenched within the two dominant categories. Auxiliary beliefs, in this instance, included conspiracy theories suggesting that political and scientific organizations had an ulterior motive which was peddled through mainstream media (Priniski and Holyoak 2022).

A further analysis of 'auxiliary beliefs' highlights the religious connections to Covid-19 denialism. Perhaps this is best exemplified by QAnon, a prophetic political movement following the posts of an anonymous observer named 'Q'. Adherents of 'Q', who vary in political and religious background, believe that 'Q' is unearthing the covert war that Donald Trump is raging against the 'deep state' (Hughey 2021). Of course, Donald Trump enjoyed substantial support from evangelical Christians throughout his nomination and election as the president of the United States (Margolis 2020). Unsurprisingly, QAnon belief also found purchase among evangelical Christians during the Covid-19 pandemic, connecting evangelical concerns with anti-mask and anti-vaxxers conspiracy theories (Beauchamp 2022).

The eclectic mix of distrust and belief embodied by QAnon members is a contemporary example of how health, political and religious narratives are threaded together with the use of 'cult' rhetoric (Graham-Hyde 2023). With the terminology no longer being purely 'religious' in popular vernacular, it begs the question: Is scholarly work, emerging out of the study of religion, using terminology without this wider frame of reference, academically robust enough to forward the body of literature in a meaningful way? We think the answer is a resounding no.

The 'cult wars' of the past and scholarship to this date has been foundational in avoiding reductive binaries of 'what religion is' that subsequently 'others' that minority religions. The creation of Inform (Information Network Focus on Religious Movements), for example, is testament to the amount of work that was (and sometimes still is) needed to ensure the phenomenon of minority religions is understood, providing expert advice to judges, governments and members of the public. To be clear, this scholarly activity is helpful in establishing a scrupulous and sapient body of literature about religions that would otherwise go unresearched. However, with the exception of recent insider/outsider discourse and bespoke in-depth analyses of specific minority religions, the field seldom moves beyond the scaffolding of 'cult wars' and dominant typologies – with much contemporary scholarship operating within the confines of this space.

When the terminology in popular vernacular fails to match the way in which scholars are using the term then, at best, we risk becoming irrelevant. At worst, we are in danger of totally missing a new phenomenon in the development of normative cultic language and the rhetoric therein.

Forget 'atrocity stories': Listening to ex-members

While preparing the manuscript for this book, we chaired a roundtable panel on 'cult' rhetoric at the 2022 British Association for the Study of Religions conference at the Open University. While the discussion covered a range of topics and prompted lively debate among the audience, one common critique of the study of NRMs stood out: the field's historical hesitance to meaningfully engage with the testimonies of ex-members. The audience, consisting mostly of scholars from the wider study of religion, largely expressed concerns that overlooking (or dismissing) ex-member testimonies resulted in survivor narratives and instances of abuse being marginalized or muted in the field. Indeed, the wider study of religions is making strides towards studies of spiritual abuse, notably the ongoing Abuse in Religious Contexts project (Abuse in Religious Contexts, n.d.), which places the lived experiences of survivors at the centre of its research. The study of NRMs, at least from the perspectives of many of our panel's audience, is lagging far behind.

Such perceptions of the field are rather widespread beyond the academic community, with the study of NRMs often being framed as 'cult apologism'. Such framing is often dismissed as not truly understanding the nuanced and 'neutral' approach to NRM studies – but do these accusations point at an uncomfortable truth for NRM scholars? Does the study of NRMs prioritize the 'insider' experience? Has the field, in its attempt to rightfully combat prejudice and misinformation surrounding certain new religions, allowed the valuable testimonies of ex-members go unnoticed? These questions point directly to the relationship between the 'ivory tower' of academia and popular discourse.

As George D. Chryssides (2019) notes, insider accounts have typically been prioritized in the study of religion beyond the field of NRM studies. On face value, this seems an understandable perspective. Who better to ask for insider experiences than the insiders themselves? The origins of the study of new religions is particularly embedded in this approach, attempting to provide an account of new religions that is free of sensationalism. Rather than maintaining a critical and careful balance of data from member/ex-member sources, however, the study of NRMs has typically swerved hugely in favour of current members. Accusations of the field's 'cult apologism' often concern scholars dismissing ex-member testimony as biased and distorted accounts, with ex-members being categorized as 'apostates' and often depicted as having axes to grind. For many ex-members who have become vocal opponents of the groups they have left, being dismissed due to their 'ex' status is viewed as an insult and a devaluing of their lived experience. While it is erroneous to accuse all scholars of new religions of this framing (particularly more recent scholarship which has benefited greatly from the information provided by ex-members), it is clear that strands of distrust in ex-member narratives have existed in the field, often shaping the ways in which scholars set out to understand the groups they engage with.

Perhaps the most damaging framework for the dismissal of ex-member testimony is Bryan R. Wilson's (1990) model of 'atrocity stories', in which vocal ex-members are characterized as 'rehearsing' a narrative in which they are coerced and manipulated by duplicitous religious leaders, even suggesting that ex-members 'have sometimes sought to make a profit from accounts of their experiences in stories sold to newspapers or produced as books' (Wilson 1990: 19). Wilson (1994) would subsequently frame such financial gain as part of a pattern of motivations for ex-members' dissemination of personal testimonies. While it is clear that publications of ex-member narratives have become a popular market and even a career for some (see Bromley 1998; Cusack 2021; Gregg and Chryssides 2017), Wilson's dismissal of the validity of such narratives based on accusations of profiteering seems overly cynical. Moreover, the popularity of ex-member biographies highlights a significant disconnect between the sociological study of new religions and wider public discourse, in which ex-member narratives are valued and understood to be rich sources of insider knowledge.

These sources and the communities from which they emerge are fruitful areas of research in themselves. A considerable 'ex-member scene' has emerged in the digital age, as Chryssides outlines in Chapter 3 of this volume. Anticult testimonies have grown far beyond exposés and memoirs – the internet has allowed ex-members to gather, share stories and form friendships beyond the economic and geographical boundaries faced in previous decades. The increasing influence of social media, which allows networked publics of like-minded individuals to emerge through the collaboration of sharing experiences, news and events (see Papacharissi 2016), has also played a significant role in this shift. Both current members and ex-members of NRMs use social media to not only share their own views but also interact with one another, creating an often heated (and attention grabbing) debate. Despite the now easily accessible nature of ex-member testimonies via Tweets/X posts, Facebook posts and YouTube videos (among others), we are faced with another methodological question – how representative are these accounts of the overall ex-membership? In their study of ex-member testimonies, in which they also reinforce the importance and value of ex-member accounts, Gregg and Chryssides (2017) estimate that roughly 0.23 per cent of former NRM members in the United Kingdom are publicly critical of their respective movements. This, they conclude, leaves open the possibility that most former members have quietly left with mundane accounts of their time within the movement and their departure. These accounts, while no less valuable in terms of accumulating a broad picture of lived religion, are more difficult to obtain for the scholar.

Ex-member accounts are likely to maintain a greater popularity with a public market than scholarly analyses of new religions. While academic verbiage is often off-putting for non-academics, alternative sensational accounts of new religions perceived as 'cultic' or 'strange' fare well in terms of sales, particularly when authored by a former member who can attest to insider knowledge. However, there is a bigger issue at play than mere sensationalism or entertainment. Ex-member narratives, whether circulated online or published as memoirs, can be valuable sources of data for scholars on the one hand, but also an opportunity for ex-members to share instances of malpractice or abuse on the other. These are incredibly serious issues, ones that must be considered carefully by scholars of religion – both within the study of NRMs and wider study of religion.

As already established, the issue that is often raised when concerning ex-member narratives is their lack of objectivity. If an ex-member harbours ill feelings towards their former group, then can they be trusted as reliable accounts of insider information (Wilson 1990, 1994; Kliever 1995; Johnson 1998)? This approach seems short-sighted, however, as it does not appear to be applied with the same level of scrutiny to current members, who are *also* subjective in their narratives. Indeed, in his account of conducting fieldwork with the Church of

Scientology, Stephen E. Gregg observes that it is not uncommon for scholars of religion to witness 'represented religion' – 'the ways in which religious people and organizations present themselves and their traditions, in "official" materials or in the ways in which they engage with visitors to their communities' (2021: 133). He argues that scholars can be 'stage managed' in the field, in which they are introduced to enthusiastic current members and presented with an 'ideal' vision of the movement. This has also been the case in our own experiences of fieldwork (Thomas 2020). This is not intended as a criticism of the groups that kindly (and often very generously) welcome scholars of religion to their sites and organizations, but rather to acknowledge that all communities we study, whether regarded as insiders, outsiders, members, ex-members (among others), will display tendencies of bias. It is understandable that religious communities would want us to see them 'at their best', but while we acknowledge that ex-member testimonies can be problematic, current member narratives (particularly those through institutional and 'official' channels) can be equally problematic. The key for scholars, as Chryssides (2019) correctly notes, is the 'need to "manage" their informants, as is customary with all research data, evaluating the available evidence' (2019: 389–90). In other words, we should critically triangulate our sources across parties in an attempt to assemble what we view as an accurate account (see Carter 1998: 234).

These challenges are closely intertwined with notions of insiders and outsiders, a key methodological debate in the study of religion (see McCutcheon 1999; Gregg and Chryssides 2019). The framing of ex-member narratives as entirely unreliable presents a problematic binary between insiders on the one hand and outsiders on the other. The reality is far more complex. Carole M. Cusack (2019) demonstrates blurred boundaries between insiders/outsiders in a study of communities of ex-members from two separate groups: Kerista Commune and the School of Economic Science. By considering the narratives of ex-members found online, Cusack notes that Kerista Commune acts as a particularly interesting example, wherein all members are 'ex-members' due to the formal disbandment of the group in 1991. Nevertheless, members have been able to utilize online spaces to develop and maintain relationships based on a past belonging, thus ex-members 'continue to "believe" to a certain degree, but the sense that they still belong is stronger' (Cusack 2019: 403). In other words, complexities of insiders/outsiders in the study of new religions points to a number of potential publics under the 'ex' umbrella. These binaries are blurred further by recent NRM schismatics, such as Free Zone Scientology, wherein ex-Church of Scientology members have broken away from the CoS and rejected the need for institutional/hierarchical leadership (Cusack 2019). While these Scientologists may be categorized by the CoS as 'ex-members', they do in fact identify as Scientologists and practise L. Ron Hubbard's spiritual technology, albeit outside the institution Hubbard himself created (Thomas 2021). The Free Zone accordingly acts as an example of how breaking down problematic categories of 'outsiders' or 'ex-membership' to include more than those who entirely reject their former movement/community can lead to a more rich holistic picture of contemporary new religions. Moreover, while Free Zone Scientologists uphold the value of Scientology as a spiritual practice, it is not uncommon for some Freezoners to frame the Church of Scientology as a 'cult' (Graham-Hyde 2024), demonstrating nuances of cult discourse in popular vernacular.

Moving forward: Framing the discussion

Removing agenda from dialogue

Scholars, authors and individuals with long-term interest in this field will not be surprised to yet again hear a call for de-agenderizing, as robust peer-reviewed research must always aspire to such pedigree. Most are not blind to the controversy that often surrounds this field; the passionate, sometimes emotive, arguments that emerge are often met with rejection and hostility from 'the other side' of the argument. Regardless of the perspective we have when approaching the study of minority religions, all 'sides' of the argument often intentionally or unintentionally peddle agendas.

Critical analysis should avoid becoming embroiled in tit-for-tat discussions – defending religious organizations that can speak for themselves, while simultaneously worrying about what aspects of our collected data are 'too controversial' for publication. If scholars wish to avoid the label of 'cult apologist' then it stands to reason that they need to speak freely on all issues that concern minority religions and the lived reality of adherents.

Leaving the ivory tower

The majority of what is written about minority religions does not emanate from scholarly positioning. As academics we risk relevancy if we continuously ignore what is being published in the popularly accessed domain, more so when we label it as unnoteworthy, under researched or merely 'spam'. We believe that proverbial olive branches need to be extended to those that we might starkly disagree with, especially if they operate outside of academia. Those that have been labelled 'apostates', publishing in a way that circumvents academic scrutiny and rigour, often possess lived experience and/or listened to the lived experience of many who have been involved in minority religions. While we might disagree with their overall approach or potential misrepresentation of a religious group, it would be remiss to ignore the wealth of lived experience that they embody. We have engaged with an increasingly popular podcast called 'The Cult Vault',[5] an endeavour of Kacey – the host of The Cult Vault, who is fascinated by minority religions and wants to document her journey of learning about them. Overtime, Kacey has engaged with 'survivor' interviews and has often collaborated with those that heavily critique the work of scholars in the field of NRMs. While we might not always agree with the conclusions drawn by Kacey (or those that team with her), she has a high degree of access that we have not replicated, consistently ascertaining the lived experience of those who have left minority religions. Engaging with Kacey has been beneficial to our developing approaches towards the use of 'cult' rhetoric and we encourage academics to reach out to additional sources of information and access as opportunity arises.

Scholarly use of terminology must be justified

In previous publications we have argued that the use of 'cult' rhetoric must be avoided altogether (Thomas and Graham-Hyde 2021; Graham-Hyde 2023; INFORM 2021). However, in the process of collecting contributions for this volume we have come to accept that 'cult' rhetoric is an immovable fixture. While we largely agree with Zeller's (2022) recent assertion that the term 'cult' has little utility in scholarly contexts, it does possess utility for survivors of abuse and trauma, as argued elsewhere (Dubrow-Marshall, see Chapter 6 in this volume). It is important that scholarly research attempts to unpack the meanings intended by ex-members/leave-takers of minority religions when using 'cult' rhetoric. Furthermore, it is not the remit of scholars to make value judgements on the effective use of terminology when used by participants. Therefore, we argue that it is entirely justifiable to use the terminology when directly referring to the ideology of participants and those that have a lived reality that criticizes their previous religious identity/affiliation using 'cult' rhetoric.

Unfortunately, the use of terms such as 'cult' can sometimes be 'throwaway' in that the terms are used flippantly in other fields with little consideration given to the consequences. Therefore, where justification for the use of terms such as 'cult' or 'brainwashing' is not evidently necessary, we argue that scholars should refrain from usage unless particular care is given to articulating their definitional position. We do not wish to draw attention to articles where usage of the term is seldom justified; however, we do suggest that specific fields (and their derivatives) such as health, business, social work, political science and history pay particular attention to the vernacular they are choosing to implement – ensuring that the way in which they label groups/'others' is academically rigorous and evidence-based. Our reasons extend beyond agreeing with Zeller (2022); we argue that the mis-informed usage of terminology weakens academic research in other fields and can lead to further discrimination against those who live a minority religious reality. Ultimately, even without the publication of this volume, there is a plethora of publications in existence that highlight the issues of 'cult' rhetoric and it is lazy (if not wilfully ignorant) to lack attention to detail when labelling social groups and further obfuscates the issues within our field(s).

The purpose of this volume

This book has been assembled to revisit the notion of 'cults' and to reconsider the academic study of new religious movements as it faces the new paradigms and societal shifts of recent decades. We believe that this is best achieved with a multidisciplinary focus. Accordingly, we invited a variety of contributors to discuss aspects of 'cult rhetoric' in relation to their own scholarship and reflect on its impact. As this is the first volume in a new Inform book series with Bloomsbury, we wanted our contributors to reflect the organization's emphasis on diverse perspectives, thus demonstrating a breadth of opinions and scholarly approaches to the notion of 'cults'. The response was greater than we had anticipated and we are pleased with the rich contributions provided within this book.

These diverse contributions are an attempt to steer the ship in the direction of multidisciplinary approaches to the study of religion, beginning with a fresh and innovative discussion about the terminology we use to frame our discussions. We aim for this to be the beginning of a conversation about how the study of NRMs can move both beyond its historical foundations and archaic understandings of religion more generally, while also aiming to potential scholarly avenues which we believe will be helpful to all who study minority religions irrespective of disciplinary positioning. As with any book offering diverse perspectives, it is likely that there may be disagreement between both contributors and our readership, but we promote this in the spirit of productive dialogue. The term 'cult' is an often vague and highly subjective term – a multidisciplinary approach moves us towards a broader understanding of its deployment in contemporary discourses.

In an attempt to not retread old ground, this book is not intended as a 'guide' to various NRMs, nor a broad history of the field. Rather it is intended as a collection of contemporary and contextualized analyses of 'cult rhetoric', and the nuanced (and often unexpected) roles it plays in twenty-first-century society.

The book is divided into two parts. Part I, 'Approaches to cult rhetoric', aims to explore critical and scholarly approaches to the category of 'cult'. Suzanne Newcombe and Sarah Harvey (Chapter 2) provide a contextual account of both Inform's history and its approach to the term 'cult'. In Chapter 3, George D. Chryssides critically explores the history of anticult rhetoric and demonstrates that 'cult' controversies further entrenched pejorative connotations towards such groups, and little re-evaluation of how these religious groups have responded has occurred. William Sims Bainbridge (Chapter 4) also historically contextualizes 'cult' rhetoric through examining the intersection of religion and psychiatry over the last two centuries. Bainbridge then develops his analysis in light of the 'cult' conversion model he helped develop with Rodney Stark, before identifying the pervasiveness of 'cult' rhetoric and identity construction in Massively Multiplayer Online games. In Chapter 5, Douglas Cowan explores the new religious tropes in popular culture and provides an analysis of how the usage of terms such as 'cult' or 'brainwashing' have become metonyms for religious violence. Cowan uses an innovative methodology for analysing 'cult' rhetoric, using a propaganda model of information theory, and demonstrates how such an approach adds value to the field. Roderick P. Dubrow-Marshall (Chapter 6) completes Part I by providing a rationale for the continued use of the term 'cult', arguing that the word has utility for survivors of abuse. Durbow-Marshall further argues that the term should only be applied to groups that have unhealthy and damaging psychological impact upon members. Therefore, the term 'cult', as Dubrow-Marshall argues, refers to specific harmful practices rather than denoting a belief system as the term can be levied against any harmful group, not just religious.

Part II, 'Contemporary "cultic" issues', aims to deepen the conversation by exploring 'real-world' and contemporary issues pertaining to the term 'cult'. In Chapter 7 Donald A. Westbrook draws from his fieldwork with La Luz del Mundo ('The Light of the World') to assess the opportunities and limitations of an 'NRM' approach to a Mexican Christian movement which has previously been understood through Pentecostal frameworks. Bethan Juliet Oake, in Chapter 8, explores the contemporary 'Satanic Cult Conspiracy' (SCC). With the apparent resurgence of 'The Satanic Panic' in the previous decade, Oake's chapter deconstructs the anticult rhetoric and stereotypical image of a 'cult' deployed by the SCC to explore the broader issues at play in constructions of 'satanic cults'. Chapter 9, written by Susannah Crockford, turns its attention towards the QAnon movement and the 'cult' accusations surrounding it. Drawing from a variety of discourses, including interviews with former members, Crockford explores how the term is used with a variety of meanings and interpretations both within and outside QAnon, and how contemporary American politics resulted in the emergence of this movement that has been connected to the controversy of the Capitol riots (and more). In Chapter 10, Vivian Asimos unpacks the relationship between 'cult' rhetoric and popular culture, considering the notion of cults in terms of fandoms and communities emerging around 'cult TV' and 'cult films', among others. By positioning popular culture as a form of religious and spiritual engagement, Asimos demonstrates how 'cult' rhetoric is directly tied to shifting paradigm(s) of what religion is (and is not) for the everyday individual. Finally, in Chapter 11, Catherine Wessinger reflects on media depictions and documentaries of the Waco tragedy, and her experience of educating/advising journalists on 'cults' and issues pertaining to 'cult essentialism' from the position of a minority religion researcher.

W. Michael Ashcraft contextualizes the entire volume with an afterword that critically reflects on the deconstruction of the study of new religious movements with historical perspective. This afterword provides a helpful connection to the previous Inform book series, with this volume being the launch of a new and innovative Inform book series entitled 'Religion at the Boundaries'.

While these chapters may be diverse in nature, they are by no means comprehensive; several other areas exist as fruitful areas of discussion. However, it is our hope that this volume begins a renewed discussion of minority religions, 'cult' rhetoric and future directions for the field. This book was initially conceived as a method of moving beyond former typologies and the 'cult wars', yet it is not possible to give a simplistic answer to such a complex issue. Accordingly, the chapters from all our contributors provide a number of angles and methodologies that will help illuminate a variety of paths forward.

Notes

1 As well as all derivatives of the term that have been used, such as 'mind control'.
2 For a full methodology, see Graham-Hyde (2023).

3   While 'new religious movements' has enjoyed frequent use as a scholarly category, the subjective nature of 'new' and subsequent generations of NRMs has resulted in a reconsideration of the term (see Barker 2014).
4   A full methodology for how the survey was conducted has been written (see Graham-Hyde 2023 for more detail).
5   The full podcast episode can be found at: https://www.cultvaultpodcast.com/podcast/episode/279aa5df/104-bonus-episode-discussing-todays-academic-studies-of-cults

References

Abuse in Religious Contexts (n.d.), 'Abuse in Religious Contexts'. Available at https://research.kent.ac.uk/airs/ (accessed 16 January 2023).

Barker, E. (2014), 'The Not-So-New Religious Movements: Changes in 'the Cult Scene' Over the Past Forty Years', *Temenos: Nordic Journal of Comparative Religion*, 50 (2): 235–56.

Beauchamp, J. D. (2022), 'Evangelical Identity and QAnon: Why Christians are Finding New Mission Fields in Political Conspiracy', *Journal of Religion and Violence*, 10 (1): 17–36.

Bromley, D. G., ed. (1998), *The Politics of Religious Apostasy: The Role of Apostates in the Transformations of Religious Movements*. Westport: Praeger.

Carter, L. F. (1998), 'Carriers of Tales: On Assessing Credibility of Apostate and Other Outsider Accounts of Religious Practices', in D. G. Bromley (ed.), *The Politics of Religious Apostasy: The Role of Apostates in the Transformations of Religious Movements*, 221–38. Westport: Praeger.

Chryssides, G. (2019), 'Moving Out: Disengagement and Ex-Membership in New Religious Movements', in G. D. Chryssides and S. E. Gregg (eds), *The Insider/Outsider Debate: New Perspectives in the Study of Religion*, 371–92. Sheffield: Equinox.

Cusack, C. (2019), 'Both Outside and Inside: "Ex-members" of New Religions and Spiritualities and the Maintenance of Community and Identity on the Internet', in G. D. Chryssides and S. E. Gregg (eds), *The Insider/Outsider Debate: New Perspectives in the Study of Religions*, 393–415. Sheffield: Equinox.

Cusack, C. (2021), 'Apostate Memoirs and the Study of Scientology in the Twenty-First Century', *Implicit Religion*, 23 (2): 148–55.

Deslippe, P. (2023), 'Past the Pejorative: Understanding the Word 'Cult' Through its Use in American Newspapers during the Nineties', *Implicit Religion*, 24 (2): 195–217.

Graham-Hyde, E. (2023), 'From Bad to Worse: The Evolving Nature of "Cult" Rhetoric in the Wake of COVID-19 and QAnon', *Implicit Religion*, 24 (2): 135–59.

Graham-Hyde, E. (2024), 'Empowerment & Conversion: An Explanation for Minority Religious Recruitment in Contemporary Society'. Unpublished PhD thesis, University of Central Lancashire.

Gregg, S. E. (2021), 'Researching and Teaching Scientology: Perception and Performance of a New Religion', *Implicit Religion*, 23 (2): 129–39.

Gregg, S. E. and G. D. Chryssides (2017), '"The Silent Majority?" Understanding Apostate Testimony Beyond "Insider / Outsider" Binaries in the Study of New Religions', in E. V. Gallagher (ed.), *Visioning New and Minority Religions: Projecting the Future*, 20–32. Oxon: Routledge.

Gregg, S. E. and G. D. Chryssides (2019), 'Relational Religious Lives: Beyond Insider/Outsider Binaries in the Study of Religion', in G. D. Chryssides and S. E. Gregg (eds), *The Insider/Outsider Debate: New Perspectives in the Study of Religions*, 3–29. Sheffield: Equinox.

Hughey, M. W. (2021), 'The Who and Why of QAnon's Rapid Rise', *New Labor Forum*, 30 (3): 76–87.

Information Network Focus on Religious Movements (INFORM) (2021), *Inform Seminar: 'Cult' Rhetoric in 21st Century Thursday 24 June 2021*. Available at https://www.youtube.com/watch?v=gtPGNevfXyQ&t=155s (accessed 23 April 2023).

Johnson, D. C. (1998), 'Apostates Who Never Were: The Social Construction of *Absque Facto* Apostate Narratives', in D. G. Bromley (ed.), *The Politics of Religious Apostasy: The Role of Apostates in the Transformations of Religious Movements*, 115–38. Westport: Praeger.

Kliever, L. D. (1995), *The Reliability of Apostate Testimony About New Religious Movements*. Los Angeles: Freedom Publishing.

Margolis, M. F. (2020), 'Who Wants to Make America Great Again? Understanding Evangelical Support for Donald Trump', *Politics and Religion*, 13 (1): 89–118.

McCutcheon, R. T., ed. (1999), *The Insider/Outsider Problem in the Study of Religion: A Reader*. London: Cassell.

Olson, P. J. (2006), 'The Public Perception of "Cults" and "New Religious Movements"', *Journal for the Scientific Study of Religion*, 45 (1): 97–106.

Papacharissi, Z. (2016), 'Affective Publics and Structures of Storytelling: Sentiment, Events and Mediality', *Information, Communication and Society*, 19 (3): 307–24.

Pfeifer, J. E. (1992), 'The Psychological Framing of Cults: Schematic Representations of Cult Evaluations', *Journal of Applied Social Psychology*, 22 (7): 531–44.

Priniski, J. H. and K. J. Holyoak (2022), 'A Darkening Spring: How Preexisting Distrust Shaped COVID-19 Skepticism', *PLOS ONE*, 17 (1): e0263191.

Thomas, A. (2020), 'Engaging with the Church of Scientology and the Free Zone in the Field: Challenges, Barriers, and Methods', *International Journal for the Study of New Religions*, 10 (2): 121–37.

Thomas, A. (2021), *Free Zone Scientology: Contesting the Boundaries of a New Religion*. London: Bloomsbury.

Thomas, A. and E. Graham-Hyde (2021), 'Seeking New Approaches to the Alternative: The Merging of New Religious Movements and the Study of Religion', *Rogue: Journal for Alternative Academia*, 1 (1): 4–16.

Wilson, B. R. (1990), *The Social Dimensions of Sectarianism*. Oxford: Clarendon Press.
Wilson, B. R. (1994), *Apostates and New Religious Movements*. Los Angeles: Freedom Publishing.
Zeller, B. E. (2022), 'Cult', in G. D. Chryssides and A. Whitehead (eds), *Contested Concepts in the Study of Religion: A Critical Exploration*, 27–31. London: Bloomsbury.

2

Balancing pragmatism and precision
Inform's approach to cult rhetoric

Suzanne Newcombe and Sarah Harvey

Founded in 1988, Inform (Information Network Focus on Religious Movements) is an educational charity that was formed in the crucible of the 'cult wars'. Its central purpose is to provide accurate information about new and minority religious movements. It has sought to prevent harm based on misinformation about minority religions and sects by bringing the insights and methods of academic research into the public domain. While the guiding principles of Inform over this period have remained constant, our understandings have been refined and the context in which we have been working has changed dramatically. This chapter will cover Inform's positionality in regard to the word 'cult' and how its approach has been consistently defined by a concern for both pragmatics and precision, working within the framework of the law.

This chapter is written by the current director and senior research officer at Inform, both of whom have been working at Inform for over twenty years. We will argue that Inform's approach to the word 'cult' has largely been driven by pragmatism and a desire for precision in description. Inform attempts to maintain dialogue with all of those active around minority religions – academics, critics and former members, as well as current and prospective members, legal professionals, social workers, police officers, civil servants, journalists and students (among others). Drawing on the methodological principle of triangulating research evidence, we believe that the quality of information we can offer will only be improved by the more perspectives and experiences which we can draw upon.

Inform's founder, Eileen Barker (2013), and our former deputy director, Amanda van Eck Duymaer van Twist (2015), have described our research positioning as being that of a 'professional stranger' based on the pioneering sociologist Georg Simmel's description (1971 [1908]). It is based on the principles of methodological agnosticism (Barker 1995) where questions about the ultimate veracity of super-empirical claims are bracketed in exchange for a curiosity and exploration of the recordable testimonies and observable effects of those claims on individuals and communities. However, this is not the same positionality as methodological atheism advocated by strict social constructivists (e.g. Berger and Luckman 1966; Berger 1967). Rather, as van Eck Duymaer van Twist explains:

> methodological agnosticism allows for an open mindedness that enables engagement with possibilities. It allows a level of 'what if . . .' rather than a pre-emptive negation of the beliefs, which encourages *verstehen*. (2015: 33)

In its research method, Inform has always nurtured *verstehen*, an attempt to do more than simply 'objectify' and observe an object of research. As Max Weber argued, empathic and participatory understanding of social phenomena – although never complete and involving inferences – was nevertheless crucial to understand meaning in social context (Turner 2019). As a matter of principle, Inform has always attempted to understand the meaning-perspectives of all the different competing interest groups within the 'cultic field' in as verifiable and objective extent as possible. This describes a methodological orientation rather than any kind of perfect practice, but having ideals and standards upon which to be judged against is an important element of integrity.

To an extent, Inform has avoided using the word 'cult' to describe the organizations it researches because it wants to be able to empathetically describe, to 'translate' the beliefs, practices and worldviews of the particular minority religion to those outside the tradition. This is the *verstehen* of field research, qualitative interviews and ethnography with the religious groups themselves. No one ever decides to join a cult – and those affiliated to groups labelled as cults do not use 'brainwashed cult follower' as a self-description. It is an important element of Inform method to talk to affiliates of minority religions, to read their literature, to consider other material artefacts and to attend ritual and community events if possible. This is an important element of understanding the internal logic, the meaning appeal and the context in which any potentially objectionable, problematic and harmful behaviours might occur.

But it is also Inform's principle to attempt the same kind of *verstehen* and methodological agnosticism when approaching panicked and concerned friends and family and hurt and abused former members of minority religious groups. During interactions with those voicing these experiences, Inform training requires those responding to enquirers not to correct the use of the word 'cult' or try to minimize experiences or concerns voiced. Where there is evidence of illegal behaviour or prosecutable crimes, we take this information to the police while protecting the anonymity of informants unless this is expressly waved. In the last twenty years, Inform has assisted with ensuring criminal convictions against leaders of two minority religious groups (see Harvey Forthcoming).

However, often the abuse experienced within the context of minority religions falls below the threshold of criminal prosecution but can still be very problematic and cause harm (van Eck van Duymaer van Twist 2014). In this case Inform can help by keeping records of complaints, former member insights and other alternative testimony. When others' come for information about a particular group, Inform can alert new enquirers about these reports in a contextualized, anonymized format. For example, we could report that five people have voiced concerns about a particular religious teachers' propensity to be sexually promiscuous, or two people have complained that Y group has put pressure on young people to move into communal housing and abandon promising study or career plans in favour of promoting the group. We contextualize and balance some beliefs and practices, such as prosperity theology, or communicating with the spirit world, as being perhaps more pervasive than some enquirers have first assumed based on their own background. Sometimes we can also offer perspectives on what groups and individuals have done in the past when faced with similar situations, what the outcomes were and give some evidence-based inferences about what pitfalls there might be to a particular course of action. Inform also seeks to ensure that people are alerted to groups who are associated with controversial beliefs and harmful behaviours, and are able to make as fully informed decisions as possible about the nature and extent of involvement they want with a particular group. Indeed, once Inform gave exactly the same information about the group then known as The Children of God to two enquirers within the same week. One enquirer concluded that the group was 'all right' and would seek further contact; the second enquirer found their worst fears of a dangerous and harmful cult confirmed.

In general, when faced with an enquirer who wants to know whether or not a particular group is or is not a 'cult', Inform seeks to clarify and specify what beliefs and behaviours are of particular concern to that individual or organization. Our guiding principle is to steer the conversation back to more specific behaviours and beliefs which may or may not be present in any specific time or place. No human community, religious or otherwise, is ever immune to the potential of abusive and harmful behaviour. Therefore, no community can ever be given a clean bill of health. Conversely, a religious group considered to be a 'cult' in popular culture might be experienced as beneficial and an important source of meaning and purpose in life to its members.

Inform seeks to avoid unjustified moral panics and witch-hunts against perceived heretical beliefs. In this Inform was heavily influenced by LSE professor Stanley Cohen's work *Folk Devils and Moral Panics* (1972). In this role Inform most influentially contributed to the pacification of the moral panic around Satanic Ritual Abuse in the 1990s that implicated the growing pagan community of largely peaceful Wiccans as baby-sacrificing murderers (La Fontaine 1994 and 2003). Inform has acted in accord with Cohen insights' that moral panics inhibit rational debate as well as the development of solutions to the real problems represented in the apparent crisis.

As this volume explores, cult rhetoric has changed substantially since the founding of Inform. There have been more recent attempts to articulate the specific harm caused by betrayals of trust within religious and spiritual contexts with references to the concepts of 'spiritual abuse' (e.g. Langone 1994; Oakley and Kimond 2013; Oakley and Humphries 2019) and coercive control. We will explore how Inform has engaged with some of these more recent understandings in the cultic field in more detail after first expanding a bit more on Inform's history in relation to the use of the word 'cult'.

Founding of Inform – what to do about the 'cult problem'?

In Britain in 1984, moral panics about the brainwashing of youth by new and dangerous religious and ideological movements had reached the point of being debated in the UK Houses of Parliament. In the first substantive parliamentary debate on this subject the government was challenged about what it was doing 'to monitor the activities of so-called religious cults'. Several members of the House of Lords were concerned specifically about the ability of 'cults' to register as religious charities, as well as their reported illegal activities and harm to both individuals and families. Fear that adherents to these movements were 'brainwashed' was rife. In response to the concerns raised, the then Under Secretary of State, Lord Elton emphasized the equality of all citizens and organizations under the law and the appropriateness of media exposés in highlighting areas of harm and bad practice of organizations. The debate on 11 July 1984 concluded with a discussion about the definitional problems of the world 'cult' in law (Hansard HL 1984). Differential treatment under law based on religious affiliation alone was considered by government representatives to be a 'witch hunt' and not a foundation of successful government policy 'since The Reformation'. Over the years, this continued to be the position of the UK government despite further challenges to 'do more' to oppose dangerous cults. When asked by the Baroness Macleod of Borve if the government knew 'how many cults are operating in the country', Lord Williams of Mostyn responded: 'No, my lords. It is not a question that is capable of a rational answer because one man's religion is another man's cult and one man's orthodoxy is another man's [hetero]doxy. I really do not think that I can offer a sensible or helpful answer' (Hansard HL 1988).

The same year as this debate, Professor Eileen Barker, the founder of Inform, published her acclaimed study of brainwashing *The Making of a Moonie: Brainwashing or Choice?* (1984) based on seven years of research analysing to what extent conversion to the Unification Church could be attributed to individual choice (free will), environmental manipulation (social pressure) or inherent psychological characteristics (vulnerable psychology). Her research on this matter was described in *Sociological Analysis* as being conducted 'with exceptional objectivity, rigor, and thoroughness' (Bird 1985: 466). Although not easily reproducible due to its scale, it was also described as having a high degree of internal validity and essentially disproving the idea that conversion to a cult was irresistible or irreversible, noting the high percentage of people approached, but not ultimately associating with the movement for more than a weekend (95 per cent). Another reviewer highlighted how 'Eileen Barker identifies, explains, and then systematically discredits the simple-minded answers offered by pop journalism [for joining a cult]' (Smith 1985: 998).

The analysis offered in *The Making of a Moonie* was complex and did not offer any simple answers. Barker's work acknowledged that social pressure played a role in conversion. However, this more neutral description did not go far enough for many in condemning the extreme changes in lifestyle and priorities that marked many early Unification Church members. That the Unification Church took *The Making of a Moonie: Choice or Brainwashing?* as a *carte blanche* endorsement of their approach to recruitment[1] did not encourage those committed to addressing the 'cult problem' to reframe their questions. But the final paragraph of *The Making of a Moonie* offers a rather more sober conclusion:

[those who stay Moonies for some time] . . . will also find that they are presented with a wide range of problems, disillusionments and disappointments, and the majority will, without the need of outside intervention, leave (or at least cease to be full-time members) within a couple of years of joining. The rest may also have problems but will remain convinced that, despite these, the Unification Church is still a better place in which to be than any of the other alternatives open to them. (Barker 1984: 259)

The vision of being inside the new religion of the Unification Church offered by Barker is not one which is particularly rosy and certainly not a theological or organizational endorsement. But Barker is respectful of individual choice around beliefs and practices. Her conclusions emphasize the potential for (or inevitability of) both individual and collective change as well as the unique pushes and pulls which attract an individual to and keep them within a given religious context in comparison with other apparent life choices. Revealing and elucidating these complex and contextual insights are what drove Barker to found Inform and continue to form the bedrock of its *raison d'être*, despite a greatly changed milieu and discourse around 'cults' in the past thirty-five years.

The information and social environment around 'cults' has changed a great deal since the 1980s. It's worth remembering the social context in which Inform was founded. This was summed up succinctly with a sympathetic article in *The Guardian*:

> If your son or daughter gets caught up in a religious cult you have never heard of – and there are hundreds of them – it is surprisingly hard to get objective information. You might finish up having your child kidnapped and forcibly deprogrammed – a costly and illegal remedy that often fails and is in many ways worse than the disease.
>
> You can ring Cultists Anonymous – a secretive group of women, all called Janet, at the end of telephones around the country, who will probably confirm the worst of your fears.
>
> Another cult-watching organisation, Family Action Information Rescue (Fair) is also doggedly 'anti-cult'; it is officially against deprogramming but disinclined to envisage the possibility that your child might have found something positive. (Schwartz 1987)

In the pre-internet age in which Inform was founded, basic information on many of these minority religious groups' beliefs and practices was hard to find. In response to continuing public outcry, Barker successfully petitioned the UK's Home Office for a three-year start-up grant in 1988. With a public information line and walk-in premises, Inform offered academic access to libraries, encyclopaedias and networks of scholars as well as a growing database of groups about which it had received enquiries from which one could build an understanding of new and minority religious groups from triangulated and contextualized reporting. Inform never sought to create a list of 'bad' religions, recognizing from its establishment that bad and abusive behaviour occurs in both established, traditional religious contexts as well as those with charismatic leaders and first-generation membership (Barker 2004).

In contract to the position of some countries which allow for the registration and official recognition of some religious groups, and the blacklisting of others, the approach taken by the UK (and generally also taken by the governments of North America, the Netherlands and Scandinavian countries) has been that members of all religious groups should be treated without prejudice in the same way as other citizens of the country.

Barker, alongside representatives of mainstream churches and other supporters, registered Inform as an education charity (No. 801729). The representatives of mainstream churches, that is the Church of England, the Catholic Church and Methodist Church among others, were mindful of the dangers of legislating against religious belief and practice. However, the founders of Inform were all supportive of the principle that where illegality occurs in religious contexts members of religious organizations should be fully prosecuted without exception. Inform's foundational aim remains:

> To advance public knowledge and understanding by the promotion of study and research into religions and those movements concerned with the exploration of spiritual life or philosophies including, but without prejudice to the generality of the foregoing, cults, alternative and non-conventional religions, sects, human potential movements and new age movements, and the dissemination of the useful results of such study and research to the public. (Charity Commission 1989)

The founding brief for Inform also recognized that the boundaries between religious and secular are often porous, recognizing a variety of 'new age' and 'human potential' contexts which might be usefully considered within this context of research. In practice, Inform has always been happy to consider enquiries and keep information on any group concerned with questions relating to meaning and purpose to life – whether or not the group self-describes as religious or spiritual in their interests. Barker's 1989 book, *New Religious Movements: A Practical Introduction*, was published by Her Majesty's Stationary Office (i.e. the UK government) and sought, to the objection of some concerned about the harm caused in new religious contexts, to shift the terminology more objectively to that of 'new religious movement' or NRM.

Is this group a 'legitimate' religion (or a cult)?

Inform's approach has been to try to avoid labels which provide immediate value-laden binary categories, for example, is this group a 'good/bad' or 'real/fake' religion (Barker 2006)? In the early years of Inform, these value judgements obscured the actual harm or potential complex attractions to new movements, were pervasive, and continued throughout the 1990s. The tragedy at the Branch Davidian property in Waco, Texas, in 1993 highlighted to scholars the dangers of uninformed, heavy-handed interventions on the part of government agents (Wessinger 2000, 2009). At the other end of the spectrum, the crimes of Aum Shinrikyo brought to light with the release of sarin gas on the Tokyo subway in 1995 underscored the potential damage minority religious groups could cause to both their own members and wider society (Reader 2000). Mindful of the dangers of action based on inadequate information, Inform has always sought to provide as specific, balanced and up-to-date information as possible in response to an enquirer's particular question.

In the days before widespread use of the internet people contacted Inform pretty much as they would now use Google – as the first port of call – and enquiries reflected that – straightforward and quick to answer. There has also been something of a change in the typical questions Inform has received over time. At the founding of Inform and into the 1990s, there were many quick and simple questions such as contact details. In the early years many friends and relatives got in contact in hopes of deciding if a group was dangerous, or how to deal with their relative who had joined. Inform still receives these enquiries, but they no longer take up the majority of our time. Enquirers to Inform are varied – reflected in the 'other' category in Figure 2.1 which includes those requesting information on minority religions from diverse perspectives such as academics, chaplains, church networks, other 'cult watching groups', lawyers, medical practitioners, students, teachers and writers (see Figure 2.1 and Table 2.1).

In twenty-first-century Britain, we have seen a changing context in terms of the public recognition of religious groups, governance and regulation. There has been a general trend towards recognizing a broader spectrum of religious beliefs (and non-beliefs). Inform's enquiries also relate to these changes – from government departments, religious groups, media, as well as the 'concerned public'. The UK has no single official way of recognizing a religion – with the exception of the Church of England, being established in law and having special legal privileges in England, and the Church of Scotland in Scotland (Wales and Northern Ireland have no established church). However, there are several ways

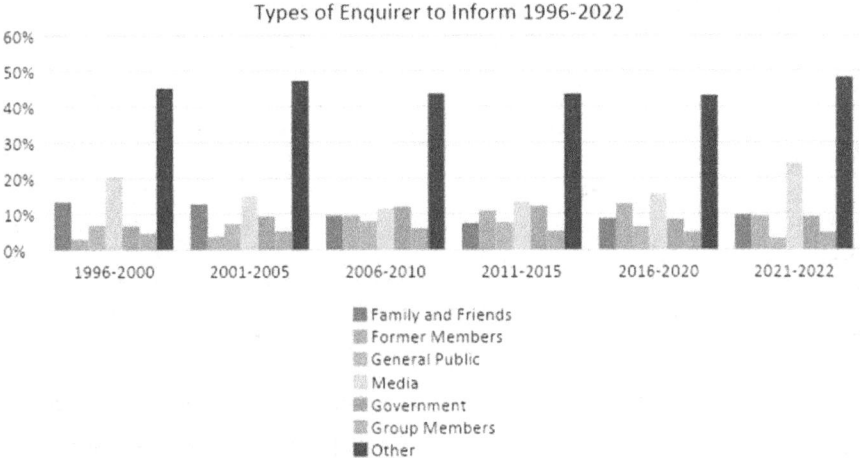

Figure 2.1 Types of enquirer to Inform 1996–2022.

for the government to recognize – and therefore 'legitimize' a religious group. Some of the most significant of these include registration as a registered charity, registration for certain tax-exempt statuses, registration of places of worship to conduct legally valid weddings, being recognized as partners in 'interfaith dialogue', state funding of religious schools and by the courts in a variety of contexts including asylum and custody decisions.

Many of the enquiries to Inform in the period 2006–15 reflected the need for in-depth information about a particular religious group for these complex decisions. This shift reflects the impact of changing government policy around the Equalities Act 2010 seeking to prevent religious discrimination as well as reflecting broader social changes of the diversity of British society in both its laws and in social expectations. Alongside this, Inform has had more enquiries about the diversity and new movements within the 'big faith groups', leading to a shift in conceptual focus towards 'minority religions' as much as NRMs or 'cults'. In this public discourse, the word 'cult' did not feature strongly. The debate was instead about the criteria for legitimate religions in different contexts, as well as reputable recipients of public funds and other forms of recognition. However, often the groups concerned positioned themselves as minority groups within mainstream religions.

In twenty-first-century Britain, public understanding of religion has become broader. And the way Inform has framed its area of research interest has shifted in reflection to these changes, putting a greater emphasis on 'minority religions' rather than NRMs or 'cults'. Inform has been asked to respond by various parties

Table 2.1 Types of Enquirer to Inform 1996–2022

	Family and Friends	Former Members	General Public	Media	Government	Group Members	Other
1996–2000	13%	3%	7%	20%	7%	5%	45%
2001–5	13%	4%	7%	15%	9%	5%	47%
2006–10	10%	10%	8%	11%	12%	6%	44%
2011–15	7%	11%	8%	13%	12%	5%	44%
2016–20	9%	13%	6%	16%	8%	5%	43%
2021–2	10%	9%	3%	24%[2]	9%	5%	48%

who have had interest in these changes – from groups themselves seeking legitimacy through registering for a particular privilege or in a court case, or by the government seeking to obtain an objective briefing in response to a challenge led by a religious organization. Inform's remit requires a flexible pragmatism and sense of judgement (Barker 1995 [1989]: 148). However, Inform's responses to these more complex enquiries are based on the same principles of its founding – to provide comprehensive, accurate and relevant information to help the enquiring parties come to their own informed decisions based on their own criteria.

In the same year that Inform was founded (1987), the Inter Faith Network was also founded as a registered charity (No. 1068934) with a government grant to 'advance public knowledge and mutual understanding of the teachings, traditions and practices of the different faith communities in Britain . . . and to promote good relations between people of different faiths' (Pearce in van Eck Duymaer van Twist 2020: 208–9). The Inter Faith Network originally accepted institutional membership representing nine major faith communities (Buddhist, Christian, Hindu, Jain Jewish, Muslim, Sikh and Baha'i and Zoroastrian). The Inter Faith Network's remit and membership structure has always been contested – who can be represented? Which organizations are accepted to represent 'Hindus' or 'Muslims'? – are not easy questions to settle. Some groups were unhappy to be excluded and the membership criteria was reviewed and adjusted in 2014 in response to a legal challenge under the Equalities Act 2010's prohibition of religious discrimination (van Eck Duymaer van Twist 2020: 214–15). At this point the Druid Network, the National Spiritualists Union and the Church of Jesus Christ of Latter-Day Saints were admitted as provisional members, while some other groups who sought membership continued to be excluded. But the existence of the government funded Inter Faith Network reinforces the idea that some religious groups receive greater legitimacy in the form of government recognition, access and status than other groups. That is to say, some religious groups are 'acceptable' and 'legitimate', while others do not enjoy this kind of status.

In contrast, Inform was set up as a network based on social scientific scholarship and not a membership-based organization within which new and minority religious could receive 'official' recognition (however much some minority groups and individuals might have wished Inform to act as such an organization). Inform keeps a record of every enquiry and every group enquired about or that comes across our network which, in our professional judgement, addresses questions of meaning and purpose to life or behaves in a way that could be illuminated using the conceptual categories and comparative context of new and minority religious movements. This has meant that although the number of enquiries has decreased in recent years, those we do take on tend to be more complex and require this analytical, comparative insight, drawing upon our database of over 5,000 different groups and movements and history of over 13,500 enquiries since 1996 (when Inform began keeping computer records).

Inform is sometimes asked if a particular group 'is a cult' – we tend to respond by deflecting this to questions about particular concerns in relation to the group and/or situation in question. Inform has been criticized by some cult critics and former members for 'blacklisting' the terms 'cult' and 'brainwashing' with straw man arguments considering these as simplistic value judgements (e.g. Zablocki 1997). It is accurate to say that Inform's approach consistently eschews the use of the terms 'cult' and 'brainwashing' as having limited utility in recognizing or preventing harm within or against minority religious groups. In the words of Eileen Barker (2009b):

> No one is likely to say that they themselves belong to a cult – what makes it a cult is that other people call it a cult. We know it's bad and wrong, but we don't know exactly what it is that is bad or wrong, which can vary quite dramatically between individuals, from place to place, and from time to time.
>
> Perhaps most significantly, throughout history new religions have been treated with fear and suspicion – they are, after all, challenging the status quo with their new beliefs and practices . . . unpopular religions can be discriminated against with relative ease throughout the world when they are labelled, and thus made into, 'cults'.

Inform is making an ideological and value-laden decision with its policy of redirecting conversation away from a focus on these two value-laden and emotionally driven terms. However, it also does try to address harm and illegal activity within minority religious groups, and we do recognize that the term 'cult' in particular has a broader use in popular discourse. Many of those associated with Inform have used the term as a teaching tool – Eileen Barker, Amanda van Eck Duymaer van Twist and Marat Shterin have taught undergraduate courses entitled 'cults, sects and new religions' in which each of these terms is opened to discussion around a variety of definitions and their social contexts (as well as involving field visits to religious groups and explorations of case studies of violence relating to new religions). We also recognize that as a term of self-description for someone who has left a group in which they experienced harm and abuse, it can be a useful tool for beginning to unpick the processes of socialization by which they adhered to beliefs and behaviours which they now find abhorrent (Barker 2009b).

Contemporary concerns – harm in religious contexts

Inform has always positioned itself primarily as an information resource closely connected with active, academic social scientific research. It never has been primarily an organization offering support for those injured by religious groups. However, over time, a significant minority of our enquiries have come from former members of religious groups who have experienced harm. This has been particularly true since 2006, when there were several clusters of former members of specific groups with grievances. Inform was successfully able to share information with the police and Crown Prosecution Service which assisted in the eventual conviction of a religious leader and alternative healer, Singh, on charges of rape and sexual assault in 2010. As part of this case, Inform was forced to successfully defend the confidentiality of its enquirers (we had received 131 enquires between 1997 and 2010) who did not want to be involved in a criminal case nor their details released to the defence attorney (Katz 2018). The rape trial was a gruelling process for the women who chose to give their testimony and many more reported harm within this group than those willing to be cross-examined in court.

In a second case from around the same period, a tightly knit community discovered their religious leader had been manipulating them sexually and financially; the group began talking to each other and left *en mass*, giving their testimony and much theological and historical material to Inform for safekeeping. In the aftermath of this event, the leader incited one of the few followers to remain to cause grievous bodily harm against another former member; Inform was able to provide briefings to the trial judge in the sentencing process which caused the leader to be imprisoned alongside his deputy. Yet there are difficulties in naming this leader as he is now out of prison and has resumed teaching; the former members who left have no obvious criminal path to further prosecution and are reluctant to have their own reputations damaged. They simply want to get on with their lives and recover. While Inform does not have a remit to proclaim the name of this group and its leader, when it is specifically asked about this individual, it can share the background, carefully anonymizing the former members and providing public domain information about the leader's past convictions and historical publicity material. While this situation is less than satisfactory for many, it highlights the legal complexities involved with protecting individuals from harm in religious contexts – the interests of both former members who wish to move on with their lives and any future followers should be safeguarded (see Harvey Forthcoming).

Meanwhile, cultural awareness of harm in religious contexts has become much more pervasive since when Inform was first founded. Accusations of sexual abuse of minors against respected members of the clergy only began to be discussed by the media in the 1980s. Inform used to have to explicitly point out that abuse happens in traditional religious contexts as well as in 'new religions' or 'cults'. In 1995, Anson Shupe needed to explicitly justify how any situations of power inequity – especially those of religious traditions – can easily create environments in which abuse, exploitation and manipulation occur (Shupe 1995: 30). The aftermath of recent Royal Commissions into the sexual abuse of children in Australia (2017) and the UK (Jay et al. 2022) have put into place more stringent 'safeguarding practices' to help protect children in all institutional settings, including those within a religious context, against future abuse. While these changes are very important, they do little to prevent the abuse and manipulation of adults within religious and other high-demand communities.

There has been growing recognition of the unique psychological harm caused by those who feel betrayed and abused within a religious context. The psychologist Michael Langone, previous executive director of the International Cultic Studies Association in the United States, included 'spiritual abuse' in the title of his edited book, *Recovery from Cults: Help for Victims of Psychological and Spiritual Abuse* (1994). However, most of the abuse described in the chapters is delineated as physical, sexual or psychological, and 'spiritual abuse' as a concept was not well defined. In the UK, Lisa Oakley has developed the use of this concept, primarily within mainstream Christian contexts, pointing towards the unique sense of betrayal when abuse is perpetrated by trusted authority figures and necessitates a subsequent potential reframing of an entire worldview (Oakley and Kimond 2013; Oakley and Humphries 2019). The inclusive framework of harm, covering all religious contexts and particularly more mainstream 'Christian' ones, helps move the debate onwards from the 'cult-wars' in which Inform was founded and helps 'survivors' pinpoint exactly the reasons for their feelings of profound betrayal when abuse happens in religious contexts.

Inform has been participating in several constructive conversations which aim to recognize and prevent harm in religious contexts. Inform has been part of regular discussions with Lisa Oakley in the context of her chairmanship of the national working group for abuse linked to accusations of witchcraft and spirit possession (formally the national working group for child abuse linked to faith or belief) which was set up in response to the death of a child of African origin in London (Department of Education 2012). Inform has also worked closely with the National FGM Centre in its expanded remit around Child Abuse Linked to Faith or Belief (CALFB), sharing information, and giving workshops at conferences (National FGM Centre 2022).

Inform's founder Eileen Barker has been attending conferences and actively seeking dialogue with those involved in raising awareness of the harms caused by 'cults' since 1998.[3] Although there are still differences of opinion in this vast and varied milieu, there is much more dialogue and agreement between those operating in this area than there was in the early 1980s. In recent years, Inform has continued this tradition in having online bi-annual meetings with organizations active in the 'cult-watching' field in the United States, Canada, Switzerland and Belgium. Inform's senior research officer Sarah Harvey is a research associate on the AHRC-funded project, Abuse in Religious Contexts, led by professor Gordon Lynch at the University of Kent and which runs from 2022 to mid-2024. She is analysing Inform materials in relation to abuse in new and minority religious movements.

Inform gave official feedback on new legal recognition for coercive control which became a criminal offence in family and intimate contexts in 2015 (Home Office). Although the UK government declined to broaden this offence to institutional and religious contexts, it is now widely recognized and discussed as an aspect of domestic violence and control. As such, the specific mechanisms of coercive behaviour are being more widely discussed as both recognizable and socially inappropriate. This can only help those who have been subject to similar pressures in the context of religious and ideological groups. The public discourse around gaslighting as a method of manipulation in both religious and secular contexts has the potential for moving on old discussions of 'brainwashing' and highlighting the continuing and unique problems of gender inequality and problems of 'survivorship' after leaving highly controlling relationships (Sweet 2021 and 2022).

Popular books like Amanda Montell's *Cultish* (2021) have usefully played on both positive and negative associations of the word 'cult' while pointing out how linguistic moves like the 'thought terminating cliché' (originally coined by Jay Lifton in 1961) are commonly found in 'cultic' contexts. Montell shifts this specific aspect of Lifton's work (which focuses on the treatment of American POWs in North Korean prisons) subtly away from the more pervasive metaphor of 'brainwashing' and the criteria for 'thought control' which are rarely if ever fully met in contexts other than those involving physical imprisonment. That Montell plays on her own 'cult appeal' within social media contexts only adds to the shifting of the public discourse around 'cults', at least in Anglophone contexts. Yet, elsewhere in the world, the idea of 'cult' still serves the interests of authoritarian states which seek to repress ideological dissent, including those associated with groups which are not considered particularly problematic in other contexts (Barker 2010; Introvigne 2018).

The current public discussion around 'cult' in the Anglophone world is less focused on minority religious groups and more generally concerned with harmful patterns of behaviour; this can only be welcome as a way to help individuals in our society be less susceptible to social pressure wherever it is found.

Conclusion

Inform has always sought to contribute to the 'cult debate' in ways that could reduce harm and promote more informed decision-making based on accurate information. While the use and social context of the world 'cult' has shifted significantly since Inform's founding in the 1980s, the need for providing accurate and up-to-date information from a variety of perspectives on specific religious and ideological groups remains. The type of information required in the twenty-first century for good decision-making is much more complex. Inform continues to be uniquely placed as being able to contribute research-based comparative and contextualized information from which a variety of individuals and organizations can make more informed decisions about minority religions.

The 1987 article in the *Guardian* announcing the founding of Inform also contained a tongue-in-cheek invitation for applications for a director of Inform who 'can handle research academically, distraught parents sympathetically, rabid anti-cultists diplomatically and cult officials with polite scepticism' (Schwartz 1987). This rather difficult job description continues to be the one that Inform attempts to live up to – and its approach to the word 'cult' reflects this position. It is hardly surprising though, that considering the audiences involved it is impossible to please all these audiences, all of the time. In seeking to keep dialogues and discourse as constructive as possible, Inform has traditionally sought to sidestep the definitional debate of 'cult' but instead to more pragmatically concentrate on moving the debate forward and mitigating incidences of harm within specific contexts.

Notes

1 'The Moonies' recognition of INFORM is one of the major reasons why I feel that Government funding of the organisation should immediately cease' (Hansard 1988).
2 The higher proportion of media enquiries in 2022 (38 out of 132 enquiries in the year) is largely down to Inform's working relationship with the Religion Media Centre – https://religionmediacentre.org.uk/ – and the assassination of former prime minister of Japan Shinzo Abe by a man whose mother had made significant donations to the church.
3 When she first attended the annual conference of the International Cultic Studies Association (then called the American Family Foundation). ICSA's current philosophy of dialogue has been influenced by Barker's approach of engagement – see https://www.icsahome.com/aboutus/benefitsofdialogue

References

Barker, E. (1984), *The Making of a Moonie: Brainwashing or Choice?* Oxford: Blackwell.
Barker, E. ([1989] 1995), *New Religious Movements: A Practical Introduction*. London: HMSO.
Barker, E. (1995), 'The Scientific Study of Religion? You Must Be Joking!', *Journal for the Scientific Study of Religion*, 34 (3): 287–310. https://doi.org/10.2307/1386880.
Barker, E. (2004), 'What Are We Studying? A Sociological Case for Keeping the "Nova"', *Nova Religio*, 8 (1): 88–102.

Barker, E. (2006), 'What Should We Do About the Cults? Policies, Information and the Perspective of INFORM', in P. Cote and T. J. Gunn (eds), *The New Religious Question: State Regulation or State Interference?*, 371–94. Oxford: Peter Lang.

Barker, E. (2009a), 'In God's Name: Practising Unconditional Love to the Death', in M. Al-Rasheed and M. Shterin (eds), *Dying for Faith: Religiously Motivated Violence in the Contemporary World*, 49–58. London and New York: I.B.Tauris.

Barker, E. (2009b), 'One Person's Cult is Another's True Religion', *The Guardian*, 29 May. Available at https://www.theguardian.com/commentisfree/belief/2009/may/29/cults-new-religious-movements (accessed 4 April 2023).

Barker, E. (2010), 'The Cult as a Social Problem', in T. Hjelm (ed.), *Religion and social problems*. Routledge Advances in Sociology, 198–212. New York: Routledge.

Barker, E. (2011), 'Stepping Out of the Ivory Tower: A Sociological Engagement in 'the Cult Wars'', *Methodological Innovations Online*, 6 (1): 18–39.

Barker, E. (2013), 'Doing Sociology: Confessions of a Professional Stranger', in T. Hjelm and P. Zuckerman (eds), *Studying Religion and Society: Sociological Self-Portraits*, 39–54. London: Routledge.

Berger, P. (1967), *The Sacred Canopy: Elements of a Sociological Theory of Religion*. Garden City: Doubleday.

Berger, P. and T. Luckman (1966), *The Social Construction of Reality: A Treatise in the Sociology of Knowledge*. Garden City: Doubleday.

Bird, F. (1985), 'Review of: The Making of a Moonie: Brainwashing or Choice? by Eileen Barker', *Sociological Analysis*, 46 (4): 466–7.

Charity Commission (1989), 'Information Network Focus on Religious Movements Governing Document'. Available at https://register-of-charities.charitycommission.gov.uk/charity-search/-/charity-details/801729/governing-document (accessed 4 April 2023).

Cohen, S. (1972), *Folk Devils and Moral Panics: Creation of Mods and Rockers*. London: Routledge.

Department of Education (2012), 'Child Abuse Linked to Faith or Belief: National Action Plan', HMSO. Available at https://www.gov.uk/government/publications/national-action-plan-to-tackle-child-abuse-linked-to-faith-or-belief (accessed 4 April 2023).

Hansard (1984), HL Deb. vol. 454, 'Religious Cults', 11 July. Available from: https://www.parliament.uk/ (accessed 9 December 2022).

Hansard (1988), HL Deb. vol. 584, 'Religious Cults: Advice in Schools', 13 January. Available at https://www.parliament.uk/ (accessed 9 December 2022).

Harvey, S. (Forthcoming), *Abuse in Minority Religions*. London: Routledge.

Home Office (2015), 'Statutory Guidance Framework: Controlling or Coercive Behaviour in an Intimate or Family Relationship'. London: HMSO. Available at https://www.gov.uk/government/publications/statutory-guidance-framework-controlling-or-coercive-behaviour-in-an-intimate-or-family-relationship (accessed 4 April 2023).

Introvigne, M. (2018), '*Xie Jiao* as "Criminal Religious Movements": A New Look at Cult Controversies in China and Around the World', *The Journal of CESNUR*, 2 (1): 13–32. Available at https://cesnur.net/wp-content/uploads/2018/02/tjoc_2_1_2_introvigne.pdf (accessed 4 April 2023).

Jay, A., M. Evans, I. Frank and D. Sharpling (2022), 'Report of the Independent Inquiry into Child Sexual Abuse'. Available at https://assets.publishing.service.gov.uk/government/uploads/system/uploads/attachment_data/file/1112123/the-report-independent-inquiry-into-child-sexual-abuse-october-2022.pdf (accessed 4 April 2023).

Katz, P. (2018), 'Mohan Singh Case: What is the Price of Confidentiality?', in J. T. Richardson and F. Bellanger (eds), *Legal Cases, New Religious Movements, and Minority Faiths*, 57–71. London: Routledge.

La Fontaine, J. (1994), *The Extent and Nature of Organised and Ritual Abuse: Research Findings*. London: HMSO.

La Fontaine, J. (2003), '"Satanic Abuse" – Lessons from a Controversy', in J. Beckford and J. J. Richardson (eds), *Challenging Religion*, 83–92. London: Routledge.

Langone, M., ed. (1994), *Recovery from Cults: Help for Victims of Psychological and Spiritual Abuse*. London: W. W. Norton & Co.

Lifton, J. (1961), *Thought Reform and the Psychology of Totalism*. London: University of North Carolina Press.

Montell, A. (2021), *Cultish: The Language of Fanaticism*. New York: HarperWave.

National FGM Centre (2022), 'Child Abuse Linked to Faith and Belief (CALFB)'. Available at http://nationalfgmcentre.org.uk/calfb/ (accessed 4 April 2023).

Oakley, L. and J. Humphries (2019), *Escaping the Maze of Spiritual Abuse: Creating Healthy Christian Cultures*. London: SPCK Publishing.

Oakley, L. and L. Kinmond (2013), *Breaking the Silence on Spiritual Abuse*. London: Palgrave Macmillan.

Reader, I. (2000), *Religious Violence in Contemporary Japan: The Case of Aum Shinrikyo*, London: Routledge.

Royal Commission (2017), 'Institutional Responses to Child Sexual Abuse'. Available at https://www.royalcommission.gov.au/child-abuse/final-report (accessed 4 April 2023).

Schwartz, W. (1987), 'Society Tomorrow: Tracking the Single Truths', *Guardian*, 16 September.

Shupe, A. (1995), *In the Name of All That's Holy: A Theory of Clergy Malfeasance*. London: Praeger.

Simmel, G. (1971 [1908]), 'The Stranger', in D. Levine (ed. and trans.), *Georg Simmel on Individuality and Social Forms* (Heritage of Sociology Series), 143–9. London: University of Chicago Press.

Smith, K. B. (1985), 'Barker, "The Making of a Moonie - Brainwashing or Choice?" (Book Review)', *Social Science Quarterly*, 66 (4): 998–9.

Sweet, P. (2021), *The Politics of Surviving How Women Navigate Domestic Violence and Its Aftermath*. Oakland: University of California Press.

Sweet, P. (2022), 'How Gaslighting Manipulates Reality', *Scientific American*, 1 October. Available at https://www.scientificamerican.com/article/how-gaslighting-manipulates-reality/ (accessed 4 April 2023).

Turner, S. P. (2019), 'Causation, Value Judgments, Verstehen', in E. Hanke, L. Scaff and S. Whimster (eds), *The Oxford Handbook of Max Weber*, Oxford Handbooks (2020; online edn, Oxford Academic, 11 February 2019).

van Eck Duymaer van Twist, A., ed. (2014), *Minority Religions and Fraud: In Good Faith?*. London: Routledge.

van Eck Duymaer van Twist, A. (2015), 'On Being a Stranger in their Midst', *Diskus: The Journal of the British Association for the Study of Religions*, 17 (1): 30–6.

van Eck Duymaer van Twist, A. (2020), 'Who Can We Dialogue With? Seeking Effective Interfaith Development: The Inter Faith Network for the UK', in K. Knott and M. Francis (eds), *Minority Religions and Uncertainty*, 207–22. London: Routledge.

Wessinger, C. (2000), *How the Millennium Comes Violently: From Jonestown to Heaven's Gate*. New York and London: Seven Bridges Press.

Wessinger, C. (2009), 'Deaths in the Fire at the Branch Davidians' Mount Carmel: Who Bears Responsibility?' *Nova Religio: The Journal of Alternative and Emergent Religions*, 13 (2): 25–60.

Zablocki, B. (1997), 'The Blacklisting of a Concept: The Strange History of the Brainwashing Conjecture in the Sociology of Religion', *Nova Religion*, 1 (1): 96–121.

3

A history of anticult rhetoric

George D. Chryssides

Cult opposition and rhetoric is by no means new. Hebrew scripture records a continual struggle between the supporters of Yahweh and the proponents of the rival Canaanite religions. When Elijah meets the prophets of Baal and Mount Carmel and challenges them to light a sacrificial fire by calling on the respective gods, he taunts them, suggesting that Baal might be asleep or away on a journey (1 Kings 18.27). Elijah, of course, wins the contest, and the failure of the Baal priests is followed by their seizure and slaughter. The majority of English-speaking and European countries have moved on from slaughtering their opponents, but opposition to new religions remains high. In what follows I aim to show how prejudice against new religious movements (NRMs) has developed, and the various forms it has taken.

In his seminal work *The Nature of Prejudice* social psychologist Gordon W. Allport defined five progressive stages of prejudice: (1) antilocution; (2) avoidance; (3) discrimination; (4) physical attack and (5) extermination. Although written in 1954, it continues to find wide acceptance, without major opposition. It would be inappropriate to suggest that the opposition between the Yahwists and the Baal worshippers went through all of Allport's five stages; we only have part of the story in the Bible, and we do not know for sure how reliable the story of this opposition is. Nonetheless, several decades later King Jehu (reigned 841–814 BCE) tricked the supporters of Baal into attending a large ceremony, while the king's supporters waited for them to emerge, and slaughtered all of them, both laity and priesthood. To add insult to injury, they destroyed the temple and its images and converted the site into a latrine (2 Kings 10.18-28).

The precise grounds for confrontation with the Baal and Asherah religions remain unclear, but a large part of the opposition was doctrinal. Yahwism was aniconic and demanded exclusive allegiance, as the religion of the Jews remains today. The first two of the Ten Commandments are, 'You shall have no other gods before me' and 'You shall not make for yourself an image in the form of anything' (Exod. 20.3-4). Doctrinal opposition has been the ground of prejudice and discrimination throughout the history of religious conflict. The persecution of Christians by the Jewish authorities had much to do with the fact that they were proclaiming Jesus as the messiah. Subsequently the Roman persecution of Christians related to the latter's refusal to practise emperor veneration, and their insistence that only Christ was divine and worthy of worship. After Constantine converted to Christianity, the tables were turned, and those who accepted the doctrines of Athanasius, as defined in the Creed of Nicaea, could pronounce anathemas (curses) against those who denied that Christ was eternally begotten of the Father, created rather than begotten, mutable, of 'like substance with the Father' rather than 'of one substance', and part of the penalty was excommunication, which involved being barred from participating in the Eucharist, or having one's baptism acknowledged as valid – forms of avoidance, in Allport's terminology.

Contemporary opposition to NRMs has two strands: the countercult movement and the anticult movement. The former is religious and essentially Christian in character, while the latter is predominantly secular. The countercult movement is principally Protestant and evangelical, and its modern expression parallels the rise of Christian fundamentalism and mission. Christian mission was essentially triumphalist in character, preaching the superiority of the Christian faith over the various religions with which it came into contact. Although the Protestant countercult movement largely focuses on the so-called cults, some of its missionary zeal is still directed against major faiths such as Hinduism, Buddhism and Islam, reflecting a continuing supremacist and colonialist view of other faiths. The missionary heyday began with William Carey, who founded the Particular Baptist Society for Propagating the Gospel among the Heathen in 1792, and undertook work in India, together with Joshua Marshman and William Ward. Carey wrote a pamphlet titled *An Enquiry into the Obligations of Christians to Use Means for the Conversion of the Heathens* (1792), in which he referred to 'the barbarous and savage manner of their living', and described their spirituality as 'heathen darkness'. William Ward's *A View of the History, Literature, and Religion of the Hindoos* (1817) displays a failure to empathize with the ideas of the religions, and uses rhetoric that would have no place today in the study of religion. To give one sample:

> It is difficult to restrain one's indignation at the shocking violation of every thing decent in this image; nor can it be ground of wonder, that a chaste woman, faithful

> to her husband, is scarcely to be found among all the millions of Hindoos, when their very temples are polluted with filthy images, and their acts of worship tend to inflame the mind with licentious ideas. (Ward 1817: xxix)

Fundamentalism took its rise in the late nineteenth century as a reaction against Darwinian evolution theory and critical biblical scholarship, and reaffirmed the Protestant Reformation principle of *sola scriptura* – scripture alone as the source of authority. Although the inerrancy of scripture was only one of its principles, it is the one that is most usually associated with the fundamentalist movement. Even today, many Protestants cannot understand the Roman Catholic attitude to scripture, which regards it as one of two sources of authority, the other being the church's tradition. R. A. Torrey's series of pamphlets titled *The Fundamentals: A Testimony to the Truth*, compiled from 1901 to 1915, contained two chapters directed at Roman Catholicism (by T. W. Medhurst and J. M. Foster, UK and US authors respectively), as well as the earliest critiques of Charles Taze Russell's *Millennial Dawn*, Mormonism, Christian Science and Spiritualism. Medhurst and Foster make several reasoned criticisms of Catholicism: these authors argue variously against papal infallibility, the Immaculate Conception, the number of sacraments, transubstantiation and the sacrifice of the Mass, and the church's historical association with temporal power.

The rise of modern opposition to 'cults' was couched in terms like heresy, idolatry and infidelity to scripture. Just as the Canaanite religions were judged to be contrary to Hebrew teaching, involving the use of material representations of their deities, the emerging countercult movement drew attention to differences between Roman Catholic teaching and their own understanding of the Bible. Medhurst writes:

> Can that be truly called Christianity, then, which is the reverse of it? Can that be fitly treated as Christianity which hates it, denounces it, and tries to destroy it? Can that be Christianity which forbids liberty of conscience, and the right of private judgement? Which commands the Bible to be burned? Which teaches the worship of saints and angels? Which makes the Virgin Mary command God? Which calls her the Mother of God, and the Queen of Heaven? Which sets aside the mediation of Christ, and puts others in His place? Which makes salvation depend on confession to man, and this is a confessional so filthy that Satan himself might well be ashamed of it? Can that be Christianity which condemns the way of salvation through faith, as a damnable heresy? Can that be Christianity which, by the bulls of its Popes, and decrees of its councils, requires both princes and people to persecute Christians? Which actually swears its bishops and archbishops to persecute them with all their might? Can that be Christianity which has set up, and

still maintains, the Inquisition? That which has been so cruel, so bloodthirsty, that the number slain by it of the servants of Christ, in about 1,200 years, is estimated at fifty millions, giving an average of 40,000 a year for that long period? No, it cannot be! With a voice of thunder, let Protestants answer, 'No!' (2013 [1910]: 766)

Amidst the somewhat hectic language in which this critique is couched, a number of Medhurst's concerns are worth noting, and which continue to form part of the Protestant countercult movement. One important issue is the concern for consistency with Christian scripture. Medhurst finds it impossible to understand why Roman Catholicism should be founded on anything other than the Bible. He expresses amazement that 'Romanism does not even profess to be founded on Scripture only' (Medhurst 2013 [1910]: 760), adding 'unwritten traditions'. Medhurst appears to think that the practices to which he objects were later additions to scripture, whereas, as I have argued elsewhere (Chryssides and Wilkins 2011: 197), one important difference between Roman Catholicism and Protestantism is the issue of whether the authority of scripture or the authority of the church came first, since it was the early church who defined the canon of scripture. Medhurst lays emphasis on Jesus' words 'Search the scriptures' (Jn 5.39), but ignores the fact that the scriptures to which Jesus was referring could not have been the totality of scripture, as defined by the church. When referring to scripture, Jesus mentions 'the Law and the Prophets' – not even the complete totality of Jewish scriptures, which in all probability was not formally defined until 90 CE.

Another concern relates to the necessity for direct access to God – a Reformation principle spearheaded by Martin Luther and his doctrine of the 'priesthood of all believers'. Medhurst mentions worship of saints and angels, although his portrayal of them as objects of worship is inaccurate: Roman Catholics do not invoke them directly, but request them to act as support to the worshipper. Part of the Protestant antagonism towards saints relates to their portrayal in statues, which are notably absent in Protestant churches, and are considered to be violations of the scriptural prohibition on 'graven images' – the same problem that the ancient Yahwists found in Canaanite religion. Yet another important concern is the doctrine of justification by faith. Protestant evangelicals typically express concern that one gains salvation through works, or by any other means other than faith.

Apart from such misunderstandings and inaccuracies, much of the language in which the opposition is couched is highly pejorative. The church itself is referred to as 'Romanism', and its practices as 'popery' and 'satanic delusion'.

'Heresy' as cult rhetoric

The countercult movement is principally concerned with maintaining true doctrine, and identifying what its supporters regard as false teachings which have emerged in new attempts to express the Christian faith. It is therefore understandable that the word 'heresy' should feature largely in the countercult critique of NRMs. In the history of Christianity, heresy largely has a very precise meaning. Thomas Aquinas defined heresy as 'a species of infidelity in men who, having professed the faith of Christ, corrupt its dogmas' (Aquinas, II-II:11.1), and defined two ways of embracing heresy: refusing to believe in Christ himself, and selecting one's beliefs at will, without accepting the whole 'deposit of faith'. To make heresy a formal misdemeanour, the accused heretic must obstinately adhere to his or her false teaching; simply to misunderstand one's faith and to accept correction is forgivable, but it is not acceptable to maintain erroneous belief once it has been pointed out. 'Heresy is the obstinate post-baptismal denial of some truth which must be believed with divine and catholic faith, or it is likewise an obstinate doubt concerning the same' (*Codex Iuris Canonici 1983*; quoted in Vatican 1994: para. 2089). The *Encyclopedia of Christianity* identifies three important components of heresy: it must go against formally defined Christian teaching, as expressed in formulated doctrinal statements; there must be formal criteria that distinguish faith that is necessary for salvation from 'sinful falsification'; and – importantly – in order to establish that heresy has been committed, there must be a court which has the authority to determine heresy and to exclude it (Mühlenberg 2022).

While there are clearly defined heresies within Christian history, the so-called heresies imputed to 'cults' have seldom, if ever, been subjected to ecclesiastical courts, since the majority of new religious movements have already separated themselves from the church, and in many cases do not wish to be part of it. In order to determine that these new expressions of Christian faith are heretical, their critics therefore require to locate an ancient heresy that has been formally defined by the church, and to demonstrate the consonance between that heresy and the 'cultic' tenets. One early attempt to do this is worth mentioning: Lewis B. Radford's *Ancient Heresies in Modern Dress* (1913). Unlike many more recent cult critiques, it is a scholarly publication: it is a collated written version of his Moorhouse Lectures, which were delivered at Saint Paul's Cathedral in Melbourne, and his material is closely argued. Radford focuses on the ancient heresies of gnosticism and Pelagianism, arguing that theosophy and Christian science in particular are new expressions of the former. Modern versions of Pelagianism (the heresy that exalts human effort above divine grace), he believes, can be found in the writings of Unitarians such as James Martineau and James Freeman Clarke (Radford 1913: 280-1). Radford also targets Adventist millenarianism, but not the Watch Tower organization, which had not yet established a significant presence in Australia.

Although the church's historical treatment of heresy has been unpleasant, the fundamental aim of weeding out heretics was to maintain the unity of the church and to maintain the 'deposit of faith' as defined within the church's tradition, without deviation. When the Protestant Reformers broke away from the Roman Catholic Church, the dependence on the church's tradition was severed, and there was no unified set of teachings to serve as a standard of authority. Each tradition defined its own set of doctrines, such as the Church of England's 39 Articles, the Westminster Confession of Faith and various other confessions throughout Europe. This did not necessarily mean that there was less concern with heresy: the Unitarians were a particular target, as was evidenced by the treatment of Michael Servetus, who was burnt at the stake in Geneva by order of John Calvin.

With the passage of time, heresy was dealt with more humanely, although not sympathetically, with each denomination having to determine how it would deal with the offender. Less formally, however, individual authors took it upon themselves to deal with perceived heresies, and some countercult organizations cross denominational boundaries to oppose what they regard as teachings that are judged to be contrary to scripture, which they uphold as the sole and supreme standard of authority. One early attempt at combatting 'false teachings' was William C. Irvine's *Timely Warnings* (1917), subsequently retitled *Modern Heresies Exposed* (1919), and later *Heresies Exposed* (1921). Writing in the introduction, Lewis T. Talbot argues that the rise of the various movements covered in the volume confirms Jesus' claim that false teachers would arise, and that their presence was a sign that humanity was living in the last days:

> If any man shall say unto you, Lo, here is Christ, or they are; believe it not. For there shall arise false Christs, and false prophets, and shall show great signs and wonders; insomuch that, if it were possible, they should deceive the very elect. (Matthew 24.23-24; quoted in Irvine 1960 [1917]: 3)

Associated with the concept of heresy was the word 'denial': the heretic is judged to have denied essential truths of the Christian faith. Talbot lists six: (1) 'denial of God and the Saviour'; (2) denial that Christ came in the flesh; (3) denial that Christ 'bought' sinners by his Atonement; (4) 'denial of the power of godliness'; (5) denial of sound doctrine, substituting 'fables' for truths; (6) denial of authority (Irvine 1960 [1917]: 4–5). Essentially mainstream Christianity has taken exception to movements that have added to scripture, since the canon of scripture is judged to be complete, and any belief that Christ has not completed his atoning work, requiring a new messiah or prophet. Thus, the Church of Jesus Christ of Latter-day Saints has been reckoned to be heretical since it has added the Book of Mormon to the Old and New Testaments; the Unification Church has taught that Jesus' mission was incomplete, and needs to be fulfilled by a new messiah, namely Sun Myung Moon, whose *Divine Principle* appears to be an additional scripture.

Two other pieces of vocabulary are worth noting: 'deviation' and 'counterfeit'. Horton Davies, an Anglican clergyman, wrote a short book titled *Christian Deviations*, which mainly targeted New Christian groups whom he believed to have deviated from mainstream Christian teachings. The word 'counterfeit' also gained momentum, although its application has gone beyond Christian-derived NRMs. The Spiritual Counterfeits Project was initially targeted at students at the University of California, and the notion of the spiritual counterfeit has been taken up by a number of countercult campaigners, such as the Reachout Trust in the UK. The word 'counterfeit' draws attention to the claim of certain emergent groups to be Christian, despite the fact that they deny certain key teachings of mainstream Christianity. By claiming to be Christian, these groups are purportedly counterfeiting the real Christian message, and arguably their followers are in greater danger than those who simply do not accept the Christian faith. Those who hold counterfeit currency think that they have the real thing, while those who have no money at least know that they are insolvent!

From countercult to anticult

The late 1960s saw a change in cult rhetoric, with the rise of the anticult movement (ACM). The ACM is different from the countercult movement (CCM) in a number of respects. The ACM was predominantly secular; although some of its members had their own religious affiliations, the critique of NRMs made no attempt to substitute some other form of religion in place of cult affiliation, and it professed to offer a critique of practices rather than doctrines. Much of the critique related to the belief that the so-called cults 'brainwashed' their members, initially at the stage of recruitment, and subsequently, following acquaintance with the organization, by a process of indoctrination.

The ACM took its rise in response to a new wave of new religions, which emerged in the 1960s and 1970s, much of which related to an emergent counterculture in the United States and Europe. There are numerous factors that affected their rise. Processes of secularization took their toll of Christian allegiance, and therefore fewer people were interested in theological truth and error. Additionally, many of the new religions made no claim to a Christian identity, for example the Hare Krishna movement, Scientology and new expressions of Buddhism, such as the New Kadampa Tradition. It was self-evident that adherents to these forms of spirituality did not accept the fundamental teachings of the Christian faith and, although organizations like the Spiritual Counterfeits Project originated from ex-members of non-Christian groups, any attempt to demonstrate that such organizations departed from mainstream Christianity was superfluous. Indeed, in many cases these NRM members deliberately sought alternatives to the Christian faith.

The decisive event in shaping public attitudes to NRMs was Jonestown: Jim Jones was a pastor in the Disciples of Christ who brought around 1,000 followers to Jonestown, Guyana, where 918 perished in the notorious mass murder-suicide of 18 November 1978. In everyday circumstances it is, of course, impossible to persuade even a small group of people to take their own lives, so the obvious question arose as to how it is possible for a leader of quite a large religious group to do this. Much literature has been directed at attempting to explain Jonestown, but because participation in the massacre did not appear to have been the result of rational persuasion, it could readily be inferred that there must be non-rational influences at work on the members of the community. Hence the brainwashing theory gained momentum.

The brainwashing theory derives from R. J. Lifton's study of US servicemen who became prisoners during the Korean War of 1950–3. Lifton's term was 'thought reform' and his *Thought Reform and the Psychology of Totalism* was based on research conducted in Hong Kong in 1954–5, which examines the way in which the Chinese treated American prisoners of war. His analysis demonstrates the way in which the environment was controlled, causing them to experience a loss of identity and feelings of guilt, making them denounce family and friends, causing psychological breakdown and extracting confessions. Lifton's claim that his analysis applies to other forms of extremism has been seized upon by the ACM, finding support from cult critics such as Margaret Singer, Janja Lalich and Steven Hassan, all of whom have contended that 'cult members' undergo brainwashing. Part of the rationale for brainwashing theory is that the majority who pursue conventional life outside NRMs find it difficult to understand why anyone should be tempted to join and to accept the worldview and lifestyle that an NRM presents. The application of the word 'cult' by these authors, extending beyond religious and spiritual groups, and spanning political, psychotherapeutic, educational and commercial organizations, promotes a much exaggerated view of their prevalence and alleged brainwashing tactics (e.g. Hassan 1988: 39–40; 2019: 3–4).

Ex-member rhetoric

Much recent anticult rhetoric, including brainwashing theory, comes from ex-members. Ex-member testimony has to be regarded with some caution, and NRM scholars have characteristically been wary of it, not to say dismissive. It should be kept in mind, as Stephen E. Gregg and I have pointed out, that it is only the vociferous members that tend to get heard. They are the ones that no doubt had bad experiences, have become embittered, and want to warn others or harbour grudges which they want to avenge by recounting atrocity tales. There are many who have personal reasons for leaving NRMs that do not necessarily involve any grievance, and those who simply lose interest and fade. Researchers of NRMs characteristically come across two categories: those who maintain allegiance to their chosen NRM, and the vociferous leavers, who join ex-member groups or anticult organizations, which can be readily accessed by the researcher (Gregg and Chryssides 2017). Particularly with the advent of the internet, it is very easy for ex-members to find other like-minded people with whom to share their experiences and air their grievances. Because of the ease of finding ex-member groups, some researchers have now taken to basing their studies on them. Obviously, it would be poor research to claim that these members are typical of those who leave the organizations, but the research can be justified in the name of 'interpretive phenomenological analysis'. In other words, the researcher can claim to be studying the testimony of these particular ex-members, who may or may not be typical. While this may sound fair and reasonable, the focus on the vociferous and organized ex-members can suggest that they are indeed typical, and the fact that they are researched while 'the silent majority' are not so accessible, leaves the latter without significant academic study. It is difficult to see how the silent majority can be accessed, although Gregg and I made a rough – and admittedly somewhat unscientific – estimate that the vociferous members only account for around 0.23 per cent of those who leave (Chryssides and Gregg 2017: 23). Anecdotally, I can state that

I have come across a small number of the silent majority who have explained their departure in somewhat uninteresting ways. One hairdresser, having heard of my interest in NRMs, divulged that she had belonged to the Soka Gakkai, but stopped going to their *gongyo* meetings because she did not like being out at night. Another acquaintance had undertaken a single Scientology course, which she rated as 'quite good', but declined to engage in any further study since she could not afford it. Yet another member of a Japanese Buddhist group told me he left because he did not like having to wear white robes in public, which he considered to be 'culturally inappropriate'.

Bryan R. Wilson and Lonnie D. Kliever have dismissed ex-member testimony almost entirely. Kliever writes, 'apostates from new religions do *not* meet the standards of personal objectivity, professional competence, and informed understanding required of expert witnesses' (Kliever 1995: 12; italics original). Wilson makes the following assertion, which understandably has angered some ex-members:

> Neither the objective sociological researcher nor the court of law can readily regard the apostate as a creditable or reliable source of evidence. He must always be seen as one whose personal history predisposes him to bias with respect to both his previous religious commitment and affiliations, the suspicion must arise that he acts from a personal motivation to vindicate himself and to regain his self-esteem, by showing himself to have been first a victim but subsequently to have become a redeemed crusader. As various instances have indicated, he is likely to be suggestible and ready to enlarge or embellish his grievances to satisfy that species of journalist whose interest is more in sensational copy than in a [*sic*] objective statement of the truth. (Wilson 1994: 4; punctuation as original)

James Beckford has suggested that ex-members typically devise a scenario after leaving an NRM to account for how they came to join the organization. Perhaps embarrassed by having spent time and money on a cause they have now rejected, it is understandable that they want to exonerate themselves from blame, and thus want to persuade others that they were lured into the movement by deception, or accepted the movement's teachings involuntarily through brainwashing, thus implying that the conversion was not a matter of personal choice (Beckford 1978: 112).

Both Wilson and Beckford should not be accepted uncritically, however. Particularly in the case of the older new religions, there are now second- and third-generation members who never actively joined in the first place, but were brought up in the organization. They have therefore no need to exonerate themselves, since any responsibility lies with their parents. Although the ex-member characteristically does not portray their former NRM in a favourable light, this does not imply that their testimony is worthless. On the contrary, particularly if they have held office within the organization that enables them to recount experiences that are not accessible to the public, their testimony can be valuable. One example is former Jehovah's Witness Brock Talon (pseudonym), who provides a very detailed description of what life was like in the Watch Tower Society's former headquarters in Brooklyn; another is Raymond V. Franz, who defected from the Society's Governing Body, and who gives some important insights into its workings and decision-making processes which would otherwise be completely inaccessible to any researcher (Franz 2000; Talon 2013).

First-generation converts and subsequent generations

Both the countercult and anticult movements include first-generation converts and second- (and subsequent-) generation members. Their situations differ somewhat, and present different issues if they decide to leave. Those who have been brought up in an NRM can find difficulties that do not apply to first-generation converts. Where the organization involves community living, or – as is the case with Jehovah's Witnesses – where interpersonal relationships are primarily forged within the organization, children and adolescents can experience difficulties in relating to the world outside the community. As is well-known, Jehovah's Witness children do not participate in traditional mainstream festivals or celebrate birthdays; and career expectations within the Watch Tower organization are less ambitious than average, hence difficulties can arise if they contemplate higher education. Finding a compatible marriage partner can be difficult within the congregation whose membership is between 100 and 150, and it is not surprising that adolescents sometimes seek nonbelieving partners. Additionally, both first-generation and subsequent-generation members can find difficulty in living up to an organization's required standards, resulting in withdrawal, suspension or expulsion. Since many new religions are typically highly demanding, members' lives are very much defined by the community, and therefore leaving can not only be a traumatic action but leave the former member without a community of friends and acquaintances. It is therefore understandable that these ex-members should wish to find a new community to forge new human relationships. With the advent of the internet, ex-member communities are very easy to find, and do not only provide instant new friendships, but a forum in which they can acknowledge their past experiences – a topic that they may feel embarrassed to mention in conventional circles.

However, every community has its own rules of engagement, and belonging to an ex-member group can play a major role in shaping or intensifying attitudes, which are almost invariably negative, causing reappraisal of one's past experiences, and even shaping one's past memories. This is not to deny the veracity of some ex-member accounts. There is little doubt, for example, that those who joined the Unification Church in the 1970s experienced poor living conditions, were asked to work unduly long hours, and in many cases experienced insufficient sleep. There is certainly substance to stories of members in some NRMs being made to fast for long periods, being subjected to physical violence from more senior members, soliciting or contributing substantial sums of money to the organization's funds, and to sexual abuse. Nonetheless, peer pressure plays an important role in determining which past memories one is encouraged to recount, and embellishing details can help to secure one's acceptance within the community.

Tactics

The grounds of cult criticism have developed in accordance with public concerns and particular periods. As I have mentioned earlier, countercult concerns with heresy became eclipsed by brainwashing theory. In more recent times, concern has extended to sexual impropriety, and accusations of sexual misconduct, particularly child abuse, have been applied to a wide range of NRMs. To a substantial degree, such criticism has been justified, and such reports have become a very serious concern. Accusations began with the Children of God (now The Family International) and have been proved justified in the case of Satya Sai Baba, Sogyal Rinpoche's Rigpa organization, Yogi Bhajan's Healthy Happy Holy community and the Triratna Buddhist Order. To learn of such activities within spiritual communities is of course shocking; nevertheless, it is important to ensure that the facts are accurately represented, and information properly interpreted.

Given the amount of publicity given to sexual abuse in a wide variety of organizations, some religious and some secular, it was inevitable that critics turned their attention to new religious movements. Jehovah's Witnesses have been particularly targeted by ex-member organizations and in the media. Sexual abuse is of course a highly sensitive topic, and academic researchers can easily be construed as 'cult apologists', who attempt to exonerate NRM leaders and their organizations, to minimize the extent of the abuse, or to be concerned with the perpetrators rather than the victims. It should therefore be emphasized that I have no wish to cover up the sexual abuse that has been perpetrated within NRMs. It is inexcusable, and even a single instance is one too many. Of course we should be concerned about the victims, who often are left with lifelong scars, and are very much in need of help and counselling support. Nonetheless, it is important that such abuses should be reported accurately, and neither exaggerated nor minimized, and it should not be suggested without firm evidence that what is true of one NRM is true of many. It should also be borne in mind that paedophiles are notoriously proficient at concealing their predilections, and there are no doubt many that have not been discovered, and will always remain undetected.

Having said this, it is easy for opponents, and for the media to seize on allegations and present a picture that arouses panic, and is at times unfair to the organizations about which comment is made. One recent example involves Jehovah's Witnesses. During the period 2014–17 numerous cases were brought before the courts, causing the Watch Tower Society to pay millions of dollars in compensation to victims. In 2015 the Australian Royal Commission reported about sexual abuse in a number of religious organizations, including Jehovah's Witnesses. Lloyd Evans, a vociferous ex-member and critic of Jehovah's Witnesses, provides the following summary:

> When Australia's Royal Commission did this, it found that 1,006 perpetrators from among Jehovah's Witnesses stretching back to 1950 had amassed around 1,800 victims, with not a single accusation of abuse reported to Australian authorities. Based on these figures, I scoured the Jehovah's Witness yearbook data and extrapolated a likely figure of 2,300+ perpetrators and 4,100+ victims for the entire UK. (Evans 2021)

The report does not in fact state that there were 1,006 perpetrators, but rather *alleged* perpetrators. Evans assumes that they are guilty until proved innocent. Of course, there may be unreported cases, and Evans's calculation for the UK would be roughly correct if one assumes that the ratio between perpetrators and members is the same in both countries. However, it should be remembered that the figure of 1,006 relates to a long period of time – 65 years in fact – which would mean that on average there were just over 15 perpetrators per year. Contrary to Evans, the report also states that 'there was no evidence before the Royal Commission that there were 1,800 victims' (Royal Commission 2016: 59).

Sociologist of religion Holly Folk clarifies the report's findings more accurately, as follows:

> We can now clarify the '1,006 perpetrator' statistic. It reflects the sum of all disciplinary reports and referrals, proven and unproven, that had been submitted to the Jehovah's Witness organization in Australia over a 65-year period. Half of those cases dealt with incest within the family household, committed by parents or siblings. Additional cases within that statistic concerned relatives other than parents or siblings, and others reported on abuse by friends of the victim's family. In other words, the vast majority of these 1,006 disciplinary reports concerned family sexual abuse and not 'institutional' abuse, done by anybody who could be considered clergy or a religious worker for the Jehovah's Witnesses organization.

She continues:

> Of the 1,006 case files that the Jehovah's Witnesses provided to the Royal Commission, 383 had been reported to the police at the time they had happened, and 161 had resulted in convictions. (Folk 2021)

There are issues concerning the reporting of sexual abuse in the media, at times encouraged by the anticult movement. Media reports have at times implied that sexual abuse has taken place on the Jehovah's Witnesses' premises, when in fact the Watch Tower organization does not organize events exclusively for children, who attend all meetings in the company of their parents. Jehovah's Witnesses may not have always handled sexual misconduct as they should, but a Kingdom Hall is certainly not a 'pedophile paradise', as one organization has claimed (Silentlambs n.d.) and, since becoming a baptized member involves stringent requirements, it is unlikely, as one critic suggests (Cutrer 2001), that a paedophile would deliberately join the organization for the purpose of molestation. The media frequently recycle stories, giving the impression of recurring sexual abuse incidents, when in fact the same story is being reproduced. Beckford calls these 'negative summary events', whereby readers or audiences are reminded of the same past event, but may believe it is a report of a fresh incident (Beckford 1985: 235). This practice is facilitated by the use of name anonymity, making it hard for the public to recognize that this is happening.

Spiritual abuse

In recent times attention has focused on the phenomenon of spiritual abuse, a concern which has proved to be shared by critics and academics alike. Attention to the phenomenon began in the early 1990s with David Johnson and Jeff VanVonderen's *The Subtle Power of Spiritual Abuse* (1991) and Ronald Enroth's *Churches That Abuse* (1992). Both books are popular rather than academic in style, and both direct attention to Christian churches rather than to NRMs more widely, although Enroth makes mention of the Churches of Christ and the phenomenon of discipling. Lisa Oakley and Kathryn Kinmond's *Breaking the Power of Spiritual Abuse* (2013) is a more substantial piece of academic research, although again focused on Christian churches. More recently, *Wounded Faith* (2021), a collection of essays edited by Neil Damgaard, former senior pastor of the Dartmouth Bible Church in North Dartmouth, Massachusetts, is prominently promoted by the International Cultic Studies Association (ICSA), and contains an introduction and a chapter from Michael D. Langone, a former president of ICSA.

The concept of spiritual abuse goes wider than sexual abuse, which is a definable category, and which has legal redress in many countries. Spiritual abuse, as understood by writers on the concept, involves dominating or manipulating others, and is usually, but not always, done by a spiritual leader. Lisa Oakley and Kathryn Kinmond offer the following definition:

> This abuse may include: manipulation and exploitation, enforced accountability, censorship of decision making, requirements for secrecy and silence, pressure to conform, misuse of scripture or the pulpit to control behaviour, requirement of obedience to the abuser, the suggestion that the abuser has a 'divine' position and isolation from others, especially those external to the abusive context. (2013: 4–5)

In *Wounded Faith* Langone writes:

> Spiritual abuse may be defined as injury to or mistreatment of the soul, of the deepest and most intimate aspects of a person's being. Spiritual abuse often results when a human being sets himself or herself up as a kind of selfish 'god' in another person's life, treating that person as an object that must be manipulated to serve the god's needs, agendas, and goals. (in Damgaard 2021: 40)

As portrayed in *Wounded Faith*, spiritual abuse is perpetrated primarily, although not exclusively, by overbearing spiritual leaders, who exercise undue control over their members' lives, and lack accountability, since they often belong to independent churches who are not subject to any external supervision, and who often lack any formal theological credentials or training. Spiritual abuse typically takes the form of asserting theological certainty, asserting that their teachings are divinely inspired, often misusing scripture to legitimize their authority, and disallowing any questioning or divergences of opinion. Some may intrusively demand disclosure of members' actions, even marital practices and secrets. They may make onerous demands on attendance, sometimes impacting on younger members' education, and impose financial obligations on their supporters. Spiritual abuse thus encompasses psychological, emotional and financial abuse, among other malpractices.

ICSA has applied the concept of spiritual abuse beyond Christian and Christian-related organizations, and has fostered a keen interest in the phenomenon. Indeed, in 2020 it established a new journal titled the *International Journal of Coercion, Abuse and Manipulation*. Its second edition carries two articles, by Stephen A. Kent and Phil Lord respectively, discussing alleged abuses of various kinds within the Church of Scientology. Kent deplores the way in which Scientology can circumvent labour law, claiming 'ministerial exception', defining itself as a religion. He criticizes what he regards as Hubbard's fabricated autobiographical details, and its internal legal system, which at least in the past has caused harsh punishments to be meted out to members of its Sea Org. Its vehement opposition to psychiatry, Kent argues, has caused numerous members to avoid conventional mental health treatment.

Here we are on difficult territory. Having esoteric teachings which are only disclosed to those who are in a state of readiness is not in itself a form of abuse. Nor is it inherently abusive for a spiritual community to have its own disciplinary system: religious organizations typically have ecclesiastical courts, sharia law, Beth Din and others. It is therefore important that proponents of the concept 'spiritual abuse' do not employ the term exclusively to NRMs, or allude to activities that are merely demanding or unusual. Should one really regard it as abusive if a leader uses soothing music and repetitive words to encourage greater spiritual commitment, as Maureen Griffo maintains (Damgaard 2021: 16)?

Many situations in the context of religion are clearly abusive or exploitative. Some years ago a prosperity gospel preacher gave a seminar in my area, which was attended by a sizeable audience of people who identified themselves as being in debt. The preacher averred that Jesus was rich rather than poor, and that their faith could make them debt free. This could professedly be achieved by sowing financial 'seeds' – in other words, making a generous contribution to his organization – and by buying his materials. He conceded that he was wealthy himself, but attributed this to practising what he preached.

However, it can be argued that we do not need the concept of spiritual abuse to characterize such situations. Writing in *Christianity Today*, Krish Khandia (2018) questions whether 'spiritual abuse' as a special category is really needed. Might we not classify the prosperity preacher's actions as financial abuse or, more generally, abuse of power, or simply exploitation? Khandia argues that, while abuse is found in a variety of contexts, we would not normally consider talking about football abuse or film producer abuse. She writes, 'the term *spiritual abuse* has been around in the UK for about 20 years. The difficulty has always come in its definition' (Khandia 2018; italics original).

Research and debate on spiritual abuse are likely to continue. The term has the advantage of not being pejorative, but its boundaries are unclear. Arguably the term serves to highlight areas in which abusive situations are likely, just as we talk about elder abuse, domestic abuse and child abuse. However, if it is to be of value as a special category, its application – in contrast to terms like 'cult' and 'brainwashing' – need to be given reasonably predictable and incontestable content.

Conclusion

Those who criticize cult rhetoric can readily be construed as 'cult apologists', but I certainly do not wish to imply that all is well within NRMs. On the contrary, much is certainly amiss, although numerous malpractices are also shared by traditional religions. Perhaps academics have been reluctant to call out abuses in NRMs, no doubt because of scholarly commitment to neutrality, and their concern to understand rather than to complain or campaign. At times apparent support of NRMs has been in the interests of religious freedom and rebutting inaccurate and unfair characterizations. It is possible that the recent interest in spiritual abuse might serve as a meeting ground between at least some anticultists and NRM scholars. Just as NRMs should enjoy freedom of religion, provided they act responsibly and within the law, critics should also be free to voice concerns. Nonetheless, as I have argued, there is a need for fair and measured criticism, and avoidance of the pejorative language and misleading information that have been characteristic of past critiques. Criticism can only have force if it is based on accurate information and reasoned argument. Once cogent criticism replaces anticult rhetoric, the various stakeholders may be able to find more common meeting ground.

References

Allport, G. W. (1954), *The Nature of Prejudice*. Reading: Addison-Wesley.
Aquinas, T. (1920), 'Summa Theologica. II', 2nd rev. edn, trans. Fathers of the English Dominican Province. New Advent [Online] Available at www.newadvent.org/summa/3092.htm (accessed 12 August 2021).

Beckford, J. A. (1978), 'Through the Looking-Glass and out the Other Side: Withdrawal from Reverend Moon's Unification Church', *Archives de Sciences Sociales Des Religions*, 45 (1): 95–116.

Beckford, J. A. (1985), *Cult Controversies*. London: Tavistock.

Carey, W. and E. A. Payne (1792), *An Enquiry into the Obligations of Christians to Use Means for the Conversion of the Heathens*. London: Carey Kingsgate Press.

Chryssides, G. D. and M. Z. Wilkins (2011), *Christians in the Twenty-First Century*. London: Equinox.

Cutrer, C. (2001), 'Sex Abuse: Witness Leaders Accused of Shielding Molesters', *Christianity Today*, 5 March. Available at https://www.christianitytoday.com/ct/2001/march5/11.23.html (accessed 26 April 2023).

Damgaard, N. (2021), *Wounded Faith: Understanding and Healing From Spiritual Abuse*. Bonita Springs: International Cultic Studies Association.

Davies, H. (1954), *Christian Deviations*. London: SCM.

Enroth, R. (1992), *Churches That Abuse*. Grand Rapids: Zondervan.

Evans, L. (2021), 'The Child Abuse Inquiry has been too Deferential to the Jehovah's Witnesses', *National Secular Society*, 25 August. Available at https://www.secularism.org.uk/opinion/2021/08/the-child-abuse-inquiry-has-been-too-deferential-to-the-jehovahs-witnesses (accessed 3 November 2022).

Folk, H. (2021), 'Jehovah's Witnesses and Sexual Abuse: 1. The Australian Case', *Bitter Winter*, 12 January. Available at https://bitterwinter.org/jehovahs-witnesses-and-sexual-abuse-1-the-australian-case (accessed 1 March 2021).

Franz, R. (2000), *Crisis of Conscience: The Struggle between Loyalty to God and Loyalty to One's Religion*, 3rd edn. Atlanta: Commentary Press.

Gregg, S. E. and G. D. Chryssides (2017), 'The Silent Majority?: Understanding Apostate Testimony beyond "Insider/Outsider" Binaries in the Study of New Religions', in E. V. Gallagher (ed.), *Visioning New and Minority Religions*, 20–32. London: Routledge.

Hassan, S. (1988), *Combatting Cult Mind Control*. Rochester: Aquarian Press.

Hassan, S. (2019), *The Cult of Trump*. New York: Free Press.

Irvine, W. C. (1960 [1917]), *Heresies Exposed*. New York: Loizeaux.

Johnson, D. and J. V. Vonderen (1991), *The Subtle Power of Spiritual Abuse*. Minneapolis: Bethany House.

Kent, S. A. (2021), 'Comparative Reflections on Scientology and NXIVM', *International Journal of Coercion, Abuse and Manipulation*, 1 (2): 3–26.

Khandia, K. (2018), 'Does The Church's First Spiritual Abuse Verdict Give Critics a New Weapon?', *Christianity Today*, 12 January. Available at www.christianitytoday.com/ct/2018/january-web-only/spiritual-abuse-church-england-guilty-verdict-ccpas-survey.html (accessed 26 April 2023).

Kliever, L. D. (1995), *The Reliability of Apostate Testimony About New Religious Movements*. Los Angeles: Freedom Publishing.

Lifton, R. J. (1989 [1961]), *Thought Reform and the Psychology of Totalism: A Study of 'Brainwashing' in China*. Chapel Hill, NC: University of North Carolina Press.

Lord, P. (2021), 'The Eternal Commitment: Scientology's Billion-Year Contract', *International Journal of Coercion, Abuse and Manipulation*, 1 (2): 82–97.

Medhurst, T. W. (2013 [1910]), 'Is Romanism Christianity?', in R. A. Torrey et al. (eds), *The Fundamentals: A Testimony to the Truth*, 759–67. Fort Collins: Delmarva Publications.

Moorehead, W. G. (1910), 'Millennial Dawn: A Counterfeit of Christianity', in R. A. Torrey et al. (eds), *The Fundamentals: A Testimony to the Truth*, vol. 4, 91–108. Los Angeles, CA: AGES Software Rio.

Mühlenberg, E. (2011), 'Heresies and Schisms', *Encyclopedia of Christianity Online*. Available at http://dx.doi.org/10.1163/2211-2685_eco_H105 (accessed 2 November 2022).

Oakley, L. and K. Kinmond (2013), *Breaking the Silence on Spiritual Abuse*. London: Palgrave Macmillan.

Radford, L. B. (1913), *Ancient Heresies in Modern Dress*. Melbourne: George Robertson & Co.

Royal Commission (2016), 'Report of Case Study No. 29'. Available at www.childabuseroyalcommission.gov.au/sites/default/fi les/fi le-list/Case%20Study%2029%20-%20Findings%20Report%20-%20Jehovahs%20Witnesses.pdf (accessed 1 March 2021).

Silentlambs (n.d.), 'Pedophile Paradise – Why?'. Available at https://silentlambs.org/news/pedophile-paradise-why (accessed 8 November 2022).

Talon, B. (2013), *Journey to God's House: An Inside Story of Life at the World Headquarters of Jehovah's Witnesses in the 1980s*. USA: Brock Talon Enterprises.

Vatican (1993), *Catechism of the Catholic Church*. London: Geoffrey Chapman.

Ward, W. (1817), *A View of the History, Literature, and Religion of the Hindoos: Including a Minute Description of their Manners and Customs and Translations from their Principal Works*, vol. 1. London: Black, Parbury and Allen. Available at www.archive.org/stream/wardshidoos00sethuoft/wardshidoos00sethuoft_djvu.txt (accessed 10 June 2010).

Wilson, B. R. (1994), *Apostate and New Religious Movements*. Los Angeles: Freedom Publishing.

4

The paradigm shift from sacred to profane

William Sims Bainbridge

Secularization may not cause religion to vanish, but traditional churches appear to be losing respect and influence, even in the United States which has always given faith a privileged status. One perplexing consequence seems to be the widespread emergence of 'cults' that do not explicitly use religious rhetoric. Carolyn Chen's (2022) study of high-tech Silicon Valley corporations documented that many of them have taken on cultic functions, for example promoting meditation and mindfulness among employees, yet avoiding religious rhetoric. One important factor shaping the cultural dynamics has been the severe anticult rhetoric that followed the proliferation of unusual religious movements in the 1960s (Robbins 1981; Robbins and Anthony 1982). Yet other factors are also at work, such as the secularization trend and so-called culture wars, so such factors must be combined in our analysis to achieve maximum understanding.

As John Horgan (1996) suggested in his book, *The End of Science*, it may no longer be possible to answer profound questions about the nature of reality through systematic discovery. Something like secularization may be eroding faith in science, perhaps resulting in repaganization (Bainbridge 2017a). Simultaneous death of faith in both religion and science could produce an explosion of cults, even while draining meaning from our terminology. However, the result may be the consolidation of many individually coherent typologies, for example the spiritual rhetoric a particular group uses to promote itself versus opponents who use 'cult' as an insult against a rival subculture.

Definitions during an age of chaos

As a cult leader once proclaimed, 'The word is not the thing. The map is not the territory.' Or, from its own perspective, that was one of the axioms of an academic discipline known as General Semantics, developed by Alfred Korzybski, that not only stressed the rhetorical aspects of linguistics but also served as an alternative form of psychotherapy (Korzybski 1941; Bainbridge 1994). Two of Korzybski's disciples illustrated how the same ideas can be framed in highly contrasting rhetorics. Science fiction author A. E. van Vogt (1948) wrote the brilliant novel *The World of Ā*, imagining a future society based on General Semantics, in which it served not only as the state religion but also its rigid system of social status. 'Ā' or 'null-A' was another radical principle of General Semantics that nothing had a stable meaning, so even in mathematics A ≠ A. Subsequently, van Vogt became a disciple of his science fiction colleague, L. Ron Hubbard, in Dianetics, the early form of Scientology. The other Korzybski disciple was S. I. Hayakawa (1949), who published the bland textbook widely used in conventional education, *Language in Thought and Action*, and who later held the respectable job of senator in the US government. Note how one subculture of innovative ideas could be described in both religious and secular rhetorics.

There are many theories of secularization, and a good deal of recent statistical research documenting the rapid decline of traditional religious organizations in many economically advanced nations, but a consensus has not been achieved. Cultural conservatives might want to read the multi-volume study *Social and Cultural Dynamics* (Sorokin 1937–41), that offered a cyclical theory of secularization, arguing that every great civilization begins as an *ideational* culture, asserting that reality is spiritual rather than material, then gradually becomes more *sensate*, abandoning supernatural beliefs and disintegrating via enlightenment ironically into a Dark Age. The very informative recent book *Beyond Doubt: The Secularization of Society* analyses two related processes: (1) *differentiation*, during which religious institutions separate gradually from other institutions of society, most significantly from government, and (2) *rationalization*, 'the ordering of society based on technological efficiency, bureaucratic impersonality, and scientific and empirical evidence' (Kasselstrand, Zuckerman and Cragun 2023: 27). *Beyond Doubt* cites a great number of surveys done across many nations, but they often measure the fraction of the population believing in God, thus measuring decline in *monotheism*, given that the particular nations are largely Christian, while ancient *polytheism* may have been more compatible with social differentiation.

In the King James version, Phil. 4.20 proclaims: 'Now unto God and our Father be glory for ever and ever. Amen.' The poetic Vulgate Latin for *forever* was *in saecula saeculorum*, referring to an age of ages, and the online Perseus Digital Library (n.d.a) defines *saeculum* as 'a race, generation, age, the people of any time'. Thus, *secularization* can be interpreted to mean retreat from eternity into the mundane culture of our current era, and religion's *secular trend* may be disintegration into fragments of various sizes and shapes. Another phrase in that biblical quote also has obscure meaning: 'our Father'. As civilization escapes from patriarchy to some form of gender equality, God may become 'our Mother', representing nurturance rather than authority. But the perplexing word in the phrase is 'our'. Returning to an even more ancient saeculum, Exodus 7 describes a fascinating episode:

> And Moses and Aaron went in unto Pharaoh, and they did so as the Lord had commanded: and Aaron cast down his rod before Pharaoh, and before his servants, and it became a serpent.
>
> Then Pharaoh also called the wise men and the sorcerers: now the magicians of Egypt, they also did in like manner with their enchantments.
>
> For they cast down every man his rod, and they became serpents: but Aaron's rod swallowed up their rods.
>
> And he hardened Pharaoh's heart, that he hearkened not unto them; as the Lord had said.

Yes, his God had given Aaron magical powers, transforming his staff into a serpent, more powerful than serpents created by 'the magicians of Egypt'. Yet the priests had supernatural powers of their own. Exodus tells the tale of a magical war between two cultures, the vast Egyptian empire with multiple conflicted gods versus the oppressed Hebrews who lacked their own land but did possess one powerful Lord. Thus, prior to appropriation by Christianity and Islam, Jehovah was the God of a particular people, eternal but not universal. As the son and grandson of Jewish rabbis, this heritage may have helped the great French sociologist Émile Durkheim, who observes in *The Elementary Forms of the Religious Life* that 'the sacred principle is nothing more nor less than society transfigured and personified' (1915: 347; Parsons 1975). Christianity and Islam seem to have failed to unify humanity, so religion may gradually disintegrate, not dying but losing power and even clarity of definition.

Perseus (n.d.b) reports that the Latin word '*religio*' meant 'conscientiousness, sense of right, moral obligation, duty'. Given that English drew upon Latin in the context of Christianity, *religion* added God to its definition, and the churches served to define and promote morality. However, Europe and the Middle East are but small parts of our world, that may no longer define *religion* globally. I was fortunate to have an aunt who belonged to the pre-revolutionary aristocracy of China, and she once exclaimed to me: 'Bill, we Chinese are not religious! We are Confucian.' The current government of China promulgates an ideology comparable to Confucianism, if not identical to its national tradition: godless, rule-oriented morality.

Perseus (n.d.c) defines *pagus* as 'a district, canton, hundred, province, region', which implies that pagan religions are local, the worship by a small community of a former resident whom legend transformed into a saint, or of a deity that metaphorically represented their local environment. Over time, the definition of the deity may evolve, becoming more cosmopolitan or aggressive. Athena, the female personification of ancient Athens, drove the military ambitions of the men who worshipped her, demanding expansion of her city and of the definition of *goddess*.

Decades ago I contemplated the goddess Sulis at her water shrine in the English town named Bath, derived from its Latin name *Aquae Sulis*, 'the waters of Sulis', whom the Romans identified with their own Minerva. A standard challenge for ancient empires was how to assemble a unified culture out of its many local cultures, and that may be the ultimate function of monotheism. Polytheism is not merely an alliance of the gods of separate tribes, but belief that multiple supernatural persons represent distinct aspects of nature, such as Neptune being the god of the sea, and also personality dimensions, such as Loki being the deception deity. Furthermore, gods may not have even yet existed at the beginning of time, only evolving like ourselves from nature, themselves worshipping the World Tree named Yggdrasil.

Repaganization need not revive polytheism specifically, as some of the following examples illustrate. Sociology has long debated the apparently curvilinear structure of society over history, beginning with simple kinship structures among hunter-gatherers, complex and formal in tribal and agricultural societies, and again simple and flexible today (Blumberg and Winch 1972). Perhaps supernaturalism will also have a curvilinear history, with well-organized state religions thriving in agriculture-based empires, encountering challenges during the Industrial Revolution, and returning eventually to small-scale social structures.

If society is a mosaic of subcultures, rather than monolithic and monotheistic, what is the meaning of 'cult'? In 1978 I published an ethnography titled *Satan's Power: A Deviant Psychotherapy Cult* that proposed: 'Cult is culture writ small'. This was a reflection of Margaret Mead's assessment that her mentor Ruth Benedict (1959) considered culture to be 'personality writ large'. I also defined *cult* as 'a culturally innovative cohesive group oriented to supernatural concerns'

(Bainbridge 1978: 14), but that left *supernatural* undefined. In order to protect the privacy of members of the group I had studied, I gave each individual a pseudonym and called the cult The Power, although soon colleagues were aware it was really The Process. It was an offshoot of Scientology and Psychoanalysis, originally named Compulsions Analysis, that consolidated into a commune, then postulated that God had divided into four competing deities to play The Game of the Gods: Jehovah against Lucifer, Satan against Christ, and each human reflecting one or two of these four competing spiritual personalities. Neither Scientology nor Psychoanalysis then postulated the existence of a god, yet The Process implied that both of its parents had the qualities of religious culture, given that its own rhetoric had evolved from secular to religious.

Sigmund Freud, the pope of psychoanalysis, pondered the resemblance between primitive beliefs and neuroticism, notably in *The Future of an Illusion*. One of his disciples, Geza Roheim (1915), went so far as to consider supernaturalism as a psychosis, not merely a neurosis. The decline of academic status suffered by psychoanalysis over the past half-century suggests that psychoanalysis may itself have been an illusion, a form of neurosis rather than a cure for it (Bainbridge 2012b). Psychoanalytic concepts like id, ego and superego, or postulation of a subconscious mind, are reminiscent of religions that conceptualized the soul as a structure of spiritually distinct components, such as the Ba and Ka of ancient Egypt (Arnett 1904; Carus 1905). Several authors have placed psychoanalysis in the Jewish mystical tradition (Bakan 1958; Berkower 1969; Fodor 1971). A very obvious cultic connection is to Mesmerism, founded by Franz Anton Mesmer, who postulated a magical force, often called *animal magnetism* (Darnton 1970), and developed the practice of hypnosis that was central to Freud's early work with Josef Breuer (1936). They used hypnosis-like methods to treat hysteria, often represented as multiple-personality neurosis, itself a fantasy pathology that may have been nothing more than ritualistic role-playing between cult magicians and their mesmerized followers.

As we were developing our rather ornate theory of religion, Rodney Stark and I contemplated terms similar to *cult* in the sociology of religious movements, notably *magic* and *sect*. Magic seems more immediate than religion, rhetorically relating to the worldly desires of humans and perhaps more susceptible to empirical refutation than exalted faith that placed God at such a distance that he could not be observed by sceptics. *Sects* seem structurally similar to cults, but less innovative, often serving as emotionally intense revivals of traditional faiths. Further contemplation suggested that cults might be divided into three subtypes, in terms of their social structure as well as beliefs and goals.

Cult movements were comparable to religious sects, competing with but modelled at least abstractly on society's major religious institutions. *Client cults* were more magical, offering cures and similar services to individual clients, thus structured more like one business in a marketplace of many. *Audience cults* resembled mass media in secular culture, promoting mythologies that often did not seem religious, such as flying saucers, for decades in periodicals like *Fate Magazine*, and today online (Bainbridge and Stark 1979, 1980a). Indeed, audience cults are mere rhetorics, lacking most of the social features of well-organized religions. In the world described by such terms, pseudoscience is practically the same thing as religious heresy.

Difficult times

Once upon a time, a novice was wandering the fifth floor of St. James Temple on Divinity Avenue, when he noticed that the local parson had placed a pile of sacrificial offerings for the students to add to their sacred archives. Or, shifting the rhetoric, when I was a graduate student at Harvard with an office on the fifth floor of William James Hall, tremendously influential sociologist Talcott Parsons gave away copies of writings by Anne Parsons, his only daughter who had died a decade earlier, a victim of suicide and/or psychoanalysis. We may hypothesize that Talcott Parsons was the leader of a post-religious cult named Structural Functionalism, in a Vatican named the Harvard Department of Social Relations that disintegrated soon after his daughter's tragic death (Bainbridge 2012a). It combined sociology with cultural anthropology and forms of social psychology often influenced by psychoanalysis, imagining that somehow society was destined to advance towards perfection (Parsons 1974).

Exactly why Anne Parsons left this life is open to multiple interpretations, but apparent factors were psychoanalysis that may have increased rather than reduced her psychological distress, and the cultural suppression of creative women in the larger society during the 1950s when psychoanalysis was popular. Sociologist Winifred Breines reports: 'She was an unusually talented intellectual, bringing passion, integrity, and insight to her research, the interdisciplinary nature of which worked against her professionally. Her studies of religion, mental illness, family dynamics and social change, and psychoanalytic theory, all from a cross-cultural and vigorously anti-ethnocentric perspective, should become part of known social scientific research, and even wisdom' (Breines 1986: 808–9). After her death, her colleagues published a collection of her writings with the deep title, *Belief, Magic, and Anomie: Essays in Psychological Anthropology* (Parsons 1969). Had she survived, I hope I would have had the courage to interview her about the possibility that her father's Structural Functionalism was a religious cult that punished her for being a heretic.

Talcott Parsons was a disciple of Max Weber, even translating Weber's (1930) classic *The Protestant Ethic and the Spirit of Capitalism* from German into English, and both saw religion as an historically significant societal institution that might eventually bequeath its functions to secular organizations. Auguste Comte argued that sociology was the positivist successor of religion, and Parsons certainly was familiar with Comte's (1883) catechism. Parsons's ambitious 1964 article, 'Evolutionary Universals in Society', considered religion to be historically fundamental, but explained how it bequeathed some of its functions to newer institutions of society as they were constructed over the centuries.

As a basis for contemplating the future of religious cults during an era of secularization that has eroded religious rhetoric, Table 4.1 lists historical movements near the border of religion, and their leaders, along with the number of times someone viewed the Wikipedia articles about them during the year 2021, a rough measure of popular interest. The fourth, New Thought, was influenced by Mesmerism through Phineas Quimby, whose Wikipedia article currently ends with the debate about the extent to which Christian Science was inspired by him, given that for a time he was the doctor of its founder, Mary Baker Eddy. Successful religious cults often combine cultural memes from multiple sources, so Christian Science can be placed at the border of the New Thought movement, if not fully inside (Bainbridge 1985, 1997b). Divine Science is listed in Table 4.1, despite having very low pageviews, to remind us that cults may come into existence as sets rather like a new generation in a family, here from the marriage of New Thought and Protestantism.

Scientology has no discernable connection to Christianity, and like many forms of Buddhism lacked a god, but was able to register legally as a religion. I first became aware of it prior to its birth, because by age eleven in 1952 I had read about L. Ron Hubbard's pre-religious version of it in the magazine *Astounding Science Fiction*, including his 1950 article 'Dianetics – The Evolution of a Science'. Only many years later did I discover my family connection, via my great uncle Consuelo Seoane, who shared a radical adventure with Joseph 'Snake' Thompson, whom Scientology considers to be a primary influence motivating L. Ron Hubbard to create Scientology. Snake mentored young Hubbard in 1923, shortly after returning 'from Vienna where he had studied Psychoanalysis with Sigmund Freud' (Church of Scientology International,

Table 4.1 Wikipedia Pageviews for Related Movements and Their Leaders

Group or Movement	Pageviews	Leader	Pageviews	Lifespan
Structural Functionalism	253,076	Talcott Parsons	137,803	1902–79
Mesmerism	110,312	Franz Anton Mesmer	87,066	1734–1815
Psychoanalysis	440,970	Sigmund Freud	2,198,101	1856–1939
New Thought	178,079	Phineas Quimby	24,698	1802–66
Christian Science	588,898	Mary Baker Eddy	145,318	1821–1910
Divine Science	13,085	Malinda Cramer	2,115	1844–1906
Scientology	2,149,295	L. Ron Hubbard	1,017,839	1911–86
The Process Church	270,012	Robert de Grimston	48,186	1935–
Thelema	634,187	Aleister Crowley	1,662,000	1875–1947
AMORC	117,334	Harvey Spencer Lewis	17,962	1883–1939
Rosicrucian Fellowship	31,931	Max Heindel	14,731	1865–1919
Sons of the Desert	29,866	Laurel and Hardy	774,634	1890–1965
Transcendental Meditation	539,721	Maharishi Mahesh Yogi	421,847	1918–2008
Oneida Community	150,955	John Humphrey Noyes	28,171	1811–86
Kiryas Joel	107,451	Joel Teitelbaum	41,596	1887–1979
Swedenborgian Church	11,663	Emanuel Swedenborg	269,556	1688–1772

n.d.). In the years 1909–11, Snake and Consuelo had been spies operating under assumed identities, charting possible invasion routes in Japan for the US military (Seoane 1960; Seoane 1968). According to family legend, Seoane and Thompson actually tricked the secretary of war into signing the approval for their amazing mission, as they succeeded in tricking the Japanese into believing they were Boer herpetologists from South Africa, enemies of England but friends of Japan, documenting the reptiles and amphibia of the coastal areas (Bainbridge 2009). Their adventure illustrated how deceptive rhetoric can be influential in real life, or how fantasies can sometimes turn out to be realities.

The connections between scientistic and religious rhetorics are well illustrated by Scientology's *e-meter*, an electronic device used to guide spiritual development interaction sessions comparable to psychotherapy between an auditor (therapist) and preclear (client), with the initial goal of *clearing* mental burdens called *engrams* from the mind of the preclear, but also used to chart memories of previous incarnations (Bainbridge and Stark 1980b). When I studied Scientology ethnographically in 1970, I obtained an e-meter, learned how to use it, and found it to be rather effective technology. Comparable to a component of the proverbial 'lie detector', it monitors galvanic skin response, indicating with a degree of accuracy the preclear's emotional reaction and thus through a display needle guiding the auditor in asking questions or giving instructions. Around 1974, near the end of my research in The Process, I used my e-meter as an interview tool, given that The Process had inherited use of the e-meter for advanced spiritual exploration sessions, but had renamed it the p-scope. Around 1983, I gave a lecture about e-meters at Harvard, indeed in the basement auditorium of William James Hall, attended by the public relations director of Scientology of Boston. I showed how it was easy to replace the display needle with an Apple II computer, visualizing the preclear's reactions via a dynamic bar graph and saving all the data. A few years later, Scientology invited me to its California branch, where I saw that in training sessions for auditors their e-meters were connected to their teacher's computer, but we did not discuss whether my experiments had contributed at all to their innovations.

Thelema inspired both Scientology and The Process, Processeans even at one point living at Aleister Crowley's Abbey of Thelema at Cefalú on the north coast of Sicily (Symonds 1958). AMORC (Ancient Mystical Order Rosae Crucis), Rosicrucian Fellowship and Sons of the Desert represent fraternal lodges I have studied that were also influential, and I would have included Masonic groups had I done research on them (Jolicoeur and Knowles 1978; Bainbridge 1985). Oh, wait: *Sons of the Desert* is a highly regarded 1933 comedy movie satirizing the then still popular secular fraternal organizations, in which Stan Laurel and Oliver Hardy struggle to attend their lodge's lascivious annual meeting, despite the opposition of their wives. Of course, fiction is a form of rhetoric that often offers metaphors of reality. Here is an example, replacing the rhetorical 'heaven' in a popular quote from Robert Brownings poem, 'Andrea del Sarto': 'Ah, but a man's reach should exceed his grasp, Or what's a metaphor?'

Two key features shared by Scientology, The Process and traditional fraternal groups are: (1) they have ritualistic cultures, (2) members are ranked up a ladder of social status and must actively adopt the culture to ascend to a higher *degree*. Colleges are artificial ladders ranking social status, that traditionally favoured men over women, so not very different from fraternal lodges. We might elsewhere explore how each school of thought in the Humanities cultivated by academics is a cult.

The last four organizations in Table 4.1 are not closely connected to the others, but make clear points. Transcendental Meditation has a cultural basis in the religious traditions of India, yet presented itself as a psychological school of thought when it came to the United States (Bainbridge and Jackson 1981). Today, the website of Maharishi International University in Iowa calls itself the 'Home of Consciousness-Based Education' and reports: 'The National Institutes of Health (NIH) have awarded over \$26 million to research TM's effectiveness on stress and stress-related conditions' (n.d.: online).

Oneida was a radical religious commune, yet its leader, John Humphrey Noyes, was a Yale graduate who published a high-quality study of comparable social movements, *History of American Socialisms* (Noyes 1870). His group marriage system, organized so children would be fathered by the most spiritually developed men, had a scientific basis, if one that science has outgrown. Noyes himself fathered thirteen children with thirteen women, following the rhetoric that he was most spiritually advanced of all, and thus his children would begin life with significant spiritual superiority, which today seems outrageous (Bainbridge 2017b). However, during his lifetime, Jean-Baptiste Lamarck's theory of inheritance of acquired characteristics was respectable within biological science, and has recently had a slight revival within the subfield of epigenetics (Balter 2000; Burggren and Crews 2014).

I am not well prepared to study Kiryas Joel, because I do not speak the languages of most residents, and am not familiar with its ancient tradition. However, I inherited a personal connection that has forced me to think deeply in recent years about what it may mean for American society more generally. Throughout childhood, I often visited Green Hollow Farm, owned by my grandfather, William E. Sims, a leading Wall Street attorney, and tended by tenant farmers. In 1939, a local newspaper noted he had bought this historic mansion 'built with stone quarried and cut on the place'. He was an expert if amateur historian, using skills that had great value for the legal profession. Among his most famous cases was his successful effort to overturn a US court decision that had awarded extensive properties of the Russian Orthodox Church in America to the puppet Archbishop in the Soviet Union, awarding them instead to their local congregations, a victory that required him to study closely the history of that denomination. His substantial library contained a few parapsychology and Occult books, and he subscribed to the series of histories about societal collapse written by Arnold Toynbee (1947–57). Motivated by simple nostalgia, in 2018 I tried to find his home by virtually driving around Monroe, New York, in the online street view version of Google Maps. I could not find it, so I checked Facebook groups devoted to the town, and my motivation shifted suddenly to the social science of religion, because Green

Hollow Farm had become the Kiryas Joel religious community (Bainbridge 2018: 278–86).

Much of their economy is collaborative and operates apart from the dollar markets that surround them. With help from controversial New York governor Andrew Cuomo, Kiryas Joel separated officially from Monroe in 2018, renamed Palm Tree, a translation of the last name of charismatic founder, Joel Teitelbaum. This may be the first step in a revolution, eventually ending the separation of church and state, encouraging creation of religiously uniform communities of many types across the nation. Oh, at first the spirit of my deceased grandfather hoped they would use his home as Teitelbaum's residence, or a very practical suite of offices, but it has been torn down, and Mr. Sims posthumously deduced that this was an interesting prophecy of what may happen to American institutions more generally in the coming years.

The reason for adding the Swedenborgian Church at the end of the table is not merely because Swedenborgianism is a rhetorical bridge between religion and astronomy. Mysteriously, the administrative offices of the Swedenborgian Church of North America are across Kirkland Street from William James Hall, and at the intersection with Divinity Avenue. William James was raised in Swedenborgianism, and after deep psychological stress, he became one of the world's first academic psychologists, promoting a view of religion that did not require faith:

> The true is the name of whatever proves itself to be good in the way of belief, and good, too, for definite, assignable reasons ... 'The true' to put it very briefly, is only the expedient in the way of our thinking, just as 'the right' is only the expedient in our way of behaving. (James 1907: 76, 222)

Thus, if a spaceship ever takes us to heaven, and we see it is devoid of gods, we may still remain devoted to God if that is pragmatically valuable, for example supporting ethical behaviour towards other human beings.

General compensators

My research on The Process was not merely a follow-up to my study of Scientology, in which Robert de Grimston and his partner Mary Ann MacLean had trained as auditors, but was inspired by reading publications like *Doomsday Cult* by John Lofland (1966). I admired Lofland's article with Rodney Stark (1965), 'Becoming a World-Saver', which is like an application of Sutherland's

(1947) differential association theory to cults, and also quite compatible with George Homans's (1950, 1974) behavioural sociology. I was a graduate student teaching assistant for Homans, who was chairman of the Harvard Sociology Department, after it broke away from Social Relations, and an opponent of Talcott Parsons. The Lofland–Stark model conceptualizes religion as a *problem-solving perspective*, mentioning that many people might respond to life's stresses from different problem-solving perspectives, such as those using political or psychiatric rhetorics. When Stark and I began collaborating it felt quite natural to conceptualize religion in terms of its pragmatic applications rather than faith in gods. We began our theory of religion (Stark and Bainbridge 1987) with seven simple axioms:

> *Axiom 1:* Human perception and action take place through time, from the past into the future.
>
> *Axiom 2:* Humans seek what they perceive to be rewards and avoid what they perceive to be costs.
>
> *Axiom 3:* Rewards vary in kind, value, and generality.
>
> *Axiom 4:* Human action is directed by a complex but finite information-processing system that functions to identify problems and attempt solutions to them.
>
> *Axiom 5:* Some desired rewards are limited in supply, including some that simply do not exist.
>
> *Axiom 6:* Most rewards sought by humans are destroyed when they are used.
>
> *Axiom 7:* Individual and social attributes that determine power are unequally distributed among persons and groups in any society.

Several of these are similar to axioms Homans proposed, but we went further by deriving, admittedly roughly, sets of propositions, which I later called *algorithms* but could have called *theorems*. Their meanings were specified by somewhat formal definitions, and here is the set relevant here:

> *Proposition 3:* In solving problems, the human mind must seek explanations.
>
> *Definition 7:* The *mind* is the set of human functions that directs the action of a person.
>
> *Definition 10: Explanations* are statements about how and why rewards may be obtained and costs are incurred.
>
> *Proposition 4:* Explanations are rewards of some level of generality.
>
> *Proposition 6:* In pursuit of desired rewards, humans will exchange rewards with other humans.

Proposition 14: In the absence of a desired reward, explanations often will be accepted which posit attainment of the reward in the distant future of in some other nonverifiable context.

Definition 18: Compensators are postulations of reward according to explanations that are not readily susceptible to unambiguous evaluation.

Proposition 22: The most general compensators can be supported only by supernatural explanations.

Definition 20: Compensators that substitute for a cluster of many rewards and for rewards of great scope are called *general compensators*.

Definition 22: Religion refers to systems of general compensators based on supernatural assumptions.

Magic employs specific compensators, while religion is defined in terms of general compensators. However, these need not involve gods, even though interaction with the supernatural realm would be facilitated by communication with residents of it. There are many kinds of supernatural explanations, not readily susceptible to unambiguous evaluation, and neither Stark nor I was prepared to undertake an expedition into heaven, Valhalla or Hades to test any out. Already by the middle of the 1980s, I was experimenting with artificial intelligence computer simulation to see how rigorously the deductions could be modelled (Bainbridge 1987, 1995, 2006).

A new ideational culture

Were Pitirim Sorokin able to communicate with us from the Afterlife, he might proclaim again his sacred truth: It is possible to avoid the impending Dark Age, but only by synthesizing ideational and sensate principles to create an idealistic culture. Such issues have been debated since the Renaissance revived interest in classical Greek and Roman society. Long ago, Edward Gibbon (1880) debated whether Christianity had caused the collapse of the Roman Empire or moderated the suffering it caused in preparation for the rise of a new civilization. Dare we speculate today that another radically new religion disguised as science may be at the heart of secularization? Perhaps its true name is Cybernetics, the science of control, that assumes rhetorical identities such as computer science and artificial intelligence (Pickering 2002; Malapi-Nelson 2017).

We can agree with Kasselstrand, Zuckerman and Cragun (2023) that rationalization of many facets of life has promoted secularization, and differentiation of religion from major institutions has had the same effect. If so, institutionalization of Cybernetics could represent a new ideational ideology, using scientistic rhetoric to obscure the possibility that a radical technocratic cult is replacing the old state church. To the extent that computer scientists abandon meaningful statistical analysis methods in favour of deep learning artificial intelligence neural nets that cannot be given human intellectual interpretations, they may unintentionally promote a new horde of cults or build the foundation for a new religious orthodoxy.

Social scientists have long suggested that religion and science are incompatible (Stark 1963), for example in the triumph of Darwin's theory of evolution and the failure of science more generally to find evidence not merely of some kind of deity, but of the particular God described in the Bible. Two centuries ago, science was seen as a way of learning more about God (Paley 1807). Yet cosmology has failed to find evidence of His existence, even as it promoted the legend of a Big Bang, has so far failed to demonstrate directly the reality of Dark Energy and Dark Matter, and may be describing a universe that is fundamentally random in nature (Bainbridge 1997a).

Medical science has slowed nearly to a halt, lacking the magic to end the pandemic instantly, yet improving vaccines, a treatment that partners with our natural immune system and was developed centuries ago (Scannell et al. 2012; Van Norman 2017; NASEM 2021). Faith that computing can render progress immortal may be nothing more than a cultic superstition. Assessing the current state of science and technology would take far more than a book chapter, yet it must be recognized that we may have neared their conclusions. Over half a century ago, on 7 December 1972, I stood on a Florida beach and watched the last Apollo launch to the moon. Using the name of a goddess rather than a god, NASA's Artemis programme is returning to Luna, but there are no serious plans to colonize Mars, and quick travel to the stars is impossible without magic.

The previous rhetoric suggests that every institution of society that experienced differentiation from religion and rationalization would now be vulnerable to their opposites, perhaps initially invisibly, following Sorokin's prediction of a future ideational dogmatism. I do ponder the future of the idealistic agency where I supported science for three decades, the National Science Foundation. Originally established in 1950 to fund pure research in the natural sciences, NSF had great difficulty including the social sciences over the years, and in recent decades has been shifting its emphasis to application-oriented engineering (England 1983; Larsen 1992; Freeman, Adrion and Aspray 2019; Solovey 2020). In 2022, the trend towards engineering took a big step forward through establishment of a new Directorate for Technology, Innovation, and Partnerships (TIP).

On 28 April 2023, the US Federal Register requested public input about an initial roadmap for TIP's development, prominently listing ten Key Technology Focus Areas, three of which seemed rather pedestrian: biotechnology, advanced energy and industrial efficiency technologies, and advanced materials science (Plimpton 2023). To someone faithful to traditional religion, the other seven Focus Areas might have seemed like Cybernetic rhetoric: (1) artificial intelligence, machine learning, autonomy and related advances; (2) high performance computing, semiconductors and advanced computer hardware and software; (3) quantum information science and technology; (4) robotics, automation and advanced manufacturing; (5) natural and anthropogenic disaster prevention or mitigation; (6) advanced communications technology and immersive technology; (7) data storage, data management, distributed ledger technologies and cybersecurity, including biometrics.

The third focus might seem especially cultic: quantum computing. Yes, calculation devices comparable to computer chips can be based upon principles of quantum physics, doing certain kinds of calculations amazingly swiftly. But recently the Congressional Research Service (2019) implied it has supernatural power:

> Combining elements of mathematics, computer science, engineering, and physical sciences, quantum information science (QIS) has the potential to provide capabilities far beyond what is possible with the most advanced technologies available today.

In 2018, the United States instituted the National Quantum Initiative Act, during the controversial Trump administration, and the legislation was introduced and promoted by Lamar Smith, who had a compatible religious orientation (Congress 2018). As the journal *Science* reported: 'He grew up steeped in the Christian Science church, which adheres to a teaching that medical ailments can be treated by prayer and faith. His current wife (his first wife died in 1991) has held a leading post at the Christian Science church's headquarters in Boston' (Mervis and Cornwall 2017).

This is not to say that enthusiasm for quantum computing was exclusively caused by Christian Science rhetoric, but for decades a few Christian scientists have been debating whether the apparently subjective nature of quantum phenomena provides scientific confirmation of Mary Baker Eddy's view of reality (Fair 1988). The general public may find quantum physics rather mystical, especially if they read popular interpretations of Heisenberg's uncertainty principle and long-distance entanglement. Whether integrated with quantum computing or not, or proclaiming revelations of future disasters, artificial intelligence may be used by a new elite class as rhetoric to control the population, in a *techno-religio*. Consider the classic science fiction scripture that describes a conversation between a computer scientist and a vast new supercomputer: 'He turned to face the machine. "Is there a God?" The mighty voice answered without hesitation, without the clicking of a single relay. "Yes, *now* there is a God"' (Brown 1954).

References

Arnett, L. D. (1904), 'The Soul: A Study of Past and Present Beliefs', *The American Journal of Psychology*, 15 (2): 121–200.
Bainbridge, W. S. (1978), *Satan's Power: A Deviant Psychotherapy Cult*. Berkeley: University of California Press.
Bainbridge, W. S. (1985), 'Cultural Genetics', in R. Stark (ed.), *Religious Movements*, 157–98. New York: Paragon.
Bainbridge, W. S. (1987), *Sociology Laboratory*. Belmont: Wadsworth.
Bainbridge, W. S. (1994), 'General Semantics', in R. E. Asher and J. M. Y. Simpson (eds), *The Encyclopedia of Language and Linguistics*, 1361. Oxford: Pergamon.
Bainbridge, W. S. (1995), 'Neural Network Models of Religious Belief', *Sociological Perspectives*, 38: 483–95.
Bainbridge, W. S. (1997a), 'The Omicron Point: Sociological Application of the Anthropic Theory', in R. A. Eve, S. Horsfall and M. E. Lee (eds), *Chaos and Complexity in Sociology: Myths, Models and Theory*, 91–101. Thousand Oaks: Sage Publications.
Bainbridge, W. S. (1997b), *The Sociology of Religious Movements*. New York: Routledge.
Bainbridge, W. S. (2006), *God from the Machine: Artificial Intelligence Models of Religious Cognition*. Walnut Grove: AltaMira.
Bainbridge, W. S. (2009), 'The Cultural Context of Scientology', J. R. Lewis (ed.), *Scientology*, 35–51. New York: Oxford University Press.
Bainbridge, W. S. (2012a), 'The Harvard Department of Social Relations', in W. S. Bainbridge (ed.), *Leadership in Science and Technology*, 496–503. Thousand Oaks: Sage.
Bainbridge, W. S. (2012b), 'The Psychoanalytic Movement', in W. S. Bainbridge (ed.), *Leadership in Science and Technology*, 520–8. Thousand Oaks: Sage.
Bainbridge, W. S. (2017a), *Dynamic Secularization*. Cham, Switzerland: Springer.
Bainbridge, W. S. (2017b), 'Historical Research: Oneida Online', in R. Finke and C. D. Bader (eds), *Faithful Measures: New Methods in the Measurement of Religion*, 227–59. New York: New York University Press.

Bainbridge, W. S. (2018), *Family History Digital Libraries*. Cham, Switzerland: Springer.

Bainbridge, W. S. and D. H. Jackson (1981), 'The Rise and Decline of Transcendental Meditation', in B. Wilson (ed.), *The Social Impact of New Religious Movements*, 135–58. New York: Rose of Sharon.

Bainbridge, W. S. and R. Stark (1979), 'Of Churches, Sects, and Cults: Preliminary Concepts for a Theory of Religious Movements', *Journal for the Scientific Study of Religion*, 18: 117–31.

Bainbridge, W. S. and R. Stark (1980a), 'Client and Audience Cults in America', *Sociological Analysis*, 41: 199–214.

Bainbridge, W. S. and R. Stark (1980b), 'Scientology: To Be Perfectly Clear', *Sociological Analysis*, 41: 128–36.

Bakan, D. (1958), *Sigmund Freud and the Jewish Mystical Tradition*. Princeton: Van Nostrand.

Balter, M. (2000), 'Was Lamarck Just a little Bit Right', *Science*, 288 (5463): 38.

Benedict, R. (1959), *Patterns of Culture*. Boston: Houghton Mifflin.

Berkower, L. (1969), 'The Enduring Effect of the Jewish Tradition upon Freud', *American Journal of Psychiatry*, 125 (8): 1067–73.

Blumberg, R. L. and R. F. Winch (1972), 'Societal Complexity and Familial Complexity: Evidence for the Curvilinear Hypothesis', *American Journal of Sociology*, 77 (5): 898–920.

Breines, W. (1986), 'Alone in the 1950s: Anne Parsons and the Feminist Mystique', *Theory and Society*, 15 (6): 805–43.

Breuer, J. and S. Freud (1936), *Studies in Hysteria*. New York: Nervous and Mental Disease Publishing Company.

Brown, F. (1954), 'Answer', in *Angels and Spaceships*. Boston: E. P. Dutton. Available at https://xpressenglish.com/our-stories/answer/ (accessed 11 December 2023).

Burggren, W. W. and D. Crews (2014), 'Epigenetics in Comparative Biology', *Integrative and Comparative Biology*, 54 (1): 7–20.

Carus, P. (1905), 'The Conception of the Soul and the Belief in Resurrection among the Egyptians', *The Monist*, 15 (3): 409–28.

Chen, C. (2022), *Work Pray Code: When Work Becomes Religion in Silicon Valley*. Princeton: Princeton University Press.

Church of Scientology International (n.d.), 'Commander "Snake" Thompson'. Available at www.lronhubbard.org/timeline/commander-snake-thompson.html (accessed 5 April 2023).

Comte, A. (1883), *The Catechism of Positive Religion*. London: Trübner.

Congress (2018), 'H.R.6227 National Quantum Initiative Act'. Available at https://www.congress.gov/bill/115th-congress/house-bill/6227 (accessed 5 April 2023).

Congressional Research Service (2019), 'Quantum Information Science: Applications, Global Research and Development, and Policy Considerations', R45409. Available at https://fas.org/sgp/crs/misc/R45409.pdf (accessed 5 April 2023).

Darnton, R. (1970), *Mesmerism and the End of the Enlightenment in France*. New York: Schocken.

Durkheim, E. (1915), *The Elementary Forms of the Religious Life*. London: Hollen Street Press.

England, J. M. (1983), *A Patron for Pure Science: The National Science Foundation's Formative Years, 1945–57*. Washington, DC: National Science Foundation.

Fair, S. L. (1988), 'Keeping a Spiritual Perspective on the New Physics'. *The Christian Science Journal*. Available at https://journal.christianscience.com/shared/view/7z4ep7yxns (accessed 5 April 2023).

Fodor, N. (1971), *Freud, Jung, and Occultism*. New Hyde Park: University Books.

Freeman, P. A., W. R. Adrion and W. Aspray (2019), *Computing and the National Science Foundation, 1950–2016*. New York: ACM.

Freud, S. (1964), *The Future of an Illusion*. Garden City: Doubleday.

Gibbon, E. (1880), *History of the Decline and Fall of the Roman Empire*. New York: Hurst and Company.

Hayakawa, S. I. (1949), *Language in Thought and Action*. New York: Harcourt, Brace.

Homans, G. C. (1950), *The Human Group*. New York: Harcourt, Brace and World.

Homans, G. C. (1974), *Social Behavior: Its Elementary Forms*. New York: Harcourt, Brace Jovanovich.

Horgan, J. (1996), *The End of Science*. Reading: Addison-Wesley.

Hubbard, L. R. (1950), 'Dianetics - The Evolution of a Science', *Astounding Science Fiction*, 45 (3): 43–87.

James, W. (1907), *Pragmatism*. New York: Longmans, Green.

Jolicoeur, P. M. and Knowles, L. L. (1978), 'Fraternal Associations and Civil Religion: Scottish Rite Freemasonry', *Review of Religious Research*, 20 (1): 3–22.

Kasselstrand, I., P. Zuckerman and R. T. Cragun (2023), *Beyond Doubt: The Secularization of Society*. New York: New York University Press.

Korzybski, A. (1941), *Science and Sanity: An Introduction to Non-Aristotelian Systems and General Semantics*. New York: The International Non-Aristotelian Library Publishing Company.

Larsen, O. N. (1992), *Milestones and Millstones: Social Science at the National Science Foundation, 1945–1991*. New Brunswick: Transaction Publishers.

Lofland, J. (1966), *Doomsday Cult*. Englewood Cliffs: Prentice-Hall.

Lofland, J. and R. Stark (1965), 'Becoming a World-Saver; A Theory of Conversion to a Deviant Perspective', *American Sociological Review*, 30: 862–75.

Maharishi International University (n.d.), 'Transcendental Meditation'. Available at www.miu.edu/about-miu/transcendental-meditation-technique (accessed 22 July 2023).

Malapi-Nelson, A. (2017), *The Nature of the Machine and The Collapse of Cybernetics*. New York: Palgrave Macmillan.

Mervis, J. and W. Cornwall (2017), 'Lamar Smith, the Departing Head of the House Science Panel, Will Leave a Controversial and Complicated Legacy', *Science*.

Available at www.sciencemag.org/news/2017/11/lamar-smith-departing-head-house-science-panel-will-leave-controversial-and-complicated (accessed 5 April 2023).

NASEM [National Academies of Sciences, Engineering, and Medicine] (2021), *High and Rising Mortality Rates Among Working-Age Adults*. Washington, DC: The National Academies Press.

Noyes, J. H. (1870), *History of American Socialisms*. Philadelphia: J. B. Lippincott.

Paley, W. (1807), *Natural Theology*. London: Faulder.

Parsons, A. (1969), *Belief, Magic, and Anomie: Essays in Psychological Anthropology*. New York: Free Press.

Parsons, T. (1964), 'Evolutionary Universals in Society', *American Sociological Review*, 29 (3): 339–57.

Parsons, T. (1974), '"The Interpretation of Dreams" by Sigmund Freud', *Daedalus*, 103 (1): 91–6.

Parsons, T. (1975), 'Comment on "Parsons' Interpretation of Durkheim" and on "Moral Freedom through Understanding in Durkheim"', *American Sociological Review*, 40 (1): 106–11.

Perseus Digital Library (n.d.a), 'Latin Word Study Tool: Saeculum'. Available at www.perseus.tufts.edu/hopper/morph?l=saeculum&la=la (accessed 4 April 2023).

Perseus Digital Library (n.d.b), 'Latin Word Study Tool: Religio'. Available at www.perseus.tufts.edu/hopper/morph?l=religio&la=la (accessed 4 April 2023).

Perseus Digital Library (n.d.c), 'Latin Word Study Tool: Pagus'. Available at www.perseus.tufts.edu/hopper/morph?l=pagus&la=la (accessed 4 April 2023).

Pickering, A. (2002), 'Cybernetics and the Mangle: Ashby, Beer and Pask', *Social Studies of Science*, 32 (3): 413–37.

Plimpton, S. H. (2023), 'Request for Information (RFI) on Developing a Roadmap for the Directorate for Technology, Innovation, and Partnerships at the National Science Foundation', *Federal Register*. Available at www.federalregister.gov/documents/2023/04/28/2023-08995/request-for-information-rfi-on-developing-a-roadmap-for-the-directorate-for-technology-innovation (accessed 20 September 2023).

Robbins, T. (1981), 'Church, State and Cult', *Sociological Analysis*, 42 (3): 209–25.

Robbins, T. and D. Anthony (1982), 'Deprogramming, Brainwashing and the Medicalization of Deviant Religious Groups', *Social Problems*, 29 (3): 283–97.

Roheim, G. (1915), *Magic and Schizophrenia*. Bloomington: Indiana University Press.

Scannell, J. W., A. Blanckley, H. Boldon and B. Warrington (2012), 'Diagnosing the Decline in Pharmaceutical R&D Efficiency', *Nature Reviews: Drug Discovery*, 11: 191–200.

Seoane, C. A. (1960), *Beyond the Ranges*. New York: Robert Spellar.

Seoane, R. L. (1968), *Uttermost East and the Longest War*. New York: Vantage.

Solovey, M. (2020), *Social Science for What? Battles over Public Funding for the 'Other Sciences' at the National Science Foundation*. Cambridge, MA: MIT Press.

Sorokin, P. A. (1937–41), *Social and Cultural Dynamics*. New York: American Book Company.

Stark, R. (1963), 'On the Incompatibility of Religion and Science', *Journal for the Scientific Study of Religion*, 3: 3–20.
Stark, R. and W. S. Bainbridge (1987), *A Theory of Religion*. New York: Toronto/Lang.
Sutherland, E. H. (1947), *Principles of Criminology*. Philadelphia: Lippincott.
Symonds, J. (1958), *The Magic of Aleister Crowley*. London: Muller.
Toynbee, A. (1947–57), *A Study of History*. New York: Oxford University Press.
Van Norman, G. A. (2017), 'Overcoming the Declining Trends in Innovation and Investment in Cardiovascular Therapeutics: Beyond EROOM's Law', *Journal of the American College of Cardiology: Basic to Translational Science*, 2 (5): 613–25.
Van Vogt, A. E. (1948), *The World of Ā*. New York: Simon & Schuster.
Weber, M. (1930), *The Protestant Ethic and the Spirit of Capitalism*. London: G. Allen & Unwin.

5

The dangerous cult exercise

Popular culture and the ongoing construction of the new religious threat

Douglas E. Cowan

Imagining the dangerous cult

When you first hear the phrase 'dangerous cult', what groups come to mind? Heaven's Gate? Scientology? The Unification Church or the Children of God? Perhaps the Latter-day Saints or Jehovah's Witnesses? Almost certainly Aum Shinrikyo or the Branch Davidians, but how about Hare Krishna or TM? And what about the Roman Catholic Church or even the United Methodists? Over the past half-century or so, all of these – and many more besides – have been cast in the role of 'dangerous cult' by a variety of social actors around the world. But how do you know, and how did you decide which groups to include in this little thought-experiment – and, at least as importantly, which not?

For many years, I have used what I call my 'dangerous cult exercise' in a number of different undergraduate courses, particularly those dedicated to the consideration of new religious movements, but also courses on religious diversity and social development, as well as various aspects of religion and popular culture. The object of the exercise is not to instruct students on whether 'dangerous cult' is a useful term, nor is it intended to inventory how various scholars of new religious movements (NRMs) have weighed in on the question. These discussions come later. Rather, this exercise is designed to confront students with the fundamental difficulty of the task of definition (see Stark and Bainbridge 1985).

Many people think that pointing out a 'cult', especially a 'dangerous' one, is a relatively simple matter, and as such are confident that they can do so when asked. For decades, the secular anticult movement has relied on a laundry list of putative 'cult characteristics', the majority of which are psychological and sociological in nature, but all of which are applied as a kind of infallible template for evaluating suspect religious movements. The Christian countercult, on the other hand, which is largely a Protestant response to NRMs and has existed far longer than its nonreligious correlative, relies less on psychosocial indicators than on theological deviance and ritual divergence from particular streams of conservative Christianity (see Cowan 2003, 2005b). Put very simply, the former is concerned with groups that they believe *do* bad things (regardless of their theological underpinnings and motivations), while the latter is focused on groups they are convinced *believe* bad things (which frequently have significant social and cultural implications).

While students are often familiar with many of these concepts in the abstract (e.g. they have heard of 'brainwashing' or 'deprogramming', or they recognize when a particular belief system is substantively different from their own faith), they too think that pointing out a dangerous cult should be an easy task. That is, they do so *until* they are faced with having to identify the criteria they use, to confront the consequences their decisions imply, and to explain the contradictions raised by problematic counterexamples. As many classes have discovered, when it comes to labelling something a dangerous cult, 'I know it when I see it' is no more adequate now than it was when Justice Potter Stewart offered it as the legal benchmark for obscenity in the landmark *Jacobellis v. Ohio* case over half a century ago. As it is so often in life, the issue is far less clear-cut and far more complicated than it first appears. Helping students to recognize this is the basic premise underpinning the exercise.

To begin, the class is divided into small groups and given a period of time to consider the following scenario:

> You and your team of human services professionals – including social workers, therapists and religious leaders – have been assembled to deal with the growing threat of religious cults in the country. Many people are calling this phenomenon a 'clear and present danger' and are demanding that 'somebody needs to do something'. The reasons for this, though, seem vague and ambiguous at best, and opinions on the subject vary widely.
>
> In order to address the problem, you and your team must answer a series of questions. Bear in mind that you will be required to justify your answers when you make your report to the Parliamentary Commission. That is, you must be able to say why you believe what you do, not simply what you believe. This is very important.

To do this, your group must arrive at consensus on the following three questions: (a) How should we define a 'dangerous cult'? What indicators should we use in our assessment of religious groups? (b) What obligations do we have to the wider society? How should we weigh civil liberties and social harmony in the balance? And (c) what are your recommendations? What measures, if any, should we implement in response to this issue?

While I want students to discuss these questions in depth and answer them as fully as possible, I caution them against simply pulling out their laptops and googling the problem. This is not a research project in that sense. Instead, the exercise is most effective as a time-bounded, in-class activity, the endgame of which is to help students appreciate (a) how *little* they actually know about new religious movements, despite (b) how much they *think* they know, and, most importantly, (c) help them recognize *where* they gained such knowledge as they do think that they have.

Explaining the questions in slightly more detail, I suggest that another way of putting the matter is: How would we know a 'dangerous cult' if we saw it or recognize one if we heard something reported on the news? And how would we tell others about it? How would you warn your family or friends? Because this exercise presumes a secular (or at least putatively secular) democracy, students then proceed to consider broader philosophical issues: What obligations do we have to fellow members of our society? Which, put differently, asks what responsibilities we have to and for each other. In terms of the specific question of the so-called dangerous cult, how do we weigh civil liberties (i.e. people's right to believe as they want, worship as they see fit, and ritually gather as they choose) in the balance with group harmony (i.e. our ongoing participation in and commitment to a common social contract)? While students often think the first part of the exercise is the most difficult, they quickly discover that questions of responsibility and obligation – what happens 'when freedoms collide', as Canadian human rights lawyer Alan Borovoy put it (1988; see also Narveson 1999) – are far more challenging.

Having arrived at something of a consensus on the first two questions, each group is then expected to come up with a set of recommendations. That is, what measures, if any, should we as a society implement in response to this issue? While this is obviously something of a contrived exercise, students are encouraged to treat it as a thought-experiment, a way of imagining what they would do if they could, then thinking through the consequences of their own choices. Finally, having done all that – identification, expectation, recommendation – I ask students to take a few minutes to list all the groups that they can think of, collectively and however they arrive at the list, which appear to fit the criteria that they established for the first question. If the government commission to which their report will be submitted ask them to identify any 'dangerous cults' on the current religious landscape, which groups would they include and, most importantly, why? Throughout the exercise, I stress that students should continually be asking themselves how they know what they know – or at least what they think they know about these groups.

I push them to consider, for example, whether groups exist that fit their criteria, but which have been excluded from their lists, either consciously or not. If so, why have these other groups not been included? What makes them different? Very often, for example, students contend that 'dangerous cults' are marked by situations in which 'members give up all free will to the group leader and are expected to follow their orders without question'. To which I often respond, 'OK, how is that any different from, say, most military units anywhere in the world'? Indeed, for many years, when called upon to serve as expert witnesses in NRM court proceedings, prominent anticult activist Margaret Singer and her colleagues at the American Family Foundation (now the International Cultic Studies Association) felt compelled to bring a series of talking points answering the question, 'Aren't the Marines a Cult by your Definition'? As I have pointed out elsewhere, however, the very fact that the secular anticult has had to clarify these differences with such regularity indicates in no uncertain terms the fundamentally ambiguous nature – and corresponding unreliability – of their definition (see Cowan 2002; Singer and Lalich 1995: 98–101). Yet, nearly half a century on from the cult panics of the 1970s and 1980s, and despite the numerous other problems inherent in their approach, this precise argument still regularly circulates both in anticult discourse and in the research materials it provides to the public.

As I point out to students, this particular problem highlights the value of comparative counterexamples when it comes to identifying so-called dangerous cults. They learn the analytic utility of looking for groups that fit the same criteria they have established – whatever those are – but which they do not categorize the same way or which they do not hold to the same standards. And then, as always, I ask them to consider, 'why not'?

Another common criterion students regularly propose is that 'a dangerous cult is a group where people who join have to give up all their possessions and they have to promise to obey their religious superiors'. 'Okay', I reply, 'then tell me how that is different from a woman who joins a Roman Catholic convent and chooses to become a cloistered nun, or a man who joins a monastery and becomes an eremitic monk? Shouldn't they be able to make those religious choices if they want'? Once students realize that they have named two groups, both of which fit the criteria, but one of which is marginalized as a 'dangerous cult' and the other not, they are forced to confront the possibility that there is something wrong with their working definition, something problematic about the means by which groups are being identified.

Finally, if time permits, I complicate this part of the exercise further by encouraging them to consider all these various questions under what is known as a 'veil of ignorance'. That is, what recommendations would they make for society if they did not know going into the process what religious tradition each of them would belong to at the outcome? In this case, I usually prepare a reasonable demographic cross-section of religious affiliation into which members of the class are randomly sorted once they have completed the tasks. Realizing that they might be members of a new religious movement themselves – raised by Scientologist parents who have loved and cared for them their entire lives, perhaps, or converted to modern Paganism after experiencing a lifetime of spiritual alienation in the Roman Catholic Church, or choosing to join the Latter-day Saints because their Mormon neighbours were the first to welcome them to their new community – I want the students to reflect on whether that would change their recommendations or their evaluation of the issue.

Over the years, I've been quite surprised at how conservative many of my students turn out to be when it comes to the question of new religious movements, especially when these young people are often archly and vocally liberal on any number of other social and cultural issues. Once they see this for themselves, though, it is often very confronting for classes to experience how limiting many of them want to be – or feel they have the right to be – in terms of what they perceive as the religious liberties of others, and how quickly they move to marginalize those they consider a faith-based threat. Despite best intentions, despite being really nice people (generally speaking), despite having convinced themselves that they just want to do the best for the world, when faced with the 'dangerous cult exercise', it is astonishing how restrictive they become.

Indeed, the results have ranged from the anticipated to the appalling, the expected to the egregious. Some students have argued for the creation of a government oversight body which must verify and validate all religions. ('On what grounds?' I respond. 'Who gets to decide and who would be a part of such a panel, and how would they make their decisions?') A few have even suggested a dedicated law enforcement unit charged with the investigation and certification of approved religious groups and organizations. ('How would this differ from the religious police in, say, Saudi Arabia or Iran or Nigeria or *The Handmaid's Tale*? And how does this respond to the issue of constitutional guarantees of religious freedom?') Not surprisingly, many students did not want to make any judgement, preferring to deflect the question with conventional pieties about liberty and freedom and the right to personal opinion. ('So', I reply, refusing to let them off the hook, 'you and your family would be fine if a sibling chose to marry, say, a Scientologist or a Mormon or a modern Druid?') Once again, the point is not to articulate the right way to approach these issues, but to expose problems which are already deeply ingrained in the ways that students think about them.

Now, of course, very little of what I've said so far will be unfamiliar to scholars of new religious movements. Much of this exercise and the class discussions that follow distil research that has been conducted over the past fifty years as regards the definition of new religions, the nature of conversion and deconversion, the function of leadership and NRM hierarchies, the question of violence, and so forth. But that is not the point. The object of the exercise is that students find themselves confronted with these issues by wrestling with them in much the same ways that prompted new religious movements research in the first place. All of which, for them, leads to the question: How do we know what we know?

Popular culture and the problem of how we know what we know

Part of the general class discussion of the dangerous cult exercise inevitably revolves around the question of 'how we know what know', a principal concern of any sociology of knowledge, and particularly salient when issues of fundamental civil liberties and human rights are at stake. While I have never encountered a class in which no one has heard of the Church of Scientology, for example, I often ask how many students know a Scientologist personally? For the purposes of the question, I define this as a person one knows well enough to identify them on the telephone simply by the sound of their voice. In all the years I've been doing this exercise, and ranging from first-year undergraduate to advanced graduate courses, no one has ever answered 'Yes' to that question.

Yet, conversely, no one is completely unfamiliar with Scientology, and many claim to be quite informed on the topic. The next question, and the second principal object of the exercise, is: 'Okay, then, since no one has any personal knowledge, then how *do* you know what you know? Where did you learn *everything* you know – or think you know – about Scientology'? At this point, I remind them, the issue is not whether what they know is right or wrong, accurate or inaccurate. I just want them to think about the stock of knowledge on which they have drawn.

While it is true that, occasionally, someone might have done a university course on new religious movements, those students are rare, the exceptions that test the rule, as it were. Far more common is the reality that, although few are willing to admit it initially, when we dig more deeply into the topic it becomes clear that many learned everything they know about the Church of Scientology from popular culture, in more than a few cases 'Trapped in the Closet', the infamous 2005 episode of the adult cartoon *South Park* (see Feltmate 2017, esp. 188–94).

Read the last part of that sentence again and think about its implications.

Put plainly, despite the best efforts and fondest delusions of the academy, far more people learn about new religious movements – whether labelled 'cults' or not – from popular culture than they do from reputable scholarship or university coursework. New religious tropes ranging from the all-powerful cult leader to the brainwashing theory to 'cult' as metonym for religious violence are ubiquitous in everything from horror movies to police procedurals and crime dramas, and from infotainment programming to situation comedies. Together, these tropes form the matrix of 'what people know' about new religious movements of all kinds, the common stock of 'recipe knowledge' on which they rely to evaluate new, alternative and unfamiliar religious movements. This is, as it were, ground zero for the problem of popular culture and how we know what we know. To take another example, it is axiomatic that orders of magnitude more people watched (or will watch in streaming syndication) Showtime's massively popular *Dexter*, in which one of the main season five plot lines revolves around the Afro-Caribbean religion of Santería, than will ever read *Creole Religions of the Caribbean* (Olmos and Paravisini-Gebert 2022) or *Cults and New Religions: A Brief History* (Cowan and Bromley 2015) or, sadly, even the book you now hold in your hands.

For many years, I have argued in favour of the power of popular culture in the social construction of knowledge and the reification of the religious imagination (Cowan 2005a, 2008, 2010, 2018, 2019a, 2022), an insight that finds support every time I run the dangerous cult exercise in class. Yet, popular culture as a principal driver of the ongoing construction of the new religious threat is often overlooked in pursuit of what are considered more important scholarly endeavours. After all, it's just a movie, right? It's just a novel or a sitcom or a comic book, and who could possibly take those seriously?

The problem, I believe, is that these are not the right questions, and that we ignore the power of popular culture to our detriment.

New religious movements and popular culture

As I was writing this chapter, a student in one of my current courses pointed out how 'binge-watching documentaries about dangerous cults on Netflix has truly got me intrigued about religion and the power of religion'. The ambiguous grammar notwithstanding, this student illustrates precisely the issue the dangerous cult exercise is intended to highlight: a tremendous amount of what students know (or think they know) about NRMs comes from watching Netflix or Prime Video or Crave, BritBox, Acorn, or any one of the growing assortment of streaming video services, all of which is augmented, of course, by the conceptual echo-chamber that is social media. Unless students have made a particular point of seeking out reliable information about new, controversial or alternative religious groups, whatever they learn comes to them osmotically through the course of their regular media diet. Contra my student, however, even documentaries, which still enjoy at least the cultural patina (if not the reality) of objectivity, are not the principal source of information.

Indeed, because so-called documentaries and infotainment television constitute such a small portion of streamed programming, I encourage students to consider the effect of more common pop culture products such as situation comedy, anime, crime drama, legal and forensic procedurals, even reality television (e.g. *Sister Wives*). Because of the vast, often international social penetration of situation comedies, for instance, we discuss their depiction of new religious movements – especially *South Park* (e.g. 'All about Mormons'; 'Trapped in the Closet'), *The Simpsons* (e.g. 'The Joy of Sect'), *American Dad* (e.g. 'Holy Scoomp'; 'Who Smarted'), *Family Guy* (e.g. 'Chitty Chitty Death Bang'), and, occasionally, *Unbreakable Kimmy Schmidt* (about a young woman who escapes an underground bunker, having been held captive by a polygamous religious leader for fifteen years). However, because of the generic framing of programmes such as legal procedurals and crime dramas, I also urge students to pay particular attention to how new religions are portrayed there. That is, although students invariably laugh at *American Dad*'s Francine reminiscing over her 'All My Cults' scrapbook, or *South Park*'s Stan confronting the Harrisons about the improbability of their Mormon beliefs, other programmes reinforce the concept of the 'dangerous cult' simply by virtue of presenting it within the context of criminal activity, legal and forensic proceedings, or murder mysteries. Consider just these few examples.

In the American police drama *Numbers* (styled *Numb3rs*) mathematics genius Charlie Epps uses his extraordinary abilities to help his brother, Don, a senior FBI agent assigned to the violent crimes unit. While a few episodes trade lightly on well-known NRM themes (e.g. 'Conspiracy Theory'), the third-season episode 'Nine Wives' is an unambiguous reference to the dangers allegedly posed by polygamous Mormonism. A young woman is found unconscious by the side of a country road and identified as Josephine Kirtland, the seventy-third wife of a self-proclaimed prophet from whom she has apparently just escaped. Her name is a conspicuous compound of Joseph Smith and Kirtland, Ohio, site of the first Latter-day Saint temple, and anyone who is even moderately familiar with Mormon history and presence in popular culture would have difficulty missing the connection. Called in the episode the Apostolic Saints (another barely concealed reference to Mormonism), the group is both polygamist and incestuous, outlier behaviours that provide further layers of narrative tension and implicate the shadowy, dangerous world of the 'cult'. As the episode enters its third act, the new religious trope shifts from the metaphorical Kirtland, Ohio, to Waco, Texas, as the leader, Abner Stone, orders his followers into a final, apocalyptic battle with federal agents. Epitomizing the superficial way in which popular culture treats NRMs, an IMDB review describes the episode's theme simply as 'one of those polygamy cults lead by a "prophet" who has been impregnating children for years in the name of his religion'. Similarly, in the fifth-season finale, 'Angels and Devils', the David Koresh trope is revisited as another putative cult leader uses a small group of women to commit a variety of crimes. As the story unfolds, though, it becomes clear that what the leader, Mason Duryea, really wants is a Waco-like shootout with law enforcement, something that he believes will bring him enduring, if posthumous, fame and recognition.

While not every NRM-related crime drama culminates in the possibility of a fiery showdown, a number of other well-known 'dangerous cult' themes are regularly pressed into service. In the *NCIS: Los Angeles* episode 'An Unlocked Mind', for instance, a title which is at least a double-entendre, federal agents are assigned to infiltrate the eponymous 'Church of the Unlocked Mind'. 'Welcome to crazy town', mutters one agent when the group is named during the briefing and he is assigned to go undercover. 'Here we go, through the looking-glass'

('An Unlocked Mind'). An intensely secretive organization that is clearly intended to remind viewers of Scientology, church members are presented as being forced into detailed acts of confession and self-mortification, and potential victims of sexual predation. Everyone except the leader, Owen Granger, is dressed in white button-down shirts and khaki chinos. Senior group members guide newcomers and are always on the lookout for someone 'special', usually an attractive young woman in whom Granger might be particularly interested. 'Welcome to the best part of your life', gushes one such leader during the initial 'love-bombing' of those who for whatever reason have found themselves at the group's palatial residence, the site of the brainwashing trope on which the principal narrative depends.

Unlike the multi-series *NCIS* franchise, *Lie to Me* was a short-lived psychological procedural loosely based on the work of Paul Ekman and his research into detecting deception leakage through studying micro-expressions (see Ekman 2009). Placed in this context, new religious movements are, by dint of the series' narrative premise, portrayed as deceptive and manipulative. In 'Truth or Consequences', for example, the episode's B-story concerns the investigation of a religious group to determine if it should be entitled to 501(c)3 status. That is, is this a 'real' religion or not – at least in terms of the US Internal Revenue Service? Since students often reject religions as 'real', 'authentic' or 'true' because they do not look like their own particular faith, aspects of this episode usefully highlight the problem of dismissing religious beliefs simply because they are unfamiliar – a gaffe that is hardly limited to undergraduates (see, e.g., Cowan 2008: 43–6, 2010: 150–2, 2019b). Not unlike 'An Unlocked Mind', though, in 'Beyond Belief' the well-known tropes of NRM brainwashing and the predatory self-help movement take centre stage. In this episode, *Lie to Me*'s main character, Cal Lightman – another tortured double-entendre – exposes the sideshow cold reading tactics of a so-called cult leader. Once again, however, the notion of an unfamiliar spiritual movement or faith group is placed in the context of de facto deception.

Across the pond from where I write, the enormously popular British crime drama *Midsomer Murders* waded into the shallow end of the new religious pool with 'The Oblong Murders'. In this episode, a young woman has gone missing while in the company of The Oblong Foundation, a group represented as a new age-style 'cult'. Asked by a family friend to investigate her disappearance, the main characters (DCI Barnaby and DS Jones) not surprisingly find more than a little malfeasance at the group's manor house estate. Though this episode was first broadcast in 2011, scholars of new religions will recognize reflections of the brainwashing/deprogramming controversy that dominated NRM discourse in the 1970s when family distress over unacceptable religious choices on the part of children or siblings often led to the involvement of law enforcement. Similar non-traditional religions have featured in at least two interrelated episodes of the reimagined *Father Brown* mysteries: 'The Eye of Apollo' and 'The Children of Kalon'. The entirety of the six-episode third series of the brooding Icelandic murder mystery *Entrapped* (2021), another narrative double-entendre, revolves around the threat of a non-traditional religious group. The IMDB tagline for *Entrapped* reads simply, 'Police investigate the disappearance of a cult member'. *Res ipsa loquitur*, it seems.

Although class time is limited, and we never have as much as we would like, I try to show short clips of many of these programmes to demonstrate how closely popular culture not only mirrors students' impressions of the 'dangerous cult' but reciprocally contributes to and reinforces those perceptions. And while a number of these programmes include an opening credit disclaimer that the storyline is fictitious and not meant to represent real people, events or groups, students quickly recognize that for the duplicitous fiction that it is. When we talk about various pop culture representations of NRMs, if the group is not explicitly named (e.g. unlike the Church of Scientology or the Latter-day Saints in *South Park*), I caution students against trying to solve the 'riddle' of the group that is presented as though that answers the problem represented by the story. For example, the *NCIS LA* episode is clearly (no pun intended) meant to represent the Church of Scientology, simply making that identification is not sufficient. It treats the episode as a simple matching exercise. Rather, I encourage students to look past the superficiality of this approach to consider what dangerous cult tropes are embedded in the narrative itself, and how they contribute to their understanding of new religions beyond the television screen. This leads us to the final aspect of the discussion.

Pattern-seeking and why we think the way we do

To their credit, students almost inevitably want to know why they think the way they do about new religious movements. It is simply not a question most of them have ever considered, and many are confused about how they arrived at such strong opinions on such a paucity of evidence. In fact, a number of people have admitted to feeling a bit ashamed by the revelation. This leads to class discussion of two interrelated conceptual schemata as ways of explaining the problem: the social psychological processes involved in pattern-seeking and pattern-making, and the reinforcing elements of newsworthiness as principal drivers of cultural antipathy towards new religious movements. Although space in this chapter allows for a brief discussion only of the former, students are also supplied with a copy of 'God, Guns, and Grist for the Media's Mill', an article outlining the effects of newsworthiness pressures and considerations (Cowan and Hadden 2004), to help them understand the force of the latter.

Because, as pattern-seeking, pattern-making and, not infrequently, pattern-manipulating creatures, we are often profoundly uncomfortable with ambiguity, ambivalence and contradiction, a number of cognitive processes have helped both select us for survival and permit us to form prosocial groups – including religious ones. Although hardly a complete list, these include the availability heuristic, source dissociation, the validity effect and the in-print fallacy, various forms of hindsight, expectation, and confirmation bias, the false-consensus effect, and the echo-chamber problem. Few, if any, of these mechanisms are deployed consciously, and none work independently of the others. Rather, together, they form an intervailing suite of perceptual algorithms, filters and prejudices that allow us to make sense of the world around us and help navigate our way through it. Curiously, although many of these cognitive processes are well-known and documented in scholarly domains such as psychology and sociology, and seem ideally suited to the analysis of religious worldviews, they have until relatively recently been all but ignored in religious studies research. Indeed, only in the last few years have results for any of these terms begun to show up in a database search of the American Theological Library Association (ATLA), one of the principal repositories of religious studies scholarship in the world.

In terms of popular culture and the perception of new religious movements, the persuasive power of these processes cannot be overlooked, and four of the most significant are the availability heuristic, source dissociation, the validity effect and confirmation bias. Put briefly, the *availability heuristic* tells us that the more easily and quickly we can draw an example of something to mind, the more likely we are to consider that thing true or significant. As I have written elsewhere, 'whatever is most "available" to us becomes "what we know" about that thing' (Cowan 2022: 90; see Begg, Armour and Kerr 1985). If all someone knows about the Church of Scientology or modern Witchcraft is what they learned from a thinly veiled *NCIS LA* episode or Robert Eggers's relentlessly depressing film, *The Witch*, then those pop culture products become the stock of knowledge on which they draw whenever these topics come up in conversation.

Having watched the *Numb3rs* episode, 'Nine Wives' (and perhaps binge-watched *Sister Wives* or *Big Love*), the availability heuristic virtually guarantees that this is the information on which viewers with no knowledge other than that will draw when trying to understand, for example, something like the 2008 raid on Yearning for Zion Ranch of the Fundamentalist Church of Jesus Christ of Latter-day Saints and the events that followed.

Source dissociation, on the other hand, describes our tendency to forget or blur where we learned something that we consider true or significant (see Schacter, Harbluk and McLachlan 1984). Thus, rather than a television episode or a movie about a suspect new religion, over time this information becomes 'something I saw somewhere' and contributes to the kind of conversational 'recipe knowledge' which Peter Berger and Thomas Luckmann (1966) argue is the most potent form of reality maintenance. This is only reinforced through the *validity effect*, which tells us that the more often we see something, especially when we encounter it in multiple sources, the more likely we are to believe that thing true or significant (see Hasher, Goldstein and Toppino 1977; Schwartz 1982). In terms of a situation such as the YFZ Ranch raid, the boundaries between fictional television and real-world events – however problematically framed by news media – become profoundly blurred.

Finally, because once we have established an understanding of something we are reluctant to relinquish it in the face of contradictory data, we tend to privilege information, explanation and evidence that *confirms our biases* – no matter how we arrived at them in the first place. That is, we tend to filter and retain information according to our degree of agreement with it (see Dardenne, Benoit and Leyenne 1995; Van Swol 2007). We confirm our bias in hindsight by recreating events to suit our recollection, and we filter new information through the lens created by our biases. Throughout the class sessions devoted to the dangerous cult exercise, students come to understand the domino effect of these interrelated social psychological processes. Indeed, taken together (and considered with a number of the other concepts noted above), they comprise the foundation of an explanatory framework both for religious belief and worldview reinforcement, and for social and cultural antipathy towards particular religious practitioners and traditions.

If these aspects of social psychology offer us explanations for how we think, the emerging field of cognitive theory and the ecology of cognition suggest intriguing reasons why. Put simply, it is a resource issue: all of these mechanisms allow our brains to function more quickly and efficiently, conserving resources that may be required for more complex cognitive tasks (see Navon and Gopher

1979; Sherman, Judd and Park 1989). As it applies to religion, though, this is a relatively new theoretical approach, though it is already yielding some fascinating (and often provocative) results (for just a few examples, see Atran 2002; Barrett 1999; Boyer 1994, 1999). Using it as a way of understanding recurring and resilient antipathy towards new religious movements is one of the fascinating areas these conceptual tools opens up for exploration.

Conclusion

By the end of the exercise, which not infrequently extends over a few class sessions, students not only discover for themselves the difficulty of defining the terms of the discussion but also come to understand some of the issues that, for more than fifty years, have driven the research of scholars of new religious movements. They wrestle with problems of the controversial brainwashing/deprogramming hypothesis (e.g. Bromley and Richardson 1983), explore the process and durability of new religious conversion (e.g. Barker 1984) or simply become exposed to the lived religious experience of those in non-traditional religious movements (e.g. Rochford 2007; Westbrook 2019). Many of them emerge from the process considerably less certain of their own opinions on the matter, and certainly less dogmatic in their approach to religions different from their own. A few students have even gone on to study and research new religions in more formal ways. Thus, in its own small way, I hope that this 'dangerous cult exercise' has contributed to forming the next generation of new religious scholars.

References

'All about Mormons' (2003), *South Park*. [TV programme], Comedy Central, 19 November.

'Angels and Devils' (2009), *Numb3rs*. [TV programme], CBS, 15 May.

Atran, S. (2002), *In Gods We Trust: The Evolutionary Landscape of* Religion. New York: Oxford University Press.

Barker, E. (1984), *The Making of a Moonie: Choice or Brainwashing?* London: Basil Blackwell.

Barrett, J. L. (1999), 'Theological Correctness: Cognitive Constraint and the Study of Religion', *Method & Theory in the Study of Religion*, 11 (4): 325–39.

Begg, I., V. Armour and T. Kerr (1985), 'On Believing What We Remember', *Canadian Journal of Behavioural Science*, 17 (3): 199–214.

Berger, P. L. and T. Luckmann (1966), *The Social Construction of Reality: A Treatise on the Sociology of Knowledge*. London: Penguin Books.

'Beyond Belief' (2010), *Lie to Me* [TV programme], 20th Century Fox, 15 November.

Borovoy, A. A. (1988), *When Freedoms Collide: The Case for Our Civil Liberties*. Toronto: University of Toronto Press.

Boyer, P. (1994), *The Naturalness of Religious Ideas: A Cognitive Theory of Religion*. Berkeley and Los Angeles: University of California Press.

Boyer, P. (1999), 'Functional Origins of Religious Concepts: Ontological and Strategic Selection in Evolved Minds', *Journal of the Royal Anthropological Institute*, 6 (2): 195–214.

Bromley, D. G. and J. T. Richardson, eds (1983), *The Brainwashing/Deprogramming Controversy: Sociological, Psychological, Historical, and Legal Perspectives*. New York: Edwin Mellen Press.

'Children of Kalon, The' (2022), *Father Brown*. [TV programme], BBC One, 6 January.

'Chitty Chitty Death Bang' (1999), *Family Guy*. [TV programme]. 20th Television, 18 April.

'Conspiracy Theory' (2008), *Numb3rs*. [TV programme], CBS, 8 December.

Cowan, D. E. (2002), 'Exits and Migrations: Foregrounding the Christian Counter-cult', *Journal of Contemporary Religion*, 17 (3): 339–54.

Cowan, D. E. (2003), *Bearing False Witness? An Introduction to the Christian Countercult*. Westport: Praeger.

Cowan, D. E. (2005a), *Cyberhenge: Modern Pagans on the Internet*. New York: Routledge.

Cowan, D. E. (2005b), 'Episode 712: *South Park*, Ridicule, and the Cultural Construction of Religious Rivalry', *Journal of Religion and Popular Culture*, 10 (1). https://doi.org/10.3138/jrpc.10.1.001.

Cowan, D. E. (2008), *Sacred Terror: Religion and Horror on the Silver Screen*. Waco: Baylor University Press.

Cowan, D. E. (2010), *Sacred Space: The Quest for Transcendence in Science Fiction Film and Television*. Waco: Baylor University Press.

Cowan, D. E. (2018), *America's Dark Theologian: The Religious Imagination of Stephen King*. New York: New York University Press.

Cowan, D. E. (2019a), *Magic, Monsters, and Make-Believe Heroes: How Myth and Religion Shape Fantasy Culture*. Berkeley and Los Angeles: University of California Press.

Cowan, D. E. (2019b), 'Science Fiction and the Imitation of the Sacred', *Journal of Contemporary Religion*, 34 (2): 386–8.

Cowan, D. E. (2022), *The Forbidden Body: Sex, Horror, and the Religious Imagination*. New York: New York University Press.

Cowan, D. E. and D. G. Bromley (2015), *Cults and New Religions: A Brief History*, 2nd edn. Oxford: Wiley-Blackwell.

Cowan, D. E. and J. K. Hadden (2004), 'God, Guns, and Grist for the Media's Mill: Constructing the Narratives of New Religious Movements and Violence', *Nova Religio*, 8 (2): 64–82.

Dardenne, B. and J.-P. Leyenne (1995), 'Confirmation Bias as Social Skill', *Personality and Social Psychology Bulletin*, 21 (11): 1229–39.

Ekman, P. (2009), *Telling Lies: Clues to Deceit in the Marketplace, Politics, and Marriage*, Rev. edn. New York: W. W. Norton.

Entrapped (2021), [TV programme], RVK Studios, 14 October–5 December.

'Eye of Apollo, The' (2013), *Father Brown*. [TV programme], BBC One, 18 January.

Feltmate, D. (2017), *Drawn to the Gods: Religion and Humour in The Simpsons, South Park, and Family Guy*. New York: New York University Press.

Hasher, L., D. Goldstein and T. Toppino (1977), 'Frequency and the Conference of Referential Validity', *Journal of Verbal Learning and Verbal Behavior*, 16 (1): 107–12.

'Holy Scoomp' (2021), *American Dad*. [TV programme], 20th Television, 28 June.

'Joy of Sect, The' (1998), *The Simpsons*. [TV programme], 20th Television, 8 February.

Narveson, J. (1999), *Moral Matters*, 2nd edn. New York: Broadview Press.

Navon, D. and D. Gopher (1979), 'On the Economy of the Human-Processing System', *Psychological Review*, 86 (3): 214–55.

'Nine Wives' (2007), *Numb3rs*. [TV programme], CBS, 5 January.

'Oblong Murders, The' (2011), *Midsomer Murders*. [TV programme], Bentley Productions, 25 May.

Olmos, M. F. and L. Paravisini-Gebert (2022), *Creole Religions of the Caribbean: An Introduction*, 3rd edn. New York: New York University Press.

Rochford, E. B., Jr (2007), *Hare Krishna Transformed*. New York: New York University Press.

Schacter, D. L., J. L. Harbluk and D. R. McLachlan (1984), 'Retrieval without Recollection: An Experimental Analysis of Source Amnesia', *Journal of Verbal Learning and Verbal Behavior*, 23 (5): 593–611.

Schwartz, M. (1982), 'Repetition and Rated Truth Value of Statements', *American Journal of Psychology*, 95 (3): 393–407.

Sherman, S. J., C. M. Judd and B. Park (1989), 'Social Cognition', *Annual Review of Psychology*, 40: 281–326.

Singer, M. T. and J. Lalich (1995), *Cults in Our Midst: The Hidden Menace in Our Everyday Lives*. San Francisco: Jossey-Bass.

Stark, R. and W. Bainbridge (1985), *The Future of Religion: Secularism, Revival, and Cult Formation*. Berkeley and Los Angeles: University of California Press.

'Trapped in the Closet' (2005), *South Park*. [TV programme], Comedy Central, 16 November.

'Truth or Consequences' (2009), *Lie to Me*. [TV programme], 20th Century Fox, 5 October.

'An Unlocked Mind' (2015), *NCIS: Los Angeles*. [TV programme], CBS, 9 November.

Van Swol, L. M. (2007), 'Perceived Importance of Information: The Effects of Mentioning Information, Shared Information Bias, Ownership Bias, Reiteration, and Confirmation Bias', *Group Processes & Intergroup Relations*, 10 (2): 239–56.

Westbrook, D. A. (2019), *Among the Scientologists: History, Theology, and Praxis*. New York: Oxford University Press.

'Who Smarted?' (2021), *American Dad*. [TV programme], 20th Television, 19 April.

6

The recognition of cults

Roderick P. Dubrow-Marshall

Introduction

The word 'cult' and its meaning and use in popular culture and in academia and professional services has a history of controversy and debate over many decades (Zablocki and Robbins 2001). In recent years the term has been recognized and applied to describe a growing variety of abusive and coercive groups and organizations whose activities have also sought the attention of law enforcement and security agencies and the intervention of prosecutorial authorities and the courts. From the 'death cult' of ISIS, to the convicted founder of NXIVM, and many more besides, the use of the word 'cult' can be seen to bring explanatory value as a designation which indicates an actuality of coercive and abusive practices which are harmful and potentially unlawful. It also has a potential unifying value in bringing together a range of related categories of harmful organizations or groups which share some key distinguishing features (such as gangs, organized crime groups, terrorist groups, oligarchies).

As this chapter will go onto illustrate, the word 'cult' thus provides a clarion call for victims as a deliberately pejorative term which is used with the intention to call out systemic abuse and coercion in groups, organizations and in societies in a similar way in which calling out specific forms of harassment, bullying and sexual assault or rape can highlight specific abuses to an individual. The fact that systemic abuse in organizations or society more widely inextricably and inevitably involves abuse perpetrated on individuals provides a clear and necessary justification for shining a zero-tolerance spotlight on such abuses whenever and wherever they occur and the legal and ethical requirement for organizations and governments to take decisive action to root out such practices and behaviours.

What is a cult?

A widely used and accepted definition of a cult (in research on cults) is provided by West and Langone:

> a group or movement exhibiting a great or excessive devotion or dedication to some person, idea, or thing and employing unethically manipulative techniques of persuasion and control (e.g., isolation from former friends and family, debilitation, use of special methods to heighten suggestibility and subservience, powerful group pressures, information management, suspension of individuality or critical judgement, promotion of total dependency on the group and fear of leaving it . . .), designed to advance the goals of the group's leaders, to the actual or possible detriment of members, their families, or the community. (1986: 119–20)

There are several elements to the West and Langone definition of a cult which align with concepts such as thought reform (Lifton 1961) and also coercive persuasion (Schein 1961) and coercive control (Stark 2007; Home Office Serious Crime Act 2015). The 'great or excessive devotion or dedication' mirrors concepts in thought reform such as 'doctrine over person' and 'demand for purity' which indicate that a tipping point can be reached, whereby the level of devotion by members, and their compliance to the group and its leader(s) and activities, becomes so encompassing in everyday life as to be potentially unhealthy (physically and psychologically) for the individuals involved. This is also similar to Zablocki's (1997) definition of a cult as 'an ideological organisation held together by charismatic relationships and demanding total commitment' (cited in Rosedale and Langone 2015).

This dominance of the group to the exclusion of other personal needs can be compared to concepts in organizational psychology such as 'work-life balance' (Sirgy and Lee 2018) where achieving a balance of focus and activity between work and other goals has been shown to be beneficial to health. In a cult the influence of a group on an individual effectively becomes a form of 'undue influence' where there is an 'overpowering or overbearing of the testator's volition, judgement or wishes by substitution of one mind for another' (Peisah et al. 2009: 8). Undue influence is a term founded and used mainly in the law of tort but whose applicability to other forms of contract, including psychological contracts and trauma bonds in coercive relationships and groups, has been widely noted (Wallace 2007; Lavy 2022).

For West and Langone this imbalanced level of devotion occurs in groups defined as cults where 'unethically manipulative techniques of persuasion and control' are used to ensure that this extent of devotion is created and maintained. The forms of manipulative persuasion listed in their definition are similar to key aspects of controlling and coercive behaviour in abusive relationships (England and Wales Serious Crime Act 2015, Section 76) which includes isolation from family and friends, monitoring of a person's time and controlling aspects of day-to-day life, and this also has much in common with the term 'milieu control' in thought reform. These actions and the resulting behaviours are intentionally 'designed to advance the goals of the group' in the West and Langone definition which illustrates how both the intent of the group and its leaders and its effects on members involve a focus and devotion towards the group, its ideas and often back towards its leader(s), in a perpetuating cycle.

It is notable that the intent of the coercive persuasion as noted by West and Langone in cults is also a feature of UK laws on coercive control in intimate relationships and families (England and Wales Serious Crime Act 2015, Section 76, Domestic Abuse Act 2021). It is also a key aspect of Biderman's (1957) Framework of Coercion, where a range of methods of coercion are used intentionally to ensure compliance and many of which have been shown to be the experience of survivors of human trafficking (Baldwin et al. 2011).

Laws on modern slavery and human trafficking (e.g. the England and Wales Modern Slavery Act, 2015) draw on the UN Protocol to 'Prevent, Suppress and Punish Trafficking in Persons' (the 'Palermo Protocol', Article 3) in defining trafficking as 'having control of another person, for the purpose of exploitation' with exploitation occurring when there is 'slavery servitude and forced or compulsory labour' (Section 3 of the England and Wales Modern Slavery Act 2015). These coercive practices are also notably the offences for which the leaders of the NXIVM cult were successfully prosecuted (in New York) and demonstrates how it is the coercive, and sometimes illegal, actions of cult members which can helpfully be used to define them as such (Boyle-Laisure 2016, 2021). There is also clear commonality in the coercive practices in trafficking groups and those observed in gangs and organized crime groups more widely thus also showing how cults can also be usefully seen as a form of gang or organized crime group, depending on the nature of coercion and exploitation which is practised (Knox 1999; Nwaogu, Weli and Mbee 2019).

How can cults affect their members?

It has been demonstrated in multiple research studies that participation in such groups in this imbalanced way, to the relative exclusion and detriment of other personal needs, interests and relationships, can have a negative impact on physical and mental health (Aronoff, Lynn and Malinoski 2000; Dubrow-Marshall and Dubrow-Marshall 2017, 2023) and can ultimately lead in some cases to a psychological 'dispensing of existence' (Lifton's [1961] final theme in thought reform). This deleterious effect on psychological functioning, including in the form of post-traumatic stress disorder (PTSD) has been widely demonstrated as a common outcome of coercive persuasion and control (Courtois 2008; Herman 2015).

As such then involvement in a cult, which, by definition, practises such methods of coercive control and persuasion, has the potentiality to lead to such negative psychological outcomes for its members and, as the West and Langone definition notes, also for its members' 'families, or the community', thus showing how a cult can have an impact far beyond its own confines. This is most viscerally demonstrated in cults which also resort to physically violent behaviours on former members (Krakauer 2003) and wider society, including in terrorist attacks in support of the group's cause (Banisadr 2009).

The evidence for harm from participation in abusive cult-like groups or movements remains an active area of research in the fields of psychology and mental health (Almendros et al. 2011; Goldberg et al. 2017; Saldana et al. 2021). Langone's statement that 'some groups under some circumstances harm some people' (2005: 161) illustrates the importance of deploying scientific methods to establish evidence for the specific circumstances and practices which lead to harm for individuals in such groups. The wider acceptance of Langone's statement and the impact of research on the harm inflicted on some individuals in cults also appears to be reflected in the definition of Otherwise Specified Dissociative Disorder in APA's Diagnostic and Statistical Manual (DSM 5-TR) (300.15 (F44.89)):

> Identity disturbance due to prolonged and intense coercive persuasion: Individuals who have been subjected to intense coercive persuasion (e.g., brainwashing, thought reform, indoctrination while captive, torture, long-term political imprisonment, recruitment by sects/cults or by terror organizations) may present with prolonged changes in, or conscious questioning of, their identity. (306)

A distinct form of psychological distress linked directly to involvement in cults or sects is therefore defined and this has also been identified in research with survivors of abuse in cults. Analysis of in-patient data collected at the Wellspring Retreat (in Ohio in the United States) reveals a significant positive relationship between extent of group identity and anxiety, depression and dissociation (Dubrow-Marshall 2010). This specific form of group-related psychological distress was also successfully ameliorated by the tailored treatment programme at Wellspring, thus indicating that treatment approaches are best focused on specific forms of psychological trauma (Herman 2015). Importantly, this research indicates that the extent of identification with the group is a significant predictor of later psychological symptoms. The 'Extent of Group Identity Scale' (Dubrow-Marshall, Martin and Burks 2003) specifically seeks to establish the level of group identification in positive and neutral terms and in this way it is not a measure of 'abuse' but instead an indicator of psychological attachment and identification which then appears to significantly relate to symptoms of psychological distress.

Overall therefore, a particular form of psychological harm linked to a person's cult identity and the extent of their beliefs in the group's teachings, leaders and its practices is suggested and this further reinforces the suggestion from Lifton (1961) and others, that the psychological dominance of such a group identity, brought on by group practices (such as milieu control), is potentially unhealthy. As such then a theory of 'totalistic identity' emerges (Dubrow-Marshall 2010), which outlines how an unhealthily dominant form of group identity, to the exclusion of other aspects of self-identity and aligned to the different aspects of thought reform, is implicated in a particular pattern of psychological distress among former cult members. This theory builds on established research regarding cognitive aspects of social identity (Tajfel and Turner 1979) and self-categorization (Turner et al. 1987) and is derived from evidence which clearly indicates that psychological totalism in cults, including in violent radical groups (Kruglanski and Orehek 2011) can be damaging to mental health. As such this work demonstrates the ongoing relevance of the term 'cult' and the need to better understand the potential psychological features and consequences of cult involvement.

Judicious noting of the 'cult' warning signs

The late president of the American Family Foundation (now International Cultic Studies Association) Herb Rosedale once said that 'judgements should rest on careful analyses of structure and behaviour within a specific context, rather than superficial classification' (ICSA Herb Rosedale Award). In this spirit of disciplined empirical inquiry, it is therefore arguably important for academics and professionals, while recognizing the relevance of the word 'cult', to be cautious in applying the term and to only do so with sufficient evidence or justification. It is broadly for these reasons that the International Cultic Studies Association (ICSA), on whose board I serve, specifically eschews the temptation to label groups as 'cults'. There are of course many groups for whom this label is applied by the media or by former members and it is also important, as this chapter will go on to argue, to hear and respond empathically and professionally to the 'survivor voice'.

It is precisely this voice, represented in the data collected in countless studies, which allows for a scientifically judicious use of the word 'cult' to apply to groups where the evidence clearly points in the direction of thought reform characteristics and the propensity for harmful psychological effects as outlined earlier. As such, then applying the pejorative term 'cult' to a particular group, implies and indicates certain features which require *a priori* evaluation and judgement. At the same time, if the evidence points in the direction of psychological totalism, then the label cult is a fitting warning sign that such a group may be best avoided and in need of reform to protect the safety and well-being of its members.

As noted earlier, using the word 'cult' to describe a particular group, based on an analysis of the evidence, does not of course mean that everyone in the group is affected in the same way or that everyone in the group is harmed. As with health and safety at work, the assessment of risk indicates that such harm may be likely and that certain practices may be responsible. It is unarguable that all organizations should be subject to this form of scrutiny and that adherences among members of particular groups to particular ideologies or leaders should not be a 'free pass' to a lack of such scrutiny and an ignoring of reported abuses and harms, whether by former members or through research. When companies, schools, universities, hospitals, government departments, the military and in fact any organization which one can think of are reported for harmful practices and abuse then the light of scrutiny is rightly shone. Where such abuses appear (from the evidence available) to emanate from cult-like practices of thought reform and psychological totalism then application of the word 'cult' may be an appropriate warning label that all is not well in the organization and that action needs to be taken to safeguard all involved.

Avoiding unhelpful comparisons and stereotypes

The understandable overlap between the meaning of the word 'cult', as defined earlier and elsewhere, and other related terms, such as 'high demand group', 'extremist group' and of course the French word 'sect' can lead to the making of broader comparisons which do not bear closer scrutiny. Two such comparative terms are 'new religious movements' (Barker 1989; Bromley 2012) and 'minority religions' (Chryssides 2018) which over many years have been unhelpfully conflated or compared with the word 'cult' (Robbins 1988). The reason that this particular comparison is unhelpful is because the broad definition of cults provided by West and Langone (1986), born from and tested across a variety of domains and among many thousands of group abuse survivors, is manifestly secular and ideology free. As such then the word 'cult' does not denote a particular form of belief system. It does, as outlined earlier, denote certain practices and resulting psychological effects which may be unhealthy and damaging to some members of the group concerned. It follows that new religious movements and minority religions should not be assumed to be more likely to be cults or to have the cult label applied, compared to political groups, terrorist groups, psychotherapy groups, businesses, colleges and so on.

It is here that media representations of cults may be decidedly unhelpful in that many fictional (and many non-fictional) accounts involve a religious or quasi-religious ideology and/or messiah figure (as in 'Wild Wild Country' or 'The Master'). The way in which such media stereotypes may negatively affect former members and can potentially inhibit their recovery is a hitherto under-researched area of inquiry (Levey and Dubrow-Marshall 2023). However, it is perhaps because of these stereotypes, and some high-profile examples in history of minority religions for whom the word 'cult' has been applied, that leads to this faulty and vastly overrated confluence. It is a terminological hybridization which essentially ignores the pan-ideological nature of cultic practice and its psychological effects and inherently implies that minority or new religions are disproportionately likely to be (allegedly) guilty of such, compared to other types of organization or social movement. Historical attempts to define 'cult' by some sociologists of religion (such as Richardson 1993) reinforce this problem by couching the term mainly within the context of religion (as the focus of their work), with the term 'emergent religion' (citing Ellwood 1986) noted as a plausible alternative (by Richardson).

Such sociological and terminological arguments could be seen to be valid within their own frame of reference (within the field of the sociology of religion) were they to stay there (Beckford 2003; Rochford 2007). However, the use of the word 'cult' is criticized and argued by the same authors as unhelpful on a wider terrain and far beyond the alleged false equivalency of cult with new or minority religions, an equivalency which has never been spelt out or argued by any writers or scholars on cults or sects. It is these false implications which, among other factors, have promulgated over decades a voluminous set of writings by a number of scholars of new religions which seek to defend the rights of new and minority religions against the use of the word 'cult' and the so-called 'anticult movement' (Dawson 1998; Melton 1992). As if to be anticult is to be anti-religion because, the fallacious logic goes, cult is a derogatory term per se for new or minority religions, which, of course, it is not.

An academic shibboleth has thus been created which obscures the utility of the term 'cult' and how it can used to helpfully identify groups and organizations of all kinds (religious granted but also political, psychological, educational, varieties of business etc.) which exert coercive influence with negative psychological consequences for some of their members (or workers). This shibboleth also masks the genuine attempts by some former members of religious cults to seek new spiritual and religious hope following spiritual abuse and coercion and its psychological effects (Damgaard 2021). While some former members of coercive groups, which are also new religions, turn decisively against religion in their recovery, some do not and to equate being anticult or anticultic abuse with a particular journey of travel theologically or ideologically is to be ignorant of the many and diverse recovery routes which survivors take (Goldberg et al. 2017).

It is precisely because these arguments about cults and new or minority religions are based on false understandings and implicated equivalencies that the debates have led to a series of circular arguments, often referred to as 'cult wars' (Langone 2000), which it can be hoped that this volume, among other efforts, will begin to positively address (as was the hope with the aforementioned book edited by Zablocki and Robbins in 2001). Importantly, to judiciously use the decidedly pejorative term 'cult' to describe a particular group and its coercive practices, should, if one follows the Rosedale edict, be based on a careful analysis of the available evidence. There are definitions and models of identity and harm which are evidence-based (as outlined earlier from research over many years), across a range of group types and domains, which also allow for the term 'cult' to be carefully applied if the evidence matches (Barker 2010).

None of that analysis says anything about the rights, per se, of the group and its members to believe what they want to believe nor does it comment in any way whatsoever about the right to hold religious and/or political beliefs more broadly. However, the definitions and models do explicitly indicate that beliefs, per se and specifically, do not provide a justification, per se or specifically, for abusive practices and the perpetration of harm to members to happen, whether the group or organization is religious, political, both, or neither. One can be, and arguably should be, both firmly pro-freedom of belief and religion, while also being firmly anti-coercion and abuse in all its forms.

When to shine the light and not defend the indefensible

The careful and judicious use of the term 'cult', to call out coercive and abusive practices which harm individuals, thus is aligned with international definitions of human rights (articles 3, 4 and 5 of the UN Universal Declaration on Human Rights), reflected and enshrined also in many national and regional jurisdictions (such as the European Convention on Human Rights, articles 3, 4 and 5). Human rights at the individual level, to not be abused or enslaved, sit appropriately alongside and do not contradict the human right to belief and faith and to such organize beliefs (religious, political etc.) into a group or movement, which will have the freedom to operate and advance those beliefs without state intervention or imposed doctrine (as enshrined in article 2 of the UN Universal Declaration of Human Rights and in the European Convention on Human Rights, article 9).

It follows that, while government interventions against groups which are reported to be coercive by their former members (such as the government prohibition on the Jehovah's Witnesses in Russia or the actions of the Chinese government with regard to Falun Gong) may be understandably welcomed by some survivors and those who work to end abuses in such groups, when this is done through defining minority religious beliefs as deviant then it is a totalitarian action which breaches those inalienable human rights to believe what one wants to believe. Such government action is thus not defensible in human rights terms, but that does not mean that abusive practices in such religious or political groups should be defended in those terms either or ignored and nor does it mean that the defining of such groups, as cults or cult-like, based on evidence and against aforementioned and established definitions of coercive practices and their effects, is also not appropriate.

When religions or political groups or businesses transgress these recognized human rights then they should rightly be held to account through the legal system. The term 'criminal religious movements' (Introvigne 2018) is thus a welcome attempt to overcome the arid and self-defeating debates of the 'cult wars'. There is rightly an acknowledgement by new religious movement scholars such as Introvigne (2018; see also Bromley and Melton 2002) that certain minority religions (and indeed religious groups per se) can, on occasions, commit crimes, including against their members. Such an acknowledgement is to recognize the obvious and manifest examples of abuse and violence perpetrated in such groups, as is also the case in what could also be labelled as 'criminal political movements' (aka extremist and radical groups) and 'criminal businesses' (aka organized crime groups). Introvigne, as with many other new religion scholars (but not all, such as Kent 1992, 2005), also deny the existence of 'brainwashing' and seek to equate that with the term 'cult' and thus seek to invalidate the latter by invalidating the former. Such semantic conflation unhelpfully deploys the relatively dated and untested concept of brainwashing as a further 'white elephant' and hence more evidence-based definitions of coercive control and persuasion and its psychological as well as physical effects in cults, as outlined earlier, go ignored. Such ignorance also obscures the benefits of explanatory terms such as 'cult', as a means of highlighting coercive and abusive practices and their effects when they occur and the need to seek remedy and redress when they do.

It is arguably well beyond time for research and discussion on cults and examples of such which are religious, political and so on to transcend such semantic straightjackets and silos. The much argued and litigated dichotomy of 'God v Gave' (Hamilton and Becker 2005) thus portrays a terrain where individual human rights to be free to believe and worship and to be free from coercion and abuse are falsely pitched against one another. Where beliefs directly lead to coercion and abuse then the right to belief does not, under law, trump the right not be abused, coerced and harmed. Defence of peaceful and beneficial religious and political ideology is therefore enhanced by scrutiny of and opposition to examples of where belief systems are abusive and harmful (see the UK government's Bloom Review; Bloom 2023).

Health and safety law and also criminal law, across many jurisdictions, does not make exceptions based on the ideology or belief system of the organization or company in question. The WHO is also clear in its secular definitions of what denotes a healthy or hazardous workplace (WHO 2010) with the following areas being highlighted, namely 'health and safety concerns in the physical work environment; health, safety and well-being concerns in the psychosocial work environment including organization of work and workplace culture; personal health resources in the workplace; and ways of participating in the community to improve the health of workers, their families and other members of the community (2010: 10). It is interesting to see how this WHO definition of a healthy organization is a direct anthesis to the carefully worded definition of a 'cult' provided by West and Langone (1986) where 'manipulative techniques' and the aforementioned imbalanced devotion and focus on the group, is potentially to the detriment of 'members, their families or the community'.

While health and safety law is commonly used to counter harmful practices in organizations who employ staff, those which rely partly or mostly on volunteers or voluntary labour, particularly in deregulated sectors (involving contractors), are sometimes subject to less scrutiny (Tombs and Whyte 2013). Abuses within the charitable and non-profit sector are also sadly well recorded (Clarke 2021) and as such there is no justifiable reason why abuses in the context of religious or political groups, who often rely heavily on congregants/members as volunteers, should be exempt from such a focus. The use of the word 'cult', when applied carefully based on an assessment of the group or organization's practices against such defined aspects of health and safety and duty of care, is a clear and timely watchword that there is a significant risk of physical and/or psychological harm and that relevant agencies (such as the Health and Safety Executive in the UK) should be invited to intervene.

Hearing and acting on the survivor voice in cult research

In research on sexual abuse and domestic or intimate partner violence, there is a long and reputable tradition of research which is survivor oriented and focused on establishing effective treatment protocols for victims of such abuses (Schechter 1982; Herman 2015). Likewise for those exiting coercive and abusive groups or cults, there is a growing corpus of work which embraces the survivor voice and which is focused on effective recovery approaches (Langone 1993; Goldberg et al. 2017).

Some of the research is led by survivors who have undertaken training and education to become professionals and academics in the field of coercive control and influence. One such education programme, the MSc in the psychology of coercive control (Dubrow-Marshall and Dubrow-Marshall 2017) at the University of Salford has, since 2017, focused on commonalities and differences in the forms of coercion and abusive practices across the domains of intimate partner violence, cults and extremist groups, trafficking gangs and organized crime. Adopting a secular position on the nature of harm, but also recognizing the ideological justification that is given at times for forms of psychological and physical violence and abuse (such as female genital mutilation, starvation, group induced suicides, isolation and servitude), programmes of this nature seek to ensure that an 'insider' perspective on research and practice is fully embraced (Voloder and Kirpitchenkom 2013).

Research and knowledge on coercion and abuse can therefore be seen to adopt a range of epistemological forms that make the research fundamentally action oriented. A transformational or transformative epistemology thus allows for research which is measuring not only the extent of harm from abusive practices (Dubrow-Marshall and Dubrow-Marshall 2015, 2023) but also the capacity of research to transform the experience of those who conduct it and who are the participants in it. The notion of co-researchers in such action focused research is operationalized, as is the rightful assumption that subjective experience, an emic-based approach to knowledge, can add heightened awareness in the process of data collection and analysis (Groot et al. 2019). By recognizing the value of survivors in research, the playing field for inquiry is levelled and democratized in fundamentally agentic ways which make the research process 'matter' for the people most affected by the subject at hand with demonstrable benefits for well-being (Scarpa, Di Martino and Prilleltensky 2021). Social and personal change thus become the potential outcomes of research in this transformational realm or what Stevens (1998) refers to as a 'tertiary mode' of enquiry (an example of which is feminist psychology). When the focus is on coercion and undue influence in cults then this enshrines a commitment to ensure that abusive practices are rooted out and that the survivors of such practices get justice.

It follows therefore that the use of the word 'cult' in research is fundamentally useful to allow an epistemological key to be turned which unlocks social change and the ending of abusive practices. In the same way as with research on 'domestic abuse' or 'sexual abuse' or 'sex trafficking', the power of the word 'cult' is in its specific intent to point to abuses and their harmful effects and to allow for the identification of evidence-based and specific interventions to prevent the harm in the future and to provide a recovery path for survivors. With such terms, including the term 'cult', comes a call to arms and which allows for survivor-led research to investigate the extent of harm perpetrated and the remedies for it, both individually and socially (within and beyond the confines of the group in question). As such then this form of action-based research (Mertens 2009) does not intend, as with some classical forms of social anthropology (Grimshaw 2001), to merely observe the happenings and ideological writings of cult-like groups and to leave them unchanged. Such a hermeneutic epistemology has its place, particularly perhaps among sociologists and anthropologists of culture, and is complimentary, not contradictory of genuine attempts at transformative research which aims to bring emancipatory and restorative change when coercion and abuse is recognized as taking place.

In all of the abovementioned ways the use of the word 'cult' provides a clear form of social empathy for those who have been coerced and abused. It recognizes that no organization is above the law and is beyond reproach, regardless of its ideology. Thus a focus on cults and a fuller recognition of the utility of the term facilitates a focus on justice for victims of cultic practices and is in alignment with approaches towards justice for victims broadly and in alignment with the UN's instrument and 'Declaration of Basic Principles of Justice for Victims of Crime and Abuse of Power' (UN 1985).

Recognizing 'cults'

The recognition of cults, as groups and organizations with coercive and abusive practices which harm some of their members, therefore engenders a progressive and transformational approach for both individuals and for the groups themselves as well. A range of groups and movements have, over the years, welcomed the scrutiny which a focus on cultic practices and potential harms brings. Whether in egregious cases in mainstream churches (such as with sexual abuse cases involving Catholic clergy Secretariat of Laity, Marriage, Family Life and Youth 2017), in newer minority religious groups (e.g. with child abuse cases in ISKCON, Rochford and Heinlein 1998) or in radical political groups (Downes 2017), the acknowledgement of abusive practice and a practical commitment to change and justice for victims and survivors, powerfully demonstrates that recognizing cults is a vital first step to addressing and combatting abuse and harm wherever it is found. The word 'cult' should be used carefully, with an assembling of evidence and an eschewing of lazy stereotypes, but its use is a powerful driver for change and justice and creates a ripple of hope that suffering is not inevitable and that something demonstrable can be done to put an end to coercion and abuse in all its forms everywhere.

References

Almendros, C., M. Gámez-Guadix, Á. Á. Rodríguez-Carballeira and J. A. Carrobles (2011), 'Assessment of Psychological Abuse in Manipulative Groups', *International Journal of Cultic Studies*, 2 (1): 61–76.

American Psychiatric Association (2023), *Diagnostic and Statistical Manual of Mental Disorders: DSM-5-TR*, 6th edn. Washington: American Psychiatric Publishing, Inc.

Aronoff, J., S. J. Lynn and P. Malinoski (2000), 'Are Cultic Environments Psychologically Harmful?', *Clinical Psychology Review*, 20 (1): 91–111. https://doi.org/10.1016/s0272-7358(98)00093-2

Baldwin, S. B., D. P. Eisenman, J. N. Sayles, K. Chuang and G. Ryan (2011), 'Identification of Human Trafficking Victims in Health Care Settings', *Health and Human Rights*, 13: 1–8.

Banisadr, M. (2009), 'Terrorist Organizations Are Cults', *Cultic Studies Review*, 8 (2): 154–84.

Barker, E. (1989), *New Religious Movements: A Practical Introduction*. London: HMSO. ISBN: 9780113409273.

Barker, E. (2010), 'The Cult as a Social Problem', in T. Hjem (ed.), *Religion and Social Problems*. Routledge Advances in Sociology, 198–212. Oxon: Routledge. ISBN: 9780415800563.

Beckford, J. (2003), *Social Theory and Religion*. Cambridge: Cambridge University Press. https://doi.org/10.1017/CBO9780511520754

Biderman, A. (1957), 'Communist Attempts to Elicit False Confessions from Air Force Prisoners of War', *Bulletin of the New York Academy of Medicine*, 33: 616–25.

Bloom, C. (2023), *Does Government do God? An Independent Review into How Government Engages with Faith*. The Stationery Office.

Boyle-Laisure, R. (2016), 'Employing Trafficking Laws to Capture Elusive Leaders of Destructive Cults', *Oregon Review of International Law*, 17 (2): 209–55. (Republished in The International Journal of Coercion, Abuse and Manipulation, 2021).

Bromley, D. G. (2012), 'The Sociology of New Religious Movements', in O. Hammer and M. Rothstein (eds), *The Cambridge Companion to New Religious Movements*, 11–28. Cambridge: Cambridge University Press. https://doi.org/10.1017/CCOL9780521196505.003

Bromley, D. G. and J. G. Melton, eds (2002), *Cults, Religion and Violence*. Cambridge: Cambridge University Press.

Chryssides, G. D., ed. (2018), *Minority Religions in Europe and the Middle East: Mapping and Monitoring*, 1st edn. Oxon: Routledge. https://doi.org/10.4324/9781315595559

Clarke, G. (2021), 'The Credibility of International Non-governmental Organizations (INGOs) and the Oxfam Scandal of 2018', *Journal of Civil Society*, 17 (3–4): 219–37.

Council of Europe (1950), *European Convention for the Protection of Human Rights and Fundamental Freedoms*, as amended by Protocols Nos. 11 and 14, 4 November 1950, ETS 5. Available at https://www.refworld.org/docid/3ae6b3b04.html (accessed 28 April 2023).

Courtois, C. (2008), 'Complex Trauma, Complex Reactions: Assessment and Treatment', *Psychological Trauma: Theory, Research, Practice and Policy*, 8: 86–100. https://doi.org/10.1037/1942-9681.S.1.86

Domestic Abuse Act (England and Wales) (2021), The Stationery Office.

Damgaard, N., ed. (2021), *Wounded Faith: Understanding and Healing from Spiritual Abuse*. Bonita Springs, FL: International Cultic Studies Association (ICSA).

Dawson, L., ed. (1998), *Cults in Context: Readings in the Study of New Religious Movements*. Oxon: Routledge.
Downes, J. (2017), '"It's Not the Abuse That Kills You, It's the Silence": The Silencing of Sexual Violence Activism in Social Justice Movements in the UK Left', *Justice, Power & Resistance*, 1 (2): 35–58.
Dubrow-Marshall, R. and L. J. Dubrow-Marshall (2015), 'Cults and Mental Health', in H. Friedman (ed.), *Encyclopedia of Mental Health*, 2nd edn, 393–401. Academic Press (Elsevier). http://dx.doi.org/10.1016/B978-0-12-397045-9.00153 (3rd edn, 2023).
Dubrow-Marshall, R. and L. J. Dubrow-Marshall (2017), *MSc Psychology of Coercive Control Programme*. University of Salford. Available at www.salford.ac.uk/pgt-courses/psychology-of-coercive-control (accessed 11 December 2023).
Dubrow-Marshall, R., P. Martin and R. Burks (2003), *Extent of Group Identity Scale (EGIS)*. Unpublished test instrument.
Dubrow-Marshall, R. P. (2010), 'The Influence Continuum – The Good, the Dubious and the Harmful – Evidence and Implications for Policy and Practice in the 21st Century', *International Journal of Cultic Studies*, 1 (1): 1–12.
Ellwood, R. (1986), 'The Several Meanings of Cult', *Thought*, LXI (241): 212–24.
Goldberg, L., W. Goldberg, R. Henry and M. Langone, eds (2017), *Cult Recovery: A Clinician's Guide to Working with Former Members and Families*. Florida: International Cultic Studies Association.
Grimshaw A. (2001), *The Ethnographer's Eye: Ways of Seeing in Modern Anthropology*. Cambridge: Cambridge University Press.
Groot, B. C., M. Vink, A. Haveman, M. Huberts, G. Schout and T. A. Abma (2019), 'Ethics of Care in Participatory Health Research: Mutual Responsibility in Collaboration with Co-researchers', *Educational Action Research*, 27 (2): 286–302. http://dx.doi.org/10.1080/09650792.2018.1450771
Hamilton, M. A. and E. R. Becker (2005), *God Vs. The Gavel: Religion and the Rule of Law*. Cambridge: University of Cambridge Press.
Herman, J. (1992), *Trauma and Recovery*. London: Pandora (2nd edn, 2015). Cambridge: Cambridge University Press.
Introvigne, M. (2018), 'Xie Jiao as "Criminal Religious Movements": A New Look at Cult Controversies in China and Around the World', *The Journal of CESNUR*, 2 (1): 13–32.
Kent, S. (1992), *Cults*, in E. Borgotta and M. L. Borgotta (eds), *The Encyclopedia of Sociology*, vol. 1, 402–4. New York: Macmillian.
Kent, S. (2005), 'Education and Re-education in Ideological Organizations and Their Implications for Children', *Cultic Studies Review*, 4 (2): 119–45.
Knox, G. W. (1999), 'Comparison of Cults and Gangs: Dimensions of Coercive Power and Malevolent Authority', *Journal of Gang Research*, 6 (4): 1–39.
Krakauer, J. (2003), *Under the Banner of Heaven: A Story of Violent Faith*. New York: Random House.

Kruglanski, A. W. and E. Orehek (2011), 'The Role of the Quest for Personal Significance in Motivating Terrorism', in J. P. Forgas, A. W. Kruglanski and K. D. Williams (eds), *The Psychology of Social Conflict and Aggression*, 153–64. London: Psychology Press.

Langone, M. D., ed. (1993), *Recovery from Cults: Help for Victims of Psychological and Spiritual Abuse*. New York: W. W. Norton.

Langone, M. D. (2000), 'The Two "Camps" of Cultic Studies: Time for a Dialogue', *Cultic Studies Journal*, 17: 55–68.

Langone, M. (2005), 'Cult Awareness Groups and NRM Scholars: Toward Depolarization of Key Issues', *Cultic Studies Review*, 4 (2): 146–68.

Lavy, L. (2022), 'Getting the Ghet: Analyzing the Need for State Intervention in Canadian Jewish Divorces', *International Journal of Coercion, Abuse, and Manipulation*, 3. https://doi.org/10.54208/1000/0003/004

Levey, D. and R. Dubrow-Marshall (2023), 'Cults and Media Stereotypes: Does Media Coverage of Current and Former Cult Members Hinder Victims' Recovery?', *International Journal of Coercion, Abuse and Manipulation*. https://doi.org/10.54208/1000/0005/003

Lifton, R. J. (1961), *Thought Reform and the Psychology of Totalism: A Study of 'brainwashing' in China*. Chapel Hill, NC: University of North Carolina Press.

Melton, J. G. (1992), *Encyclopedic Handbook of Cults*. Oxon: Routledge.

Mertens, D. M. (2009), 'A Transformative Research and Evaluation Model', in *Transformative Research and Evaluation*, 136–63. The Guilford Press.

Modern Slavery Act (England and Wales) (2015), The Stationery Office.

Nwaogu, N. R., V. E. Weli and M. D. Mbee (2019), 'Evaluation of Youth Vulnerability to Community Cultism in Selected States in the Niger Delta Region of Nigeria', *Asian Journal of Advanced Research and Reports*, 7 (4): 1–14.

Pesiah, C., S. Finkel, K. Shulman, P. Melding, J. Luxenberg, J. Heinik, R. Jacoby, B. Reisberg, G. Stoppe, A. Barker, H. Firmino and H. Bennett (2009), 'The Wills of Older People: Risk Factors for undue Influence', *International Psychogeriatrics*, 21 (1): 7–15.

Richardson, J. T. (1993), 'Definitions of Cult: From Sociological-Technical to Popular-Negative', *Review of Religious Research*, 34 (4): 348–56.

Robbins, T. (1988), *Cults, Converts, and Charisma*. London: Sage.

Rochford Jr., E. B. (2007), 'The Sociology of New Religious Movements', in A. Blasi (ed.), *American Sociology of Religion*. Leiden, The Netherlands: Brill. https://doi.org/10.1163/ej.9789004161153.i-317.69

Rochford Jr., E. B. and J. Heinlein (1998), 'Child Abuse in the Hare Krishna Movement: 1971:1986', *ISKCON Communication Journal*, 6 (1): 43–69.

Rosedale, H. and M. D. Langone (2015), 'On using the Term "Cult"', *ICSA Today*, 6 (3): 4–6.

Saldana, O., A. Rodriguez-Carballeira, C. Almendros and G. Guilera (2021), 'Group Psychological Abuse and Psychopathological Symptoms: The Mediating Role of Psychological Stress', *Journal of Interpersonal Violence*, 36 (11–12): NP6602–23.

Scarpa, M. P., S. Di Martino and I. Prilleltensky (2021), 'Mattering Mediates Between Fairness and Well-being', *Frontiers in Psychology*, 12: 744201. https://doi.org/10.3389/fpsyg.2021.744201

Schechter, S. (1982), *Women and Male Violence : The Visions and Struggles of the Battered Women's Movement.* Boston: South End Press.

Schein, E., I. Schneier and C. Barker (1961), *Coercive Persuasion: A Socio-psychological Analysis of the 'Brainwashing' of American Civilian Prisoners by the Chinese Communists.* New York: W. W. Norton.

Secretariat of Laity, Marriage, Family Life and Youth (2017), *Catholic Response to Sexual and Domestic Violence and Abuse.* The Catholic Church.

Serious Crime Act (England and Wales) (2015), The Stationery Office.

Sirgy, M. and D. J. Lee (2018), 'Work-Life Balance: An Integrative Review', *Applied Research Quality Life*, 13: 229–54. https://doi.org/10.1007/s11482-017-9509-8

Stark, E. (2007), *Coercive Control: How Men Entrap Women in Personal Life.* Oxford: Oxford University Press.

Stevens, R. (1998), 'Tri-Modal Theory', in R. Sapsford (ed.), *Theory and Social Psychology.* London: Sage.

Tajfel, H. and J. C. Turner (1979), 'An Integrative Theory of Intergroup Conflict', in W. Austin and S. Worchel (eds), *The Social Psychology of Intergroup Relations*, 33–47. Monterey: Brooks/Cole.

Tombs, S. and D. Whyte (2013), 'Transcending the Deregulation Debate? Regulation, Risk, and the Enforcement of Health and Safety Law in the UK', *Regulation & Governance*, 7 (1): 61–79. https://doi.org/10.1111/j.1748-5991.2012.01164.x

Turner, J., M. Hogg, P. Oakes, S. Reicher and M. Wetherell (1987), *Rediscovering the Social Group: A Self-categorisation Theory.* Cambridge: Basil Blackwell.

United Nations General Assembly (1948), *Universal Declaration of Human Rights.* United Nations. Available at https://www.un.org/en/about-us/universal-declaration-of-human-rights (accessed 28 April 2023).

Voloder, L. and L. Kirpitchenko (2013), *Insider Research on Migration and Mobility: International Perspectives on Researcher Positioning*, 1st edn. London: Routledge. https://doi.org/10.4324/9781315588773

Wallace, P. (2007), 'How Can She Still Love Him? Domestic Violence and the Stockholm Syndrome', *Community Practitioner*, 80: 32–4.

West, L. J. and M. D. Langone (1986), 'Cultism: A Conference for Scholars and Policy Makers', *Cultic Studies Journal*, 3 (1): 117–34.

World Health Organization (2010), 'Healthy Workplaces: A Model for Action', *WHO*. Available at www.who.int/occupational_health/publications/healthy_workplaces_model_action.pdf (accessed 28 April 2023).

Zablocki, B. (1997), 'Cults: Theory and Treatment Issues'. Paper presented to conference 31 May 1997 in Philadelphia, Pennsylvania.

Zablocki, B. and T. Robbins, eds (2001), *Misunderstanding Cults: Searching for Objectivity in a Controversial Field.* Toronto: University of Toronto Press.

Part II

Contemporary 'cultic' studies

7

The light of the world
La Luz del Mundo, liminality and NRM studies

Donald A. Westbrook

La Luz del Mundo ('The Light of the World', hereafter LLDM) is a Mexican-born new religious movement tracing back to the 1920s. According to J. Gordon Melton (2020), it is the second largest religious group in Mexico after the Catholic Church and has grown significantly in the last few decades, with population centers and temples (houses of worship) around the world and claims of millions of members spread across fifty nations. Demographically, outside Mexico, it is most successful in the United States, and in particular in California and Texas (Melton 2020; see also Westbrook 2020). In the last few years, however, LLDM has gained attention in the media, both in and outside of Mexico, due to the imprisonment and conviction of its apostle and leader, Naasón Joaquín García (1969–) on charges of sexual abuse against minors (see, for instance, Molina 2022). García, who was arrested in Los Angeles, has been sentenced to nearly seventeen years in prison, to be served in the United States. LLDM, meanwhile, has expressed its continued support and allegiance to their apostle, who will continue to remotely manage the church through the duration of his incarceration (Jany and Ormseth 2022). In fact, LLDM continues to maintain that their leader is innocent and honorable in public statements and worship meetings and to my knowledge has not acknowledged any illegalities or apologized to victims in the case.

The purpose of this chapter, in a volume about 'cult' rhetoric, is to consider some of the ways in which LLDM has been marginalized due to its cultural status as a so-called 'cult', especially in Mexico and the United States, and how this has affected church members and influenced the manner in which the church interfaces with outsiders. Rather than focusing on leaders such as the apostle Naasón, or for that matter on anticult/countercult activists, I would like to shift attention to the ways in which the LLDM church and its members have responded to internal and external challenges, such as the court case, incidents of persecution and violence, the Covid-19 pandemic, and, in particular, its central religious ritual known as the Holy Supper (*Santa Cena*). LLDM is a new religion with an increasing global reach but it also finds itself at a critical moment in its twenty-first century history. It is arguably large enough, and its followers apparently committed enough, to weather the various legal and public relations storms; but it is also clear that it is often operating from a largely defensive posture in its public relations and legal affairs, due in no small part to the lingering perception of the group as a 'cult' – an accusation and label that has been with the group long before the arrest and conviction of its third and current apostle (see Introvigne 2020).

LLDM: NRM or not?

LLDM researchers have often approached the organization from the standpoint of Latin American history and within the religious context of Pentecostalism in light of the group's early history and its continuing liturgical focus on the Holy Spirit (see, for instance, Nutini and Nutini 2014; De la Torre 2000; Greenway 1973). In the last few years, though, the apostle's arrest, imprisonment and conviction has led to renewed interest as more academic researchers consider it as a new religion or new religious movement (NRM), even as it continues to be marginalized as a 'cult' in popular culture. LLDM is almost one hundred years old and has undergone a tremendous amount of change and expansion, especially under the leadership of its second apostle, Samuel Joaquín Flores (1937–2014). *The Journal of CESNUR*, in particular, has published a number of articles related to LLDM, including a piece by the author on fieldwork conducted at sites in southern California (Westbrook 2020). In many ways, this chapter expands on this earlier analysis and includes my reflections on attending a Holy Supper (in Dallas, Texas, in February 2020) and visiting the Houston temple soon after an anti-LLDM shooting incident (July 2021).

Before proceeding, however, it should be acknowledged that LLDM is not particularly fond, as far as I can tell, of being labeled a new religion or NRM, given that the group views itself as a *restoration* of primitive Christianity. Indeed, on its official English language homepage, the group describes itself as a 'Restoration of the Early Christian Church' and a 'Christian-based faith. Its practices are based on the biblical teachings of Christian fraternity and solidarity, teaching respect for human dignity, equal treatment, and non-discrimination' (The Light of the World n.d.). As such, it is similar to another North American-born religious tradition, Mormonism, and its largest institutional expression, the Church of Jesus Christ of Latter-day Saints. For LLDM's part, I assume that the NRM designation is at least tolerated or understood from a historical perspective, and in any event is certainly preferable to the pejorative 'cult' or 'sect'. Moreover, LLDM has been discussed in sessions at CESNUR (Center for Studies on New Religions) conferences, including the 2022 meeting in Québec City, where two church spokespersons, Bigvai Estrada and Jack Freeman, participated in a panel entitled 'A Fast-Growing Religious Movement, a Global Charitable Work, and an Apostle in Jail' (CESNUR 2022).

While the NRM lens is methodologically useful and certainly less value-laden than 'cult' or 'sect', it is therefore inaccurate and misleading in the sense that it fails to fully account for the *self-identification* of its members. It also helps lay bare perennial problems in NRM studies (indeed in the academic study of religion in general) concerning insiders and outsiders and the place of *emic* versus *etic* analysis. How should a group such as LLDM be classified, labeled and understood, whether on its own terms, in comparative context, or based on a popular or non-technical understanding of what others within a particular culture or subculture perceive as 'cults' versus 'real religions'? Also, to what extent is LLDM 'new' anyhow? Or is this ultimately a relative assessment, even within NRM studies? After all, LLDM (founded in 1926) is relatively new (or newer) compared to its restorationist competitor, the Church of Jesus Christ of Latter-day Saints (founded in 1830), but older than many other groups studied by NRM researchers – organizations and movements that tend to be quite younger than one hundred years old. In the end, perhaps the point is that groups variously described as 'cults', 'sects', 'new religions', 'alternative religions' and the like find themselves in a kind of double bind, a methodological no man's land, in which neither 'cult' nor 'new religion' quite fits but a group would typically prefer to be analysed as an 'NRM' than be Othered and dismissed, delegitimized and denounced as a 'cult'. This partially explains why a group such as LLDM would seek to be better understood by NRM scholars and at a professional organization such as CESNUR, rather than seeking out historians of Christianity or presenting themselves at say the Society for Pentecostal Studies. Neither pair of shoes quite fit, but the former are a bit more comfortable – and in the process builds bridges with scholars who can interface with others in academia, and perhaps also the public, who might otherwise have no other source of information and be left with discriminatory and anticult stereotypes.

Holy Supper: Dallas, Texas, February 2020

The Holy Supper (*Santa Cena*), commemorating Jesus's last meal with his apostles, is a central LLDM event – its 'main religious act', according to Massimo Introvigne (2018) – that usually takes place at the church's headquarters in Guadalajara on 14 August (the birthday of the first apostle, Aarón). Introvigne, who has been to Guadalajara to visit LLDM sites on multiple occasions, corroborated church estimates that the 2019 Holy Supper in Mexico – the last before the apostle's arrest and restrictions due to Covid-19 – was attended by an astounding 600,000 members (Introvigne 2019). LLDM members, known simply as 'brothers' and 'sisters' among one another, travel from all across Mexico for the annual event as a form of pilgrimage, and many adherents travel internationally, all to celebrate the Holy Supper and reconnect with others in an event overseen by the apostle. My own academic investigation into LLDM did not begin until early 2020, after the apostle had been arrested (June 2019), and has so far been limited to fieldwork and trips inside the United States, in particular California and Texas. Again, my observations of LLDM life in California have been published and focus on visits to temples in Los Angeles and Long Beach (Westbrook 2020).

On 14 February 2020, I had the opportunity to attend a Holy Supper at the Dallas Fair Park. Unlike previous years, with Holy Supper activities traditionally in and around Guadalajara, festivities in 2020 were distributed around the world and the US-based ceremonies came at the invitation of the apostle.[1] In the United States, six locations were chosen based on church demographics for the February 2020 events (Washington, Dallas, Los Angeles, San Diego, Phoenix, and Chicago). This de-centralization was due most obviously to the apostle's imprisonment (precluding his presence in Guadalajara) but also the emerging Covid-19 pandemic (limiting travel and the logistics required for a single large event). It must be remembered that, at that point in early 2020, the outbreak of Covid-19 had not led, at least in the United States, to the mass shutdowns and closures that would ensue in the coming months.

Bigvai Estrada, head of American public relations for LLDM and then pastor of its Houston temple, invited me and a number of others (including NRM researchers J. Gordon Melton and Holly Folk) to the Dallas celebration. Most LLDM members speak Spanish and attend services in Spanish, as was the case in Dallas, where the vast majority of worshippers – in the low thousands, I would estimate – celebrated the Holy Supper together in the main rented indoor space. Estrada is somewhat rare in the church because he is bilingual and pastors to an English-speaking congregation (he has served English-speaking members in

Hawaii, California and Texas, among other locations). For academic research, Estrada was the main point of contact and helped interpret prayers and songs as they unfolded, over several hours. English-speaking members, or those who preferred an English service, worshipped in a separate and (somewhat) smaller space, but one that was still packed with brothers and sisters – at least several hundred, by my estimate, with hundreds more Spanish speakers scattered across the rest of the complex and in the larger meeting hall. The high point of the Holy Supper came with the breaking of bread and drinking of grape juice (alcoholic consumption is prohibited in the group), similar to other Christian groups that celebrate the sacrament of the Eucharist and its variations on a weekly basis. In LLDM, though, it must be remembered that the Holy Supper is typically an *annual* rather than weekly celebration, highlighting its soteriological significance as well as the sociological opportunity for members from different regions to reunite.

There are relatively few studies on LLDM and, aside from a handful of essays and reflective pieces from NRM scholars in recent years, much of the existing literature – from scholars and certainly from journalists – tends to approach the group with a degree of suspicion or outright prejudice in a manner apparently tainted by anticult rhetoric and assumptions. Perhaps the most recent and conspicuous academic example in my mind, at least in English, is Hugo and Jean Nutini's 2014 book *Native Evangelism in Central Mexico*. They discuss LLDM at length, referring to it as a 'destructive sect' (2014: 38) and 'basically a theocracy, geared to the exploitation of the faithful under strict control' (2014: 80). On the subject of the Holy Supper, they acknowledge but are ultimately dismissive of its religious and social value, and instead focus on the festivities and ritual in economic rather than spiritual terms: it is the 'central ritual-ceremonial event of LLDM [. . .] but also a very important economic event: the collection of the tithe and an opportunity to present the apostle with special offerings (cash, cars, and other worldly goods)' (2014: 78). This is followed by a superficial and astoundingly dismissive treatment of prayers, psalms and sermons, and even the interjection that 'the experienced researcher of Protestant and Catholic manifestations of Christianity cannot help wondering how this egomaniacal sect came into being' (Nutini and Nutini 2014: 103). The authors conclude that 'The Santa Cena [Holy Supper], in short, is the embodiment of the cult of personality that fundamentally characterizes the top leadership of a destructive sect' (2014: 105).

Jack Freeman, another spokesperson for LLDM who, like Estrada, pastors to English-speaking congregations, was interviewed in connection with the

February 2020 Holy Supper celebration in the Los Angeles area at the Pomona Fairplex. Freeman, clearly used to handling misconceptions about the church, addressed cultic stereotypes about the celebration and in particular the idea that members worshipped the apostle: 'The world's already made a decision on who we are', Freeman explained. 'They call us a cult. They call us violent. They call us brainwashers, they call us so many different things. But right here, we're in our biggest event, and we're just here happy, we're joyful. Nobody's forced. We're here with our own free will because we want to be a part of this' (cited in Schrank 2020: online). Indeed, certainly in Dallas, the mood was a mix of celebration and reverence, and often quiet and emotional, depending on the stage in the service. On many occasions that evening, brothers and sisters – separated, as customary, by gender (see figure 7.1) – could be seen praying aloud, even crying, as a given pastor spoke to the crowd. They were joyous, exuberant, animated – quite often with hands outstretched in front of their chests or lifting up to the ceiling, in ways that reminded me of meetings in any number of Evangelical and Pentecostal churches.

One refreshingly nuanced perspective on the Holy Supper comes from Patricia Fortuny (2002), an anthropologist in Mexico who wrote a chapter on her observations in Guadalajara in 1999 and 2000.² Drawing on a Durkheimian approach and extensive fieldwork, Fortuny (2002) analysed the sacrifices that members took to make the pilgrimage ('transnational activity') to Guadalajara under the church's second apostle, Samuel, and was far more value neutral in

Figure 7.1 LLDM brothers (left) and sisters (right) during the Spanish-language Holy Supper service. 14 February 2020, Dallas, Texas, Fair Park. Photograph by the author.

her analysis as she took into account the vibrant and spiritual experiences of the brothers and sisters observed:

> The atmosphere in the streets surrounding the temple was pervaded with a collective, ecstatic religious devotion. I saw women falling into a trance and many others just crying, loudly or silently. The people present were overjoyed with the ceremony. We saw a couple of young women who had collapsed in the temple being carried by two male members to the emergency center. [...] Believers from multiple locations get together in Guadalajara to participate in a common sacred meal, which revitalized their bond. The act of consuming the sacred meal allows them to remake their kinship as parts of a body made of the same flesh and blood. Samuel [the Apostle] constitutes the centerpiece of this ritual; the emotions aroused by him in the faithful do not parallel any others. The intense feelings produced by the presence of their living Apostle are strengthened by the intimate relationships existing between people who are aware of sharing them. (Fortuny 2002: 31-32)

I, too, observed the kind of individual and collective religious energy or effervescence described here, although no one, to my knowledge, fainted during the ceremony. A more striking difference, of course, is that the current apostle, Naasón Joaquín García, was absent due to his imprisonment. However, there was a powerful moment during the evening when, much to the surprise of everyone gathered, a phone call from the apostle came through and was broadcast live to the faithful in Dallas. The apostle spoke in Spanish, and his words were translated along the way by our guide, Estrada. In the short message, the apostle welcomed everyone, expressed regret for not being there in person, spoke about his spiritual bond with brothers and sisters, and emphasized the importance of the Holy Supper in their spiritual life. Members were visibly moved on an emotional level by the apostle's call and presence among them, even if remotely, and was all the more meaningful due to the church's collective sense that his imprisonment was, and is, unjust (see, for instance, Miller 2019; Molina 2020b).

Despite his absence on a physical level, the apostle was still very much in control of his church and deeply respected by members at the Holy Supper in Dallas. At the same time, pushing back a bit on characterizations from both Fortuny and the Nutini's, the fact that the event was successful without the presence of the apostle evidenced the extent to which the group has been able to adapt and survive in the face of change and perceived persecution. The apostle will continue to remain in prison for years to come, requiring others to fill his traditional role at the Holy Supper. Perhaps he will continue to make himself available remotely, whether by phone or a video conference call, or participate in other ways such as sending statements or prerecorded messages. In any event, the success of the Dallas Holy Supper, and others since,[3] supports the view that LLDM will likely continue to adapt the timing and logistics of the Holy Supper as it is held in and outside of Mexico. It also underscores, I think, a theological observation that seems to have been missed by other researchers who focus inordinate sociological and psychological attention on the role of the apostle – namely that the apostle is the present-day messenger but through whom members ultimately connect *directly with God* through the saving power and love of Jesus Christ in accordance with LLDM restorationist beliefs. The apostle is also the leader of the restored church and that church is the organizational means by which this reality is brought about for members – but ultimately the relationship is between brothers and sisters and God directly, and, on an experiential level, this is evidenced by the ways that individuals pray silently or express themselves in verbal ways that sometimes includes speaking in tongues. LLDM spokesperson Jack Freeman put the point this way when thinking about the apostle, in a way that once again seeks to counter rhetoric and perceptions about a possible 'cult' of personality and adoration at play: 'I care about him a lot. I love him. I know who he is and I respect him very much, just as if you had a pastor who looked after your soul, you would love and care for him as well because of the spiritual nature of the relationship. But you're not going to worship him. You're not going to pray to him. You're not going to throw yourself at his feet like what's being said. That's ridiculous' (quoted in Schrank 2020: online). Based on my own observations, LLDM members certainly love their apostle, miss him and pray for his release, but, in the end, they are carried forward by love for God, their church and the brethren within it – made all the more poignant at this particular Holy Supper in Dallas because it coincided with Valentine's Day. However, it appears that 14 February was ultimately chosen for another reason: it is the birthday of the church's first apostle, Aarón.

Jason H. Dormady, in his book *Primitive Revolution: Restorationist Religion and the Idea of the Mexican Revolution, 1940-1968*, analysed the evolving theology and practice of the Holy Supper since it was first introduced by the church's first apostle, Aarón, in 1931. Dormady makes the case that the ceremony began as a way to appeal to Mexicans with backgrounds in both Catholicism and Protestantism (specifically Pentecostalism). 'For those disgruntled with Catholicism but still attracted to ritual and hierarchy', Dormady contends, 'it sated those predilections with ceremonies of a holy supper, baptism, childhood blessing, and celebrations of miraculous moments in the church. However, for those attracted by the anticlericalism of Protestantism or moved by the emotional spiritualism and expression of spiritual gifts found in Pentecostalism specifically, LDM covered those bases as well' (2011: 35). Ninety years later, what Dormady describes as 'new forms of what for them were truly revolutionary spiritual innovations' (2011: 35) have morphed yet again, with the third apostle approving and orchestrating from behind the scenes. Observers will have to wait and see if more changes are in order for LLDM holidays and celebrations, especially as members become even more accustomed to their apostle's leadership on a remote basis.

It is also possible that the change and tumult caused by the Covid-19 pandemic have helped normalize an environment in which new or altered experiences are more tolerable, whether that be the absence of the apostle, holding the Holy Supper in a place other than Guadalajara, or other considerations, such as the manner in which the bread and wine (juice) were prepared. For example, I was impressed by the tremendous care taken by designated male church members – masked, gloved, and wearing hair nets – who prepared the bread and wine (juice) cups so that everyone in attendance would have their own. I should also add that, as the pandemic proceeded, the LLDM church became even more stringent in terms of its health procedures, transitioned to remote services and promoted mask wearing. The church has been outspoken in its support of Covid-19 protocols and especially the need for vaccinations, even setting up vaccination clinics at temples for members and the general public in the United States (Martin 2021). These sorts of partnerships with public health initiatives also arguably serve a public relations end: to help normalize LLDM as a 'mainstream' (i.e. non-'cultic') religious group that follows rather than protests federal and state public health guidelines.

Persecution, violence and the realities of liminality

In the wake of the apostle's arrest, imprisonment, trial and conviction, it appears that everyday LLDM members remain committed followers and continue to express their faith, even at a moment in their church's history where it is increasingly subject to persecution, discrimination and even violence. Steady or increased religious commitment in the face of adversity is not altogether surprising, especially for NRM researchers familiar with the resilient ways in which religious organizations and members cope with, and rationalize, events that conflict with expected outcomes and contribute to cognitive dissonance (Dawson 1999). Whether or not LLDM continues to retain membership in the coming years remains to be seen, but it is clear that those who choose to stay or join have faced an increase in anti-LLDM sentiment. Francisco Tenório, in a 2020 article, outlined numerous examples of discrimination against LLDM members around the world following the apostle's arrest: custody disputes, loss of employment and bullying and physical violence at schools (Tenório 2020). A more recent example occurred in Houston on 10 July 2021, when a gunman approached the main LLDM temple around midday, with members and children eating lunch on the front lawn, and fired at least twelve bullets at the building before fleeing in his vehicle (LLDM members apprehended the suspect and he was arrested by local police). Fortunately, no one was physically injured or killed, though some of the shots entered through administrative offices as well as into the pastor's office and lobby. The gunman, Josue David Cordova, was not a member of the church, but, according to court data as reported in the *Houston Chronicle*, he 'took aim at the church for believing that the church was responsible for brainwashing his family' (Gill and Hensley 2021), lending support to the idea that he was indeed motivated by anticult rhetoric and presuppositions about the influence of 'mind control'. Bigvai Estrada, who was still pastor of the Houston LLDM temple at the time, toured me around the complex about two weeks after the incident. This was the third shooting at a Houston area LLDM site within a year, and coincided with a rise in other incidents directed against LLDM temples and members.[4] In another example from Houston, on 2 July 2020 a temple was vandalized, in what was later determined to be a hate crime, with words such as 'abusive', 'mistreatment', 'pedophilia' and 'bastards' spray painted prominently on the exterior of the building.[5]

Naasón Joaquín García pled guilty to sex crimes on 3 June 2022, after close to three years of sitting in jail ahead of a trial, and was sentenced to nearly seventeen years in prison. However, his legal difficulties are not yet over, and as of September 2022 faced a sexual abuse lawsuit in California (Molina 2022).[6] Two weeks after pleading guilty, LLDM spokespersons Bigvai Estrada and Jack Freeman attended CESNUR's annual meeting, held that year at Laval University in Québec City. LLDM was the subject of a panel, where I was one of the academic speakers, and naturally the apostle's legal troubles and guilty plea were discussed in the session. After a series of presentations, Estrada and Freeman read from a prepared statement – first in Spanish, then in English – that provided the church's rationale for why he pled guilty rather than continue to trial:

> The most common question we have been asked is: Why did the Apostle plead guilty? If you recall, for the last three years the Apostle Naasón Joaquín always

pled 'not guilty'. However, the decisions taken by the court during the last three years have categorically weakened his possibility of presenting a proper defense that would prove his innocence. Trying his case before a jury under those conditions and not being able to use exculpatory evidence practically left him defenseless, risking a probable prolonged imprisonment. For those reasons, with much pain the Apostle of Jesus Christ had to accept the agreement presented to him by the California Prosecutor's Office that would allow him a reduced sentence and avoid being subjected to a trial in which he would not have the possibility of using the available evidence for his defense that would prove his innocence.[7]

Despite this legal outcome, the LLDM statement given at CESNUR also affirmed that the apostle will continue to lead the church from behind bars. 'The Apostle of Jesus Christ Naasón Joaquín García is and will continue to be the spiritual guide of The Light of the World', Freeman read to the audience in the English translation. 'We publicly express our full and complete support, our trust in him remains intact with full knowledge of his integrity, his conduct and his work.' In September 2022, the apostle spoke to followers in Mexico via phone and reiterated much the same message. 'I do not see the bars that separate me from you', García said to his faithful. 'I see your beautiful faces . . . because you are the children of God' (quoted in Lin and Jany 2022). On the subject of discrimination and persecution, the statement included the following details:

> I can report to you that since the arrest of the Apostle three years ago, members of our community around the world HAVE suffered acts of religious discrimination in various forms including: vandalism, hate speech, discrimination in school and at work, threats, bullying at school, insults on social networks, and even physical aggressions. Some of our temples have been vandalized, windows broken, people have called to threaten to burn down or shoot at our temples, and our religious services have been disrupted by people who have come into our temples to offend Church members. . . . We have reported these incidents to the appropriate authorities and we keep record[s] of these acts of religious discrimination and intolerance.

Most of the LLDM temples I have visited in southern California and central Texas are located in urban areas with dense Hispanic populations, which makes sense for a new religion with origins in Mexico and a membership base that speaks Spanish. More research needs to be conducted on the causes, backgrounds and expressions of those who target LLDM as a 'cult' but it seems to me that much of the hate speech and crimes, at least, are operationalized within a Catholic countercult culture. Massimo Introvigne (1995), for instance, has written on distinctions between *religious countercult movements* and *secular anticult movements*, and in the case of LLDM the former seems most prominent and problematic, culturally speaking. It also makes sociological sense that Catholics would be most likely to take issue with LLDM, especially given its large share of the religious market in Mexico (Fortuny 2016). Also, LLDM's restorationist claims bring it into conflict with the notion of apostolic succession in the Catholic Church that traces from the present-day pope, in his capacity as the Bishop of Rome, to the biblical Peter. Meanwhile, LLDM's restorationist theology conflicts with that of another prominent North American-born religious group, the Church of Jesus Christ of Latter-day Saints, which maintains a strong missionary presence in Mexico and throughout the world.[8]

What all of this means is that LLDM finds itself in liminal spaces on multiple fronts and – alongside other NRMs that view themselves as carrying forward older traditions – offers scholars yet another case study of the challenges involved with classification of 'cults' or new religious movements. In terms of self-identification, LLDM members do not view themselves as part of a 'new' or 'alternative' religion and indeed quite the opposite: the apostles, from their viewpoint, are continuing a tradition that extends back 2,000 years, one that itself grew out of an even older and Jewish ancestry. Being labeled a NRM rather than a cult, however, offers the group a level of neutrality or respectability, even possible legitimacy from scholars, in the face of the apostle's imprisonment and as the group's everyday members remain committed to the cause, freely participate in church life, and support their leaders. Similarly, LLDM does not want to be regarded as merely yet another Pentecostal church, since that simplification fails to account for its restorationist theology and ecclesiology. As the church continues to expand its membership base outside Mexico and the United States, that process of globalization will surely bring with it new cultural challenges and opportunities as it seeks to be understood on its own terms. These growing pains will likely lead to the need for continued public relations campaigns to address ongoing perceptions of the group as a 'cult', especially since these have had real-world consequences in the form of vandalism and violence against LLDM members and temples. Whether this confluence of anticult/countercult rhetoric and discrimination waxes or wanes remains to be seen, as LLDM brothers and sisters acclimate to the absence of their apostle, fallout from his convictions and remaining legal challenges.

Acknowledgements

I am thankful to Bigvai Estrada, who arranged for a number of scholars, myself included, to visit the February 2020 Holy Supper in Dallas, Texas. The day before the Holy Supper, I participated in an LLDM-sponsored academic forum, along with J. Gordon Melton and Holly Folk, and where I presented some observations that emerged after visiting temples in southern California. Bigvai also kindly provided the English translation of the statement read by another church spokesperson, Jack Freeman, at the June 2022 CESNUR conference in Québec City as part of panel entitled 'A Fast-Growing Religious Movement, A Global Charitable Work, and an Apostle in Jail'. I presented on this panel as did Massimo Introvigne, Sara Pozos Bravo, Rosita Šorytė and J. Gordon Melton – with Estrada and Freeman responding on behalf of LLDM, in Spanish and English, respectively.

Notes

1 According to LLDM media, members of the church in the United States received a letter from the apostle on 26 January 2020 inviting them to attend a Holy Supper (see LLDM News 2020). It should be noted that in 2018 the church 'held the first nationwide Holy Supper in the United States at Glen Helen Amphitheater in San Bernardino [California]', which also helped set the stage for events in 2020 (see Molina 2020a).
2 Another, and more recent, examination of the Holy Supper is found in Mary Puckett's (2017: 122–8) insightful dissertation that also mentions the elaborate opening ceremony in Guadalajara.
3 Berea International, the church's public relations department, posted photos and videos from the February 2020 Holy Supper events on Facebook (see Berea International 2020). It appears that in 2020, 2021 and 2022, Holy Supper events again took place outside Guadalajara, but on the traditional date of 14 August, which would make made two Holy Suppers in 2020 (i.e. 14 February and 14 August) all the more unique.
4 Bigvai Estrada provided me with police reports, photographs and documentation about crimes committed at Houston LLDM sites in 2020 and 2021.
5 Photographs and a copy of the Houston police report were provided to me.
6 In October 2023, Naasón Joaquín García was indicted in the US on federal child pornography charges.
7 The English version of the statement (read by Jack Freeman at CESNUR 2022) was provided to me by Bigvai Estrada.
8 For more on the history of the Church of Jesus Christ of Latter-day Saints in Mexico, see Dormady and Tamez (2015).

References

Berea International (2020), 'Holy Supper TLOTW'. Facebook page. Available at https://www.facebook.com/holysupper (accessed 13 April 2023).

Berea International (2022), 'Berea International'. Available at https://www.bereainternacional.com/ (accessed 13 April 2023).

CESNUR (2022), Conference Program, Laval University. Available at https://www.cesnur.org/2022/quebec-final-program.htm (accessed 13 April 2023).

Dawson, L. L. (1999), 'When Prophecy Fails and Faith Persists: A Theoretical Overview', *Nova Religio*, 3 (1): 60–82. https://doi.org/10.1525/nr.1999.3.1.60

De la Torre, R. (2000), *Los Hijos de la Luz: Discurso, Identidad y Poder en La Luz del Mundo*. Jalisco: ITESO.

Dormady, J. H. (2011), *Primitive Revolution: Restorationist Religion and the Idea of the Mexican Revolution, 1940–1968*. Albuquerque: University of New Mexico Press.

Dormady, J. H. and J. M. Tamez, eds (2015), *Just South of Zion: The Mormons in Mexico and Its Borderlands*. Albuquerque: University of New Mexico Press.

Fortuny, P. (1995), 'Origins, Development and Perspectives of La Luz del Mundo Church', *Religion*, 25: 147–62.

Fortuny, P. (2016), 'La Luz Del Mundo', *World Religions and Spirituality Project*. Available at https://wrldrels.org/2016/10/08/la-luz-del-mundo-2/ (accessed 13 April 2023).

Fortuny, P. (2002), 'The *Santa Cena* of the *Luz Del Mundo* Church: A Case of Contemporary Transnationalism', in H. E. Rose and J. S. Chafetz (eds), *Transnational Immigrant Networks*, 15–50. Walnut Creek: AltaMira Press.

Gill, J. and N. Hensley (2021), '"By the Grace of God" No One Injured when Shooter Fired into Houston Church, Spokesman Says', *Houston Chronicle*, 13 July. Available at https://www.houstonchronicle.com/news/houston-texas/houston/article/By-the-grace-of-God-no-one-injured-when-16307921.php (accessed 13 April 2023).

Greenway, R. S. (1973), 'The "Luz Del Mundo" Movement in Mexico', *Missiology: An International Review*, 1 (2), 113–24.

Introvigne, M. (1995), 'The Secular Anti-Cult and the Religious Counter-Cult Movement: Strange Bedfellows or Future Enemies?', in Towler R. (ed.), *New Religions and the New Europe*, 35–54. Aarhus: Aarhus University Press.

Introvigne, M. (2018), 'The World's Fastest Growing Religious Movement? Visiting La Luz del Mundo in Guadalajara', *CESNUR*. Available at https://www.cesnur.org/2018/lux_del_mundo.htm (accessed 13 April 2023).

Introvigne, M. (2019), 'La Luz del Mundo Alive and Growing Notwithstanding the Apostle's Detention', *CESNUR*. Available at https://www.cesnur.org/2019/lux-del-mundo-alive.htm (accessed 13 April 2023).

Introvigne, M. (2020), 'La Luz del Mundo: A Short History', *The Journal of CESNUR*, 4 (2), 3–10. https://doi.org/10.26338/tjoc.2020.4.2.1

LLDM News (2020), 'Apostle Naasón Summons to Holy Supper'. Available at https://youtu.be/B44yewg4QI0 (accessed 13 April 2023).

The Light of the World (n.d.), English homepage. Available at https://www.tlotw.org (accessed 13 April 2023).

The Light of the World (2020), 'Holy Supper: The Light of the World Church'. Available at https://web.archive.org/web/20200207223957/http://holysupper.org/ (accessed 13 April 2023).

The Light of the World (2022), 'Statement at CESNUR 2022 Conference, Laval University, Québec City' (English translation provided to the author by Bigvai Estrada).

Lin, S. and L. Jany (2022), 'From an L.A. Prison Phone, La Luz del Mundo Megachurch Leader Addresses Followers in Mexico', *Los Angeles Times*, 19 September. Available at https://www.latimes.com/california/story/2022-09-19/la-luz-del-mundo-naason-joaquin-garcia-los-angeles-prison (accessed 13 April 2023).

Martin, E. (2021), 'Mobile Clinic at Embattled La Luz del Mundo Church in East L.A. Draws Questions, but Helps Officials Vaccinate Hundreds', *KTLA*, 26 April. Available at https://ktla.com/news/mobile-clinic-at-embattled-la-luz-del-mundo-church-in-east-l-a-draws-questions-but-helps-officials-vaccinate-hundreds/ (accessed 13 April 2023).

Melton, J. G. (2020), 'The Rise of La Luz del Mundo in Texas', *The Journal of CESNUR*, 4 (2): 21–35. https://doi.org/10.26338/tjoc.2020.4.2.2

Miller, L. (2019), 'Attorneys for La Luz del Mundo Leader Accused of Sex Abuse Claim "High-Tech Hit Job"', *Los Angeles Times*, 7 June. Available at https://www.latimes.com/local/lanow/la-me-ln-la-luz-del-mundo-attorneys-20190607-story.html (accessed 13 April 2023).

Miller, L., L. Jany and M. Ormseth (2022), 'Followers of Luz del Mundo "Apostle" say They'll Wait Out His Sex-Abuse Sentence', *Los Angeles Times*, 8 June. Available at https://www.latimes.com/california/story/2022-06-08/la-luz-del-mundo-church-leader-sentenced (accessed 13 April 2023).

Molina, A. (2020a), 'La Luz del Mundo will Continue to Host US Ceremony while Leader Remains in Jail', *Religion News Service*, 24 January. Available at https://religionnews.com/2020/01/24/la-luz-del-mundo-will-continue-to-host-u-s-ceremony-while-leader-remains-in-jail/ (accessed 13 April 2023).

Molina, A. (2020b), 'La Luz del Mundo Minister Says Abuse Allegations Are False'. *Religion News Service*, 15 February 2020. Available at https://religionnews.com/2020/02/15/la-luz-del-mundo-minister-says-abuse-allegations-are-false/ (accessed 13 April 2023).

Molina, A. (2022), 'La Luz del Mundo Leader, Naasón Joaquín García, Faces New Lawsuit in Los Angeles'. *Religion News Service*, 12 September 2022. Available at https://religionnews.com/2022/09/12/la-luz-del-mundo-leader-faces-new-lawsuit-in-los-angeles/ (accessed 13 April 2023).

Nutini, H. G. and J. F. Nutini (2014), *Native Evangelism in Central Mexico*. Austin: University of Texas Press.

Puckett, M. (2017), 'The Cosmopolitanization of the Luz del Mundo'. PhD diss., University of Florida. Available at https://ufdc.ufl.edu/UFE0051664/00001 (accessed 13 April 2023).

Schrank, A. (2020), 'La Luz Del Mundo's "Apostle" Leads His Church from Inside a Jail Cell', *LAist*, 20 June. Available at https://projects.laist.com/2020/homeland/profiles/mexico/ (accessed 13 April 2023).

Tenório, F. (2020), 'Discrimination against La Luz del Mundo Members After the Arrest of the Apostle', *The Journal of CESNUR*, 4 (2): 3–10. https://doi.org/10.26338/tjoc.2020.4.2.6

Westbrook, D. A. (2020), 'Field Report: The Light of the World in Greater Los Angeles', *The Journal of CESNUR*, 4 (2): 57–71. https://doi.org/10.26338/tjoc.2020.4.2.5

Cults of conspiracy and the (ongoing) Satanic Panic

Bethan Juliet Oake

Introducing the Satanic Cult Conspiracy

The Satanic Cult Conspiracy (SCC) is a long-standing conspiracy theory that alleges the existence of secret, Satanic cults who practise 'Satanic Ritual Abuse' (SRA) – the ritualistic abuse and/or sacrifice of children. Who these so-called cult members supposedly are and what their specific goals are vary across different interpretations of the conspiracy. In its different iterations these 'cults' have comprised one or varying combinations of politicians, music industry elites, vaccine scientists, 'the media', royal families, the local police, school teachers or simply the 'Satanist-next-door' (to name a few). This conspiracy theory follows a cyclical pattern, ebbing and flowing in and out of public discourse and popularity, and periodically resurfacing in the form of mass moral panics known as 'Satanism scares'. Writing in 1970, historian Norman Cohn presented one of the first recognitions of this pattern, identifying and tracing a Satanic 'myth' dating back to the Middle Ages:

> The fantasy is that there exists a category of human beings that is pledged to the service of Satan; a sect that worships Satan in secret conventicles and, on Satan's behalf, wages relentless war against Christendom and against individual Christians. (Cohn 1970: 3)

SCC's most recent Satanism scare, and potentially its most well-known today, took the form of 'the Satanic Panic', a term coined by sociologist Jeffrey S. Victor (1996), whose research laid some of the most influential groundwork in recognizing the phenomenon as a unified moral panic. The Satanic Panic spanned from the late 1960s to late 1990s, peaking in significance over the 1980s. The Satanic Panic is most commonly recognized as a widespread moral panic about Satanic cults, driven by a series of rumours and allegations of SRA across America. Its rhetoric also spread beyond the United States, with similar 'panics' appearing in areas of Australia, Canada and the UK (Hughes 2017: 696). It led to a multitude of accusations, arrests and in some cases convictions of innocent individuals accused of SRA, a crime later concluded through various investigations to be a complete myth (see, e.g., those listed in Waterhouse 2014: 85). The dynamics and definitions of what constitutes a 'witch-hunt' can be complex; researchers for the Salem Witch Museum (2023) have offered a broad formula for helping to identify them: 'fear + a trigger = scapegoat'. Through this lens, the Satanic Panic can therefore be considered in many ways a form of modern-day witch hunt. The secret Satanic cult network of SCC, by all accounts and evidence, simply does not exist.

Despite this, over the last decade, there appears to have been a resurgence of interest in SCC, with new targets at the receiving end of new SRA allegations. This pattern has begun to be publicly recognized, raising the question: Is (Western) society experiencing another Satanism scare? Recent years have seen a surge of popular articles alleging that the Panic is back, or indeed that it never really ended at all (Yalcinkaya 2022; Shukman 2022; Zadrozny 2022; Caldwell et al. 2021; Yuhas 2021; Romano 2021).

Discourse surrounding SCC intrinsically leads into that of 'cults'. SCC theorists undoubtedly centre their narratives in anticult rhetoric, creating a representation of ultimate 'evil' through the image of the Satanic cult. With their emphasis on Satanism and Occult practice, the rumour panics and false allegations generated by this conspiracy can be seen as representative of some of the issues surrounding anticult rhetoric that have been highlighted by scholars over the years – primarily the potential for the unjustified demonization of new religious movements (NRMs) (see Gallagher 2016). SCC develops the image of the stereotypical evil 'cult' and projects it onto various communities that it seeks to demonize. Perhaps ironically, however, similarities can also be drawn between the characteristics of SCC theorists with that of the stereotypical 'cult'. The argument can potentially then be made that SCC theorists, despite their anticult focus, represent a form of 'cult' in themselves – a cult of conspiracy.

In the introduction to their *Handbook of Conspiracy Theory and Contemporary Religion*, David G. Robertson, Egil Asprem and Asbjørn Dyrendal present three perspectives on the relationship between conspiracy theory and religion: conspiracy theories *in* religion, conspiracy theories *about* religion and conspiracy theories *as* religion (2018: 3). SCC poses a particularly interesting case study when considering these three perspectives. It is derived from Christian fundamentalism (Victor 1996), concerned with theories about Satanism and the Occult, and possesses its own unique networks of followers united by its narratives. In this sense, it can be considered reflective of a conspiracy theory that is simultaneously in, about, and as religion. When considering the relationship between conspiracy theory and religion, I will be focusing in this chapter specifically on the concept of the 'cult'. Through analysing the rhetoric of SCC, this chapter will centre on discussing and comparing two potential perspectives: SCC as being *about* cults and SCC (or, more specifically, those who promote its theories and rhetoric) *as* a cult.

These perspectives, I argue, do not necessarily have to exist in contradiction to each other; someone could simultaneously recognize how SCC weaponizes anticult rhetoric in a harmful way, while also considering it an example of a harmful cult in itself. Not only this, but that the former traits can potentially be used to 'evidence' the latter. Through this example, I hope to demonstrate how rhetoric around cults can be (and often are) understood and engaged in today within complex differing motivations, ideologies and contexts. In light of this, I will then give some brief thoughts regarding how we might consider 'the cult label' moving forward within the study of NRMs, and specifically within the study of conspiracy theories.

The rhetoric of anti-Satanism

Satanic Cult Conspiracy is undoubtedly a conspiracy about cults, albeit imaginary ones. The Satanic Panic of the late twentieth century saw the spread of SCC theories, culminating in widespread accusations of SRA. Perhaps the most famous SRA case during this time was the McMartin preschool trial, which triggered a surge of similar allegations taking hold across the United States and beyond. It began in 1983, when Ray Buckey, an employee at McMartin preschool, was accused of sexually molesting a two-year-old boy who went to the school. The next few years saw Buckey and his family members stand trial for 'hundreds of counts of conspiracy and child abuse tied to cult practices that the media and alleged experts called "satanic ritual abuse"' (Hughes 2017: 691). To this day, *McMartin* remains the longest criminal trial in American history, with the case lasting seven years before Buckey's full acquittal in 1990. The *McMartin* case reflected what would become a fairly common trend across many other SRA hoaxes, the targeting of preschool teachers and other child caregivers with 'Satanic cult member' accusations.

The Satanic Panic was fuelled by a combination of factors. SRA stories were validated both by gaining support from various channels of trusted authority and their ability to build upon existing societal fears. James T. Richardson, Joel Best and David G. Bromley explain how this rhetoric became accepted by sources such as the 'secular press', psychiatrists and the 'usually antireligious therapeutic community', as well as general law enforcement (1991: 7). This reflected a very similar pattern to that of the existing anticult movement (ACM), who in the 1970s had sought out spokespersons in a variety of expertise as a means to gain support from both the courts and government agencies (Melton 2002: 298). Sarah Hughes, in her investigation of the role of tabloid media in reinforcing the Panic, discusses how 1980s tabloids had also become accustomed to reporting sensationalized content under the guise of 'news' – with stories of SRA becoming a frequent feature (2017: 699–700). While these various authority channels certainly helped drive a sense of endorsement and legitimacy to SRA claims, they were perhaps primarily driven by their ability to draw upon existing fears that existed around the threat of 'cults' that had developed over the later half of the century. Hughes notes how Reagan's election as president in 1980 brought with it a 'trend of demonizing sixties liberal types', which then intersected with concerns regarding a paranormal-populated suburbia (2017: 694). These concerns then intertwined directly with those of the ACM, who in turn 'exploited the growing attention paid to satanism' as a means to further their cause (Richardson, Best and Bromley 1991: 8):

> Satanic cults are accused of brainwashing victims, and using mind control to get their followers to commit unspeakable acts. Thus, satanism has been incorporated into the broader anticult framework promoted by the ACM for over two decades. (Richardson, Best and Bromley 1991: 8)

In combining Satanic mythology with anticult moral panic, the Satanic Panic emphasized notions of 'outsiders' as a threat to society. In some respects, it can be seen as the final pinnacle of the cult panic, where cult fears peaked in creating an entirely fictional demonic enemy. It seemingly brought together the frightening traits that had come to be associated with cult threats in the image of the Satanic cult. In championing Satan over God, these cults were evidently presented as subversive to – and actively in opposition to – the mainstream morals of Christian society. In turn, their targeting of children reflected both abusive practices and, in many ways, symbolized the destruction of the American suburban family unit (see Victor 1996: 4). Cultural anthropologist Phillips Stevens Jr. has argued that in combining this 'victimisation of children' with 'blood sacrifice' and 'supernatural evil', Satanic demonology 'comprises the worst imaginable cultural nightmare' (1991: 31). SCC therefore was, and continues to be, an ultimate template of evil that can be successfully applied on to whichever group one wishes to demonize.

Following the end of the *McMartin* case in 1990, public endorsements of the conspiracy claims began to tail off as cases were increasingly debunked. As journalists and media began openly challenging cases, mainstream public sentiment shifted to one of scepticism as the reality of SRA became dubious (see Hughes 2017: 712). By the end of the 1990s it would be fair to conclude that the Satanic Panic had finally come to its close. However, while the Satanism scare may have ended, the overall conspiracy did not. While the SCC began to be rejected by channels that had previously lent endorsement, it instead sought out new channels in the developing online social media sphere of the twenty-first century. Therefore, as current events have demonstrated, the gap between the end of one Satanic cult scare and the start of the next was to be extremely short lasting.

One of the first significant SRA cases to emerge since the end of the Satanic Panic came in the form of the 2014 'Hampstead hoax', in which it was alleged that two children had been abused by a Satanic paedophile cult operating in Hampstead, North London. Despite the internet helping aid the debunking of the hoax, it undoubtedly also played a key role in spreading it in the first place. SCC theorists circulated videos of the children's initial statements online, along with a list of the supposed Satanic cult members which consisted primarily of the children's school teachers and parents of their school (information on the case gathered from Hoaxtead Research 2021). The Hampstead hoax demonstrated how SCC theories were able to adapt and appeal in the twenty-first century, utilizing social media as a tool for online conspiracy networks to communicate and share their theories around the case. In many ways, the hoax stood as a marker of what was to come over the next few years.

While hugely significant, the Hampstead case alone was not enough to necessarily evidence the potential return of a wider Satanic moral panic. The event that triggered the escalation of SCC rhetoric came instead in the form of the 2016 Pizzagate conspiracy, which originated on 4chan. 4chan is an online anonymous imageboard which allows users to create and respond to threads centred around a variety of topics. Catherine Thorleifsson presents two of the most important features of 4chan as *anonymity* and *ephemerality* – that is, that users are not identifiable, and inactive content is routinely deleted (2021: 289). She explains how this, combined with 4chan's lack of moderation, 'has since its inception made the imageboard a hotspot for offensive humour, coalescing into political activism on multiple occasions' (Thorleifsson 2021: 288). The platform has since become increasingly associated with the far-right, conspiracy theories, terrorism, and 'cyberfascism' (see Thorleifsson 2021) – it was from this online culture that the Pizzagate conspiracy first emerged. Pizzagate claimed that Hilary Clinton, along with a cabal of Democratic Party members, held orgies in the basement of Comet Ping Pong (a Washington pizza restaurant) that involved the sexual abuse, blood-drinking, and sacrifice of children (Kaplan 2021: 918–19). It culminated with the arrest of Edgar Welch, a North Carolina resident who had taken it on himself to investigate the pizzeria armed with an assault rifle (Kaplan 2021: 919). Pizzagate then swiftly morphed into the most significant movement to bring contemporary SCC to the forefront of media attention: QAnon. QAnon began in 2017, and also originated on 4chan. Marc André Argentino and Amarnath Amarasingam define QAnon as 'a decentralized ideology rooted in an unfounded conspiracy theory that a globally active "Deep State" cabal of satanic pedophile [*sic*] elites is responsible for all the evil in the world' (2021: 19). QAnon in this sense absorbed many of the existing cultural and theoretical characteristics of the Pizzagate conspiracy, while more solidly integrating themes of Satan-worship into its accusations.

QAnon has dominated much of the recent public discourse and research attention (e.g. Robertson and Amarasingam 2022; MacMillen and Rush 2022; Uscinski 2022) when it comes to analysing contemporary conspiracy movements. It demonstrates clearly how SCC's underlying 'Satanic cult' accusation can be projected onto different communities – in this case, its enemies being primarily made up of Democratic politicians. QAnon has since dispersed into various separate but overlapping networks, which has vastly expanded its rhetoric to encompass both a broader range of conspiracy theories and a longer and more diverse list of potential Satanic enemies. Despite QAnon being the most prominent face of contemporary SCC, it is extremely important to recognize that online networks promoting similar theories and SRA myths both predate and spread far beyond those who would identify themselves with QAnon. In some cases, SCC theorists online can be seen to state their active opposition to QAnon, despite propagating similar (and sometimes near identical) conspiracy claims. Conspiracy theory networks online tend to function as interconnected webs of discourse, and thus it is not uncommon for varying interpretations, theories and ideologies to overlap and intertwine.

SCC theories may at times take a local focus – such as in the case of the Hampstead hoax, in which accusations were primarily made against members of the local community. However, even in these instances, local Satanic cults are often seen as part of a larger network, a Satanic underground led by Satanic 'elites'. A popular theory across contemporary SCC alleges that these cults of Satanic elites torture children in order to harvest a life-extending drug called 'adrenochrome' from their blood (see Friedberg 2020). Across different interpretations of the conspiracy, these 'elites' may be considered politicians, police, the music or fashion industries, media outlets, 'mainstream' medical authorities or any combination of these.

The conspiracy therefore largely represents a form of 'New World Order' (NWO) conspiracy. Michael Barkun defines NWO conspiracies as: 'Theories [that] claim that both past and present events must be understood as the outcome of efforts by an immensely powerful but secret group to seize control of the world' (2013: 39). Barkun argues that NWO theories draw on two key narratives. The first comes from fundamentalist Protestantism and speculates the coming of the Antichrist to seize and ultimately end the world (Barkun 2013: 40). The second comes from a 'secular source' of 'historical and political pseudoscholarship' that claims secret societies are responsible for plotting and/or carrying out certain major world events as a means of world domination (Barkun 2013: 40). Specifically, SCC can be seen to reflect the 'hidden masters' conspiracy theme which is derived from Western esotericism and alleges that powerful societies 'possess secret knowledge and control hidden networks' (Asprem and Dyrendal 2018). References to 'the Satanic cult' can be taken as indicative of these tropes.

In addition to their SRA claims, SCC theories allege that Satanic cults seek to coerce young people to join their ranks or carry out Satanic crimes on their behalf. A popular societal concern during the Satanic Panic was that teenagers were being influenced and indoctrinated into the Occult via Satanic symbolism in popular culture (see Best 1991). Examples of the 'Satanic material' that could influence this had included listening to heavy metal, using Ouija boards or even playing Dungeons and Dragons (Best 1991: 101–2; Victor 1996: 134). Similar concerns have arisen in recent years, perhaps the first notable example coming in response to Lil Nas X's 2021 music video for 'Montero (Call Me By Your Name)', which featured the artist sliding down a pole into hell and giving Satan a lap dance. Crowds of individuals, including 'politicians and conservative social commentators', then took to social media in outrage against the imagery of the video (Wood 2021). This growing online panic amplified when Lil Nas X announced that he was releasing 'Satan shoes' which would each contain a drop of human blood in the sole (Wood 2021). Responses alluded to a form of spiritual warfare, framing the release as both morally subversive and as a genuine spiritual attack. The intersection of demonology, spiritual warfare and Christian nationalist rhetoric has been analysed by S. Jonathon O'Donnell, who explains how 'narratives of providential political upset and the identification of alterities threatening the (Christian) fabric of the US nation . . . merge to foster an image of diabolic threat' (2020: 697). This was demonstrated in a tweet by Governor Kristi Noem which claimed that '[w]e are in a fight for the soul of our nation. We need to fight hard. And we need to fight smart. We have to win'. Since then, there have been a multitude of popular conspiracy claims surfacing online that artists, influencers, fashion brands and other figures are attempting to influence the masses with Occult imagery (see Yalcinkaya 2022).

As it did during the Satanic Panic, therefore, contemporary SCC builds its theories upon existing moral panic. Throughout the Covid-19 pandemic, for example, its rhetoric could be found intertwining within the wave of anti-vaccine conspiracies. Theories presented the pandemic as manufactured by cults of elites in order to 'pave the way for the rise of the Anti-Christ' (Sturm and Albrecht 2021: 127), with variants of the conspiracy alleging that the vaccine contained a microchip geared to control humanity which represented the Mark of the Beast from Revelations (13.17) (Sturm and Albrecht 2021: 130).

Networks who promote SRA myths and allegations are more likely to conceal 'Satanic' themes on their surface, presenting themselves primarily as activists concerned with combatting issues of child abuse or paedophilia. This was also the case during the Satanic Panic, where Joel Best noted how anti-Satanists drew upon 'images of threatened children' as a means to both gather support and obscure the religious basis of their cause (1991: 95). Victor identifies those who target Satanism and Satanic cults as 'moral crusaders', which he defines as 'people who play the roles of activists in a social movement aimed at fighting a social "evil" which they perceive to exist in society' (1996: 207–8). Presenting SRA 'activism' under the guise of a more identifiable and sympathetic cause is likely one of the main reasons for the ongoing success of its rhetoric. However, within the context of SCC, these narratives can also perpetuate moral panic with underlying prejudices.

Philip Jenkins notes how in the UK during the 1970s, moral campaigns stigmatizing homosexuality occurred alongside religious campaigns against Satanism. In the 1980s, these anti-homosexuality campaigns morphed into anti-paedophilia campaigns, and anti-Satanism into anti-ritual abuse (1992: 10). Today, similar stigmas and patterns can be seen to be re-emerging across political and conspiratorial milieus. In February 2022 Florida passed a controversial law – dubbed the 'don't say gay' bill – aimed at restricting schools from educating students about sexual orientation and gender (Woodward 2022). Proponents of the bill reframed it as an 'anti-grooming' bill, associating left-wing opposition to the bill (and in turn, homosexuality) with grooming and paedophilia in a manner that journalists have pointed out reflects Satanic Panic rhetoric (Romano 2022). This has led to a wider concerning trend of the political right associating the LGBT+ community, particularly the transgender community, with accusations of paedophilia and 'grooming', and research has found anti-LGBT+ mobilization to be on the rise in the United States (ACLED 2022). In late November 2022, a Fox News article was published entitled 'No Healthy Society Can Tolerate Paedophilia', made up of transcriptions from various news segments by right-wing news anchor Tucker Carlson. This article pivots from Carlson discussing the topic of 'shadowy' paedophile elites, to his support of the 'don't say gay' bill, to equating gender-confirming surgery with the sexualization of children which he then labels a 'dangerous cult' (2022). While SCC theorists are not politically unanimous, far-right attitudes – particularly those pertaining to antisemitism, homophobia and transphobia – can be frequently found integrated within its rhetoric.

These associations emphasize how SCC rhetoric can be used to target various communities, implicating them as direct threats to moral society and/or traditional Christian family values. The legal cases of the Satanic Panic brought to light the ways in which this conspiracy theory could also lead to real and damaging consequences for those at the receiving end of its allegations. The current spotlight on SCC rhetoric may therefore represent it becoming more widely recognized again by its potential to cause harm. The fact that Satanic cult narratives have persisted, in spite of ongoing lack of evidence, provides a foundation to analyse the characteristics and motivations of the conspiracy networks who continue to espouse its potentially harmful rhetoric.

Satan hunters: A cult of conspiracy

The cult label has often been used in popular discourse as a means to describe and categorize contemporary conspiracy groups. The spotlight on the QAnon movement in particular has led to a surge of articles, news reports and documentaries likening them, and broader conspiracy networks, to cults (e.g. BBC News 2020; Richter 2020; Badham 2020; *The Cult of Conspiracy: QAnon* 2021; Al Jazeera 2022). In this context, as with most, 'cult' is intentionally deployed as a pejorative descriptor – as a means to associate conspiracy networks with a set of recognized, negative, 'cult-like' traits. Though the imagery, traits and stereotypes associated with cults appear often to be widely presumed, there seems to be popular consensus that 'cult' is inherently negative. For the purpose of this chapter, I will be focusing on the following as examples of stereotypical 'cult' traits: harmful behaviour, subversion to the 'mainstream', community isolation, presence of 'charismatic leaders' and coercion. In order to explore the possible perception of conspiracy-as-cult, I will focus on the potential to draw parallels between these archetypal cult characteristics and case studies relating to contemporary SCC theorists. Despite their anticult narratives, SCC theorists, and their associated networks, are in several cases able to be classified by similar cult stereotypes to those that they seek to project against others.

Harmful action

Cult labels may often be intended as a means to flag specific networks or groups as possessing dangerous ideologies, espousing harmful rhetoric, or engaging in harmful action. The potential for SCC to incorporate harmful rhetoric, and harbour potentially dangerous ideologies among its theorists, has already been noted. A further point to consider is the extent to which this rhetoric may lead to harmful action perpetrated by these networks. Edgar Welch, the Pizzagate gunman, demonstrated the potential for these theories to, in their creation of imaginary enemies, perpetuate a perception of vigilantism among followers. This was further demonstrated through the storming of the US Capitol building on 6 January 2021, where numerous QAnon supporters were identified among the rioters (Spocchia 2021). Beyond this, reports of various murders perpetuated by QAnon supporters have directly cited the influence of the conspiracy's rhetoric in motivating their actions (e.g. Hernandez 2021; Sommer 2022).

In the UK in 2020, the Anglesey kidnapping saw a child abducted from their foster carer at knife point (BBC News 2021). The six individuals responsible for the kidnapping had claimed that they were saving the child from SRA, despite the fact a police investigation had already proved the allegations to be false (BBC News 2021). Despite their supposed mission to combat child abuse, this is not the only instance where SCC theorists have themselves directly put children at risk. The fact finding judgement from the Hampstead hoax case stated that the children's initial SRA stories 'came about as the result of relentless emotional and psychological pressure as well as significant physical abuse' at the hands of their stepfather Abraham Christie, adding that 'torture is the most accurate way to describe what was done' (P and Q (2015) EWFC 26). The children's personal information had also been repeatedly published and shared online by individuals perpetuating the conspiracy claims; this included the filmed police reports of their initial statements:

> As at 10 March 2015, more than 4 million people worldwide had viewed online material relating to this case.... It is inevitable that a large proportion of those have a sexual interest in children. Any rational adult who uploads film clips to YouTube featuring children speaking about sexual activity must be assumed to realise that fact. (P and Q [2015] EWFC 26)

The potential for this has been evidenced already, a recent case saw Richard Simpson plead guilty to fifteen counts of possessing child pornography, to which he claimed were part of research into sex trafficking, directly inspired by QAnon (Gangloff 2022). The central narrative of SCC theorists is that we need to '#saveourchildren' from Satanic paedophile cults, and it is therefore not uncommon for their online networks to describe and share elaborate stories of Satanic abuse in grotesque detail as 'evidence' of SRA. A further example of this comes from the 'Frazzledrip' conspiracy, which alleges the existence of a 'dark web snuff film' that shows Hilary Clinton and Huma Abedin ritualistically torturing and murdering a child (ADL 2022). Despite the video not existing, its supposed gruesome contents are frequently referenced and described by online conspiracy networks as evidence of 'elites' abusing children (ADL 2022). In creating disturbing false SRA narratives centred around saving children from child abuse and torture, SCC theorists risk subjecting children to real targeted abuse in the process.

Subversion to the 'mainstream'

Colin Campbell presented his concept of the 'cultic milieu', a 'cultural underground of society' made up of a 'heterogeneous assortment of cultural items' unified by their deviation from the dominant cultural and social narratives (2002 [1972]: 22). Victor asserts that the Satanic legend is directly derived from Christian subversion mythologies that deem Satan as the adversary, seeking to destroy God's moral order through subverting the souls of man (1996: 76–7). Satan becomes 'a collective symbol for evil forces working toward the destruction of the current moral order of society' (Victor 1996: 54). In this sense, SCC could be considered as actively rejecting the deviant status of the cultic milieu, targeting groups that it deems to be subversive opposition to the (Christian) moral status quo. Having said that, SCC today – with its emphasis on NWO theories and its integration within wider contemporary conspiracy networks – seemingly presents, or at the very least aligns itself with, a form of subversive 'anti-mainstream' ideology. Arguably, contemporary SCC today appears further distanced from dominant orthodoxies and therefore more firmly situated within the cultic milieu than during the time of the Panic.

Jesse Walker notes how theories of SRA were rarely considered a conspiracy theory at the time of the Satanic Panic (2018: 59). While literature has long mentioned Satanic myths (e.g. Cohn 1970), Satanic legends (e.g. Victor 1996) and Satanism scares (e.g. Richardson, Best and Bromley 1991), it is only fairly recently that we can see Satanic cult narratives begin to be labelled as actual conspiracies, and subsequently presented as more subversive. During Trump's presidency, he spoke of QAnon followers as simply being 'very much against paedophilia' (Trump cited in Timberg 2020), and as individuals who 'love our country' and 'like me very much' (Trump cited in Smith and Wong 2020). Trump has since begun to explicitly support QAnon, sharing their images and slogans on Truth Social (Quarshie 2022). While clearly a not-so-subtle endorsement of the movement from a mainstream public figure, Trump's QAnon references have notably steered clear from explicitly referencing any Satanic elements of their ideology. While the political and moral panics that SCC theories build upon are a common theme in contemporary right-wing discourse, SRA theories and allegations simply have not (yet) been granted the same level of wider mainstream backing that they had during the time of the Satanic Panic.

As mentioned, there is also a lot more to the landscape of contemporary SCC rhetoric than QAnon. A prominent conspiracy figure to emerge over the last few years is Jeanette Archer, a self-proclaimed SRA survivor from the UK. Independent researcher and activist James Hind, whose work centres on documenting and combatting false SRA accusations, summarizes Archer's narrative as 'an epic story of being the central victim of a Satanic cult that organised hunting, torturing, raping, murdering, the eating of babies and drinking their blood, overseen by a shapeshifting nine foot tall lizard, the Queen of England' (2022). In a speech recorded at one of her 2021 SRA rallies, Archer also claimed that it was the UK police who would transport her to Windsor Castle as a child where she would then be subjected to SRA. During the Satanic Panic, authority figures such as police were often treated as the primary source of information on Satanism (Rowe and Cavender 1991: 267); they can now be found to be implicated within the same conspiracies. Archer's narrative epitomizes a popular trend in contemporary SCC, where theorists seem to consciously distance themselves from all mainstream authorities rather than seek validation from them. SCC theorists can be seen to take on a more subversive stance, projecting the image of themselves as underdogs who the 'Satanic elites' wish to silence.

Community isolation

Similarly, SCC theorists today can also be perceived as isolated, or encouraging of isolation, from those who don't accept their theories. Created in 2019 and still consistently active today, the subreddit r/QAnonCasualties describes itself as a place 'for support, resources and a place to vent' for individuals whose friends, family and loved ones have been 'taken in' by the conspiracy. Many stories speak specifically of individuals' QAnon-supporting relatives separating from them, and ask for advice on how to try to recover their relationships. It's not uncommon for posters – including ex-Anons themselves – to refer to QAnon as a cult, or Qult. The r/QAnonCasualties description itself also takes on anticult rhetoric, reading: 'learn to heal, deal and deprogram'. This clearly demonstrates how language of the ACM has influenced both the rhetoric of SCC theorists, and those who oppose their ideology. David G. Robertson, in part referencing SRA panics, identifies how conspiracies about religions construct their group identities through 'Processes of Othering' – 'constructing group identity by distinguishing "us" from "them" along moral and ideological lines' (2015: 8). In the case of SCC theorists, however, this 'them' may not simply be perceived as the religious (and other) groups that they accuse of being Satanic cult members, but the general mass of outsiders who remain ignorant to, or actively dismiss, this perceived threat. Archer's network in many ways bridges the gap between localized SRA allegations and wider scale NWO theories. While 'satanic elites' may be considered to pose the greater threat on humanity, those in allegiance with them could be round any corner, and therefore anyone's child could be at risk. This in turn keeps the 'Satanic cult' as a very imminent threat and subsequently generates a culture of mistrust.

Charismatic leaders

From the perspective of SCC theorists, the supposed 'cult leaders' of their allegations could be seen as the NWO of Satanic elites, or even potentially as

Satan himself. When looking at SCC theorists *as* potential cults, however, it can be harder to pinpoint who their 'leader' would be. Popular conspiracy theorists can undoubtedly play an important role in influencing their theories, with individuals such as David Icke and Alex Jones having long been sources of claims about societies of evil elites. In regard to QAnon, both Trump and Q could clearly be cast within the role of charismatic leader, and this is likely a prominent reason why QAnon has been frequently attributed the cult label. Figures such as Jeanette Archer have undoubtedly also taken leader roles upon themselves. Archer organized a series of protests in 2021 and early 2022 in which she vowed to take down the Satanic elite, attracting a number of followers in the process (Hind 2022). While few have gone on to mobilize in protest like Archer and her followers, a quick search of the SRA tag on TikTok alone will bring up a multitude of videos of individuals communicating SRA testimonies, to the rallying support and praise of other theorists in their comments. Among SCC theorists, there appears to be a level of authority granted to those who claim to have been subjected to SRA, their statements taken as apparent evidence of the crime's existence.

In exploring the concept of 'the charismatic leader', Catherine Wessinger defines charisma as 'the belief that an individual . . . is imbued with the qualities of an unseen source of authority' (2012: 82). As the authority source is unseen, Wessinger argues that 'the attribution of access to that authority is a matter of faith on the part of the followers and also the leaders' (2012: 82). While self-proclaimed 'SRA survivors' do not directly draw upon external authorities as the source of their knowledge, the concept of an 'unseen authority' could arguably be provided by the accounts of experiences that they claim to have had. Belief in SRA narratives is a belief without evidence, or in spite of evidence to the contrary, and therefore there is certainly a 'matter of faith' involved. Having said this, identifying prominent charismatic leaders among the majority of SCC theorists is not possible. Many who engage with these theories do not appear to follow a particular source of authority, with much of its discourse occurring within online conspiracy networks where hierarchies are not particularly prevalent. Satanism scares have persisted without the need for any specific or continuous source of authority – when leader figures do emerge, they are less central to perpetrating the overall conspiracy narrative itself and their authority is therefore somewhat dispensable. The role of authority within the conspiracy may perhaps be better recognized as coming from its enemy; it is less driven by shared faith in a moral authority but in shared opposition to the authority of Satan and those believed to follow him. It is the image of Satan as an all-powerful evil, and the implication that he presents an ever-imminent threat, that keeps the Satanic Cult Conspiracy in existence at all.

Coercion

As discussed, a popular trope within SCC is the notion that Satanic cults not only abuse children but seek to coerce young people into their ranks, or otherwise influence people through their use of Occult imagery. However, as the Hampstead hoax case has demonstrated, where SRA cases rely on the testimony of children, instances of coercion can in fact be identified among those who promote the conspiracy themselves. Victor explains how 'moral crusades' – such as the crusade against Satanism – 'requires more than effective rhetoric to be successful in influencing the general public. It needs effective organization' (1996: 229). For SCC theorists, this effective organization involves the recruitment of others to the anti-Satanist cause.

SRA 'survivor stories' are central to providing SCC theories with a sense of credibility and were instrumental to the narrative of the Satanic Panic. Victor discusses how psychological professionals came to accept SRA testimonies through a process of 'groupthink', which he defines as 'a collective response to conformity pressures operating within ... groups which are somewhat closed to the influence of external sources' (1996: 92). These stories served 'as propaganda vehicles' for 'religious fundamentalists and conservatives', many of which worked as counsellors and therapists themselves (Victor 1996: 101). It is not a far stretch to argue that the Satanic Panic of the 1980s was hugely pushed forward by the coercion of therapy patients, encouraged by psychological professionals to reframe their experiences within the lens of SRA. This is supported by David G. Bromley, who suggests that one of the problems with survivors' accounts of SRA was that the 'Satanic material' had been introduced by their therapists, and not the clients (1991: 63). This trend was notably catalysed by the psychiatrist Lawrence Pazder in his – since discredited – book *Michelle remembers* (1980), which he co-authored with his patient Michelle Smith whose memories of SRA he claimed to have revived. Following the UK's Satanic Panic, it was also found that two psychotherapists at the Tavistock clinic had been paid a £22,000 grant from the government to try to 'produce evidence' of SRA from the reported experiences of their patients (Brindle 2000). Victor notes how despite their rationale supposedly having been 'to protect the survivors from supposed dangers of the Satanic cult conspiracy' these psychotherapeutic networks operated 'like a closed community of believers, paradoxically, much like a religious cult' (1996: 94).

I have chosen in this chapter to use the word 'theorists' over 'believers' to refer to those who engage in propagating SCC rhetoric. While I don't doubt that many – and perhaps the majority – of individuals who engage in these discourses have a level of sincere belief in the conspiracy, this is not something that is easily measurable. Engagement with conspiracy theory content online, even in the case of individuals expressing support or sharing theories themselves, is still not inherently indicative of a committed belief to any given narrative. It is not clear whether figures such as, for example, Christie, Pazder or Archer genuinely believe the claims that they are personally conceptualizing and feeding to others. 'Moral crusades' – and conspiracy theories – are built on appeals to both fear and empathy, which is something that individuals can equally inspire or exploit.

SRA theories were widely discredited as false by the end of the Panic and have not received mainstream endorsement from psychotherapeutic professionals since. While various SCC theorists have come under allegations of coercion and abuse, I will not be listing these claims directly in this chapter. These types of stories form the basis of much of the plethora of popular true crime podcasts, documentaries and articles centred around modern-day 'cults', that – just like the tabloid media of the panic – appear often to blur the line between factual and sensationalized content. Speculation without proof treads the line of when anticult rhetoric can become actively harmful, and is undoubtedly one of the characteristics that can fuel Satanism scares and wider conspiracy movements and moral panics. When identifying and criticizing the rhetoric and behaviours of SCC theorists – and especially when considering applying aspects of their own anticult framework back to them as I have in this chapter – it is important not to fall into promoting unsubstantiated claims in order to try to fit a group into the mould of what a cult should be. While there are valid reasons for concern regarding contemporary SCC-promoting networks, and certainly parallels that can be drawn between them and that of the archetypal 'cult', the existence of the conspiracy itself demonstrates the harm that arbitrary or unjustified use of cult labels can lead to. With this in mind, I will now briefly address some thoughts regarding how we consider the notion of cults moving forward in the study of NRMs, and specifically in relation to studying conspiracy movements.

Conspiracies and 'the cult label'

An underlying reason for the popular shift to the term 'NRM' in academia was the assumption that the cult label was inherently pejorative (Gallagher 2007:

205), and therefore risked stigmatizing all similar groups through automatically associating them with the most extreme cult scandals. This ultimately distracted from efforts to understand the beliefs and motivations of individual groups (Miller 2016: 37). While these risks are still relevant, the cult label today is evidently still used in popular discourse. Not only this, but it is attributed to a more diverse range of phenomenon than 'NRM' might be perceived to be an accurate label for. Eugene Gallagher notes how cult descriptors have been attributed to various phenomenon beyond 'small, alternative religious groups' such as 'direct marketing companies like Amway, various therapeutic and self-help enterprises, political groups and movements, and communes' (2007: 212). This has also been explored by popular authors, such as Amanda Montell who focuses on the presence of 'cultish' language among a broad range of different groups and movements (2021).

Looking at the Satanic Cult Conspiracy itself, its anticult rhetoric also does not seem to be exclusively targeted towards NRMs. SCC rhetoric undoubtedly stigmatizes real Satanists and other Occult practitioners due to perpetuating harmful stereotypes related to their practices. However, while Occult stigmas certainly play a key role in maintaining Satanism scares, the Satanic cults of SCC are fictional caricatures of Occult practice, and its 'cult' labels are often projected onto other communities. SCC rhetoric is regularly deployed to demonize Jewish or LGBT+ communities, as well as generally towards those in various perceived 'elite' positions. In the case of more local cases, like the Hampstead hoax, SRA accusations seem to be made against local community members based largely on the personal attitudes of those alleging them. SCC is grounded in the stigma of NRMs, but its cult allegations spread beyond them. While NRM clearly remains an accurate categorization for various religious groups, it is crucial to not consider it an all-encompassing replacement for 'the cult label'. It would be useful for research to further acknowledge (and not simply from a place of criticism and dismissal) both why cult labels persist as useful descriptors for a variety of phenomenon in popular discourse and how they are deployed in a variety of different contexts.

Understanding the phenomenon of 'Satanism scares' intrinsically involves recognition of how anticult rhetoric can be used to propagate harmful consequences. And yet, as examples have demonstrated, individuals aware of the harm caused by these conspiracy groups' use of anticultic rhetoric may still see it fit to label them as cults in themselves. It appears to be in fact directly *because* of their harmful rhetoric that SCC theorists can be perceived as 'cultlike'. Timothy Miller suggests that the quietening of the ACM may in part be due to 'overall progress toward tolerance of differences' particularly 'increased religious tolerance' (2016: 39). I agree that there is largely an increased tolerance of differences, and that these helped to challenge some of the more conservative stigmas perpetrated by the ACM. Equally, however, I would argue that the social landscape of anticult discourse is not the same as it was, but encompasses a broader range of opinions and attitudes. While use of 'the cult label' does exist today, I do not think that it necessarily reflects those still grounded in religious intolerances. In some respects it appears to instead be a means to highlight the potential cults' intolerance towards others. Many of the popular and news articles that criticize contemporary SCC rhetoric, including those cited in this chapter, directly reference its promotion of conservative and often fascist values. SCC theorists push themselves as the only 'good' side in an impending spiritual war of good and evil, scapegoating and stigmatizing outsiders in the process. Labelling SCC-promoting networks back as being cults in themselves can be seen as a direct response to their perpetration of these stigmas, emphasizing the hypocrisies of the movements through demonizing them by their own criteria, and reframing their anticultic rhetoric through a different political lens. This is not inherently equivalent to an anticult moral panic, at times quite the opposite, as notions of 'conspiracies-as-cults' can be grounded in researching and combatting the harmful effects caused by conspiratorial moral panics – such as that of SCC. Understanding the different motivations and ideologies behind cult labels is therefore also a factor that should be taken into account in research.

From any perspective, making sweeping 'anticult' stances without specifying exactly which groups are being referred to, broadly speculating around the potential activities of certain groups without evidence, or reporting unsubstantiated allegations in a seemingly factual light, has the potential to be harmful. These are how moral panics – such as Satanism scares – occur, and how communities and individuals get unjustly demonized in the process. Engagement with 'cult research', particularly in the case of researching conspiracy movements, should always ensure that its claims are grounded in fact and not speculation or stigma. Equally, though, academic knee-jerk reactions to public or researcher use of the term 'cult' can be equally presumptive and risks ignoring the bigger picture of what is trying to be conveyed about these groups and why individuals may have that perception. It both risks ignoring and belittling important research being done outside of academia and disregarding the arguments and voices of those directly affected by (and knowledgeable of) the issues being studied. There is a necessity for further communication and understanding between researchers from both within and outside of academia and, as suggested by Eileen Barker, we should seek to move towards a 'constructive cooperation' (2017).

Conclusion

The Satanic Cult Conspiracy theory represents a unique case study when considering the topic of 'cult rhetoric'. It arguably can be interpreted as a conspiracy 'about cults' and an example of conspiracy theorists 'as cult', as promoting both anticult and 'cult-like' rhetoric, and as applying cult stereotypes onto outside groups while seemingly embodying many of these stereotypes itself. In doing so, it makes a case for exploring the complexities of contemporary cult rhetoric further – particularly in the case of conspiracy theory movements. Ultimately, the contemporary landscape of cult rhetoric is far more diverse than we may currently be giving it credit for. Regarding conspiracy theorists, this is further complicated by the tendency for their narratives to stigmatize outsiders with cult stereotypes that could arguably be attributed back to them. It is therefore important to recognize and take into account how different cult rhetoric, or rhetoric about cults, may stem from a number of different motivations, ideologies and contexts.

References

ACLED (2022), 'Fact Sheet: Anti-LGBT+ Mobilization on the Rise in the United States'. Available at https://acleddata.com/2022/11/23/update-fact-sheet-anti-lgbt-mobilization-in-the-united-states/ (accessed 9 December 2022).

ADL (n.d.), 'Frazzledrip'. Available at https://www.adl.org/glossary/frazzledrip (accessed 8 December 2022).

Al Jazeera (2022), 'Trump and QAnon: The Cult and the Conspiracy', 24 September. Available at https://www.aljazeera.com/program/the-listening-post/2022/9/24/trump-and-qanon-the-cult-and-the-conspiracy (accessed 8 December 2022).

Archer, J. (2021), 'SRA Exposed', 14 October. Available at https://www.youtube.com/watch?v=PcVF1aEns6U (accessed 8 December 2022).

Argentino, M. A. and A. Amarasingam (2021), 'They Got It All under Control: QAnon, Conspiracy Theories, and the New Threats to Canadian National Security', in L. West, T. Juneau and A. Amarasingam (eds), *Stress Tested: The COVID-19 Pandemic and Canadian National Security*, 15–32. Calgary: University of Calgary Press.

Asprem, E. and A. Dyrendal (2018), 'Close Companions? Esotericism and Conspiracy Theories', in A. Dyrendal, D. G. Robertson and E. Asprem (eds), *Handbook of Conspiracy Theory and Contemporary Religion*, 207–33. Boston: Brill.

Badham, V. (2020), 'If Your Family or Friends have Fallen for an Internet Conspiracy Cult, Here's What You Should Do', *The Guardian*, 27 September. Available at https://www.theguardian.com/commentisfree/2020/sep/28/if-your-friends-or-family-have-fallen-for-an-internet-conspiracy-cult-heres-what-you-should-do (accessed 7 December 2022).

Barker, E. (2017), 'From Cult Wars to Constructive Cooperation – Well, Sometimes', in E. V. Gallagher (ed.), *'Cult Wars' in Historical Perspective: New and Minority Religions*, 9–22. London: Routledge.

Barkun, M. (2013), *A Culture of Conspiracy: Apocalyptic Visions in Contemporary America*, 2nd edn. Berkeley: University of California Press.

BBC News (2020), 'QAnon, Coronavirus and the Conspiracy Cult', *BBC News*, 23 July. Available at https://www.bbc.co.uk/news/av/world-53507579 (accessed 8 December 2022).

BBC News (2021), 'Anglesey Kidnap: Gang Jailed for Snatching Child Over Satanic Abuse Fears', *BBC News*, 30 September. Available at https://www.bbc.co.uk/news/uk-wales-58753545 (accessed 8 December 2022).

Best, J. (1991), 'Endangered Children in Antisatanist Rhetoric', in J. T. Richardson, J. Best and D. G. Bromley (eds), *The Satanism Scare*, 95–106. New York: Aldine De Gruyter.

Brindle, D. (2000), 'Satanic Abuse Row Erupts', *The Guardian*, 10 February. Available at https://www.theguardian.com/uk/2000/feb/10/davidbrindle (accessed 8 December 2022).

Bromley, D. G. (1991), 'Satanism: The New Cult Scare', in J. T. Richardson, J. Best and D. G. Bromley (eds), *The Satanism Scare*, 49–72. New York: Aldine De Gruyter.

Caldwell, N., A. Shapiro, P. Jarenwattananon and M. Venkat (2021), 'America's Satanic Panic Returns – This Time through QAnon', *NPR*, 18 May. Available at https://www.npr.org/2021/05/18/997559036/americas-satanic-panic-returns-this-time-through-qanon (accessed 8 December 2022).

Campbell, C. (2002), 'The Cult, the Cultic Milieu and Secularization', in J. Kaplan and H. Lööw (eds), *The Cultic Milieu: Oppositional Subcultures in An Age of Globalization*. [ProQuest eBook Central], 20–32. Walnut Creek, CA: AltaMira Press.

Carlson, T. (2022), 'TUCKER CARLSON: No Healthy Society can Tolerate Pedophilia', *Fox News*, 22 November. Available at https://www.foxnews.com/opinion/tucker-carlson-no-healthy-society-tolerate-pedophilia (accessed 7 December 2022).

Cohn, N. (1970), 'The Myth of Satan and his Human Servants', in M. Douglas (ed.), *Witchcraft Confessions & Accusations*, 3–16. London: Tavistock Publications.

The Cult of Conspiracy: QAnon (2021), [Documentary], Dir. Benjamin Zand, Channel 4.

Friedberg, B. (2020), 'The Dark Virality of a Hollywood Blood-Harvesting Conspiracy', *Wired*, 31 July. Available at https://www.wired.com/story/opinion-the-dark-virality-of-a-hollywood-blood-harvesting-conspiracy/ (accessed 7 December 2022).

Gallagher, E. V. (2007), 'Compared to What? Cults and New Religious Movements', *History of Religions*, 47 (2–3): 205–20.

Gallagher, E. V., ed. (2016), *'Cult Wars' in Historical Perspective: New and Minority Religions*. London: Routledge.

Gangloff, M. (2022), 'Pulaski County Child Pornography Defendant Says QAnon made Him Do It', *The Roanoke Times*, 17 November. Available at https://roanoke.com/news

/local/crime-and-courts/pulaski-county-child-pornography-defendant-says-qanon-made-him-do-it/article_c2a7f724-66a1-11ed-9f3e-9fc4e5aa91d1.html (accessed 8 December 2022).

Hernandez, J. (2021), 'A California Father Claims QAnon Conspiracy Led Him To Kill His 2 Children, FBI Says', *NPR*, 13 August. Available at https://www.npr.org/2021/08/13/1027133867/children-dead-father-claims-qanon-conspiracy-led-him-to-kill (accessed 7 December 2022).

Hind, J. (2022), 'Satan Hunter Jeanette Archer Set for a Fall?', *Satanicviews*, 29 January. Available at https://satanicviews.wordpress.com/2022/01/29/satan-hunter-jeanette-archer-set-for-a-fall/ (accessed 8 December 2022).

Hoaxtead Research (2021), 'Frequently Asked Questions: The Hoax Timeline'. Available at https://hoaxteadresearch.wordpress.com/hampstead-hoax-faq/frequently-asked-questions-the-hoax-timeline/ (accessed 8 December 2022).

Hughes, S. (2017), 'American Monsters: Tabloid Media and the Satanic Panic, 1970–2000', *Journal of American Studies*, 51 (3): 691–719.

Jenkins, P. (1992), *Intimate Enemies: Moral Panics in Contemporary Great Britain*. New York: Aldine De Gruyter.

Kaplan, J. (2021), 'A Conspiracy of Dunces: Good Americans vs. a Cabal of Satanic Pedophiles?', *Terrorism and Political Violence*, 33 (5): 917–21.

MacMillen, S. L. and T. Rush (2022), 'QAnon – Religious Roots, Religious Responses', *Critical Sociology*, 48 (6): 989–1004.

Melton, J. G. (2002), 'The Modern Anti-Cult Movement in Historical Perspective', in J. Kaplan and H. Lööw (eds), *The Cultic Milieu: Oppositional Subcultures in an Age of Globalization*. [ProQuest eBook Central], 289–312. California: AltaMira Press.

Miller, T. (2016), 'Are the Cult Wars over? And If So, Who Won?', in E. V. Gallagher (ed.), *'Cult Wars' in Historical Perspective: New and Minority Religions*, 33–42. London: Routledge.

Montell, A. (2021), *Cultish: The Language of Fanaticism*. New York: Harper Wave.

O'Donnell, S. J. (2020), 'The Deliverance of the Administrative State: Deep State Conspiracism, Charismatic Demonology, and the Post-truth Politics of American Christian Nationalism', *Religion*, 50 (4): 696–719.

P and Q (2015), EWFC 26.

Quarshie, M. (2022), 'In Trump Embrace of Qanon, Election Experts See Potential for Midterm "Chaos" and More Election Denying', *USA Today News*. Available at https://eu.usatoday.com/story/news/politics/elections/2022/09/28/trump-qanon-midterm-violence/10166422002/ (accessed 8 December 2022).

Reddit (2022), *r/QAnonCasualties*. Available at https://www.reddit.com/r/QAnonCasualties/ (accessed 8 December 2022).

Richardson, J. T., J. Best and D. G. Bromley (1991), 'Satanism as a Social Problem', in J. T. Richardson, J. Best and D. G. Bromley (eds), *The Satanism Scare*, 3–17. New York: Aldine De Gruyter.

Richter, A. (2020), 'Conspiracy Cults and the Mental Health Pandemic', *The Spinoff*, 19 September. Available at https://thespinoff.co.nz/society/19-09-2020/conspiracy-cults-and-the-mental-health-pandemic (accessed 7 December 2022).

Robertson, D. G. (2015), 'Conspiracy Theories and the Study of Alternative and Emergent Religions', *Nova Religio*, 19 (2): 5–16.

Robertson, D. G. and A. Amarasingam (2022), 'How Conspiracy Theorists Argue: Epistemic Capital in the QAnon Social Media Sphere', *Popular Communication*, 20 (3): 193–207.

Robertson, D. G., E. Asprem and A. Dyrendal (2018), 'Introducing the Field: Conspiracy Theory in, about, and as Religion', in A. Dyrendal, D. G. Robertson and E. Asprem (eds), *Handbook of Conspiracy Theory and Contemporary Religion*, 1–18. Boston: Brill.

Romano, A. (2021), 'Why Satanic Panic Never Really Ended', *Vox*, 31 March. Available at https://www.vox.com/culture/22358153/satanic-panic-ritual-abuse-history-conspiracy-theories-explained (accessed 8 December 2022).

Romano, A. (2022), 'The Right's Moral Panic Over "Grooming" Invokes Age-Old Homophobia', *Vox*, 21 April. Available at https://www.vox.com/culture/23025505/leftist-groomers-homophobia-satanic-panic-explained (accessed 8 December 2022).

Rowe, L. and G. Cavender (1991), 'Caldrons Bubble, Satan's Trouble, but Witches Are Okay: Media Constructions of Satanism and Witchcraft', in J. T. Richardson, J. Best and D. G. Bromley (eds), *The Satanism Scare*, 263–75, New York: Aldine De Gruyter.

Shukman, H. (2022), 'The Return of Satanic Panic', *UnHerd*, 12 October. Available at https://unherd.com/2022/10/the-return-of-satanic-panic/ (accessed 7 December 2022).

Smith, D. and J. C. Wong (2020), 'Trump tacitly Endorses Baseless QAnon Conspiracy Theory Linked to Violence', *The Guardian*, 20 August. https://www.theguardian.com/us-news/2020/aug/19/trump-qanon-praise-conspiracy-theory-believers (accessed 11 December 2023).

Smith, M. and L. Pazder (1980), *Michelle Remembers*. New York: St. Martin's Press.

Sommer, W. (2022), 'Latest QAnon Killer Had Murder Hit List', *Daily Beast*, 4 November. Available at https://www.thedailybeast.com/latest-qanon-killer-had-murder-hit-list (accessed 7 December 2022).

Spocchia, G. (2021), 'What Role did QAnon Play in the Capitol Riot?', *The Independent*, 9 January. Available at https://www.independent.co.uk/news/world/americas/us-election-2020/qanon-capitol-congress-riot-trump-b1784460.html (accessed 8 December 2022).

Stevens Jr., P. (1991), 'The Demonology of Satanism: An Anthropological View', in J. T. Richardson, J. Best and D. G. Bromley (eds), *The Satanism Scare*, 21–39. New York: Aldine De Gruyter.

Sturm, T. and T. Albrecht (2021), 'Constituent Covid-19 Apocalypses: Contagious Conspiracism, 5G, and Viral Vaccinations', *Anthropology & Medicine*, 28 (1): 122–39.

Thorleifsson, C. (2021), 'From Cyberfascism to Terrorism. On 4chan /pol/ Culture and the Transnational Production of Memetic Violence', *Nations and Nationalism*, 28 (1): 286–301.

Timberg, C. (2020), 'Trump's Commendts on Conspiracy Theory are Celebrated: "This Was the Biggest Pitch for QAnon I have Ever Seen:"', *Washington Post*, 16 October. https://www.washingtonpost.com/technology/2020/10/16/qanon-trump-conspiracy/ (accessed 11 December 2023).

Uscinski, J. E. (2022), 'Getting QAnon Wrong and Right', *Social Research*, 89 (3): 551–78.

Victor, J. S. (1996), *Satanic Panic: The Creation of a Contemporary Legend*, 4th edn. Chicago: Open Court.

Walker, J. (2018), 'What We Mean When We Say "Conspiracy Theory"', in J. E. Uscinski (ed.), *Conspiracy Theories and the People Who Believe in Them*, 53–62. New York: Oxford University Press.

Waterhouse, R. T. (2014), *Satanic Abuse, False Memories, Weird Beliefs and Moral Beliefs*. PhD Thesis, City University London.

Wessinger, C. (2012), 'Charismatic Leaders in New Religions', in O. Hammer and M. Rothstein (eds), *The Cambridge Companion to New Religious Movements*, 80–96. Cambridge: Cambridge University Press.

Wood, M. (2021), 'Lil Nas X's "Montero" and the Delight of Yet another Satanic Panic', *Los Angeles Times*, 29 March. Available at https://www.latimes.com/entertainment-arts/music/story/2021-03-29/lil-nas-x-montero-satanic-panic (accessed 8 December 2022).

Woodward, A. (2022), 'What is Florida's "Don't Say Gay" Bill?', *The Independent*, 21 April. Available at https://www.independent.co.uk/news/world/americas/us-politics/dont-say-gay-bill-florida-ron-desantis-b2057359.html (accessed 8 December 2022).

Yalcinkaya, G. (2022), 'Demons, Blood Harvests and Occult Rituals: Inside the New Satanic Panic', *Dazed*, 2 December. Available at https://www.dazeddigital.com/life-culture/article/57670/1/satanic-panic-doja-cat-mainstream-4chan-conspiracy-adrenochrome (accessed 7 December 2022).

Yuhas, A. (2021), 'It's Time to Revisit the Satanic Panic', *The New York Times*, 31 March. Available at https://www.nytimes.com/2021/03/31/us/satanic-panic.html (accessed 8 December 2022).

Zadrozny, B. (2022), 'Satanic Panic is Making a Comeback, Fueled by QAnon Believers and GOP Influencers', *NBC News*, 14 September. Available at https://www.nbcnews.com/tech/internet/satanic-panic-making-comeback-fueled-qanon-believers-gop-influencers-rcna38795 (accessed 8 December 2022).

9

'There is no QAnon'

Cult accusations in contemporary American political and online discourse

Susannah Crockford

Introducing QAnon

In 2019, I saw a YouTube video called 'Q – The Plan to Save the World' that was shared publicly on Facebook by Randell Standswithbear. I had met Randell in Sedona, Arizona, during my fieldwork there in 2012–14 (Crockford 2021a: 403–22). He called himself a starseed and shaman, and claimed Cherokee ancestry, while presenting as a white man from Arizona who voted Republican. The video was made by Joe M, the online identifier of a QAnon-influencer popular at that time on social media (Beverley 2020: 38–9). It explained in suspenseful tones a war between good and evil. The patriots were 'the good guys', and they were led by an anonymous poster on the image board 4chan, and later 8chan which became 8kun, known as Q, and Donald Trump. Q claimed to be a military insider, close to Trump (or a codename for Trump himself), who knew of his battle against the deep state. The deep state is a collective noun symbolizing a group of unknown criminals operating in government and other institutions, who were depicted as unequivocally evil, involved in child trafficking and satanic rituals, and included all of Trump's enemies, particularly Hillary Clinton. This battle between good and evil is the ideological core of the network of conspiracy theories that became known as QAnon (Conner and MacMurray 2022; Uscinski 2022).

QAnon spread rapidly from its origin on 4chan through influencers such as Joe M, who made videos and reposted the Q posts – known as 'drops' – on aggregator sites such as QMap.pub, as well as on Reddit, YouTube, Twitter and Facebook (Papasaava et al. 2022). It is these larger social media networks where most of the people who came to follow QAnon first encountered it (Forberg

2022). QAnon was a puzzle to solve, encouraging those who engaged in it to 'do your own research', or as Q drop 364 suggested, 'follow the crumbs'.[1] It was both mimetic and interactive; people felt involved in something larger than themselves, a battle of good vs evil in which they were 'digital soldiers',[2] fighting on the side of truth and justice by posting on Facebook.

The identity of the Q poster is a belaboured question,[3] but one which ultimately does not aid much in the analysis of the meaning and implications of QAnon as an ideology or movement. To examine why QAnon has proliferated from its chan origins, the 'Anons' are perhaps more relevant. The chans operate anonymously, anyone can post without needing to create an account (Wesch and Digital Ethnography Class of Spring 2009 2009: 90). All a user needs to do is post a comment, and they are listed as anonymous. Posters on chans therefore became known as Anons, forming a collective, amorphous, identity-free zone of speech without specified speakers. So QAnon is made up not only of the poster(s) who called themselves Q, but also substantially by the many Anons who replied, reposted and reworked the original cryptic drops to create a swirling network of ideas, theories, content, merchandise and offline political activity. Like Joe M's much-shared video, much of QAnon focuses on the plan. The plan is attributed to Trump, who figures as a saviour; he will bring 'the storm'. What the storm is varies, as a symbol it often refers to the arrest and trial of the deep state operatives, often in secret, military tribunals, leading to executions. But it semiotically refers to any possible, potential moment in which the deep state suffers and the patriots triumph. It operates as a kind of Badiouian event that will rip into the social order and transform it structurally (Badiou 2013).

QAnon is perhaps best described as a prophetic millenarian movement. Even in this brief precis of QAnon, its religious themes emerge: a Manichean battle of good versus evil, a millenarian expectation of a coming event which will save the elect and damn the unbelievers, a messianic figure who will lead the elect. These themes appeal across religious affiliations, and despite the roots in American politics, it has also spread outside the United States to Australia, Japan, the UK, Germany, Canada and elsewhere (Hoseini et al. 2021). To outside observers, QAnon is uniformly cast as harmful and violent, as a dangerous form of extremism that takes over the minds and lives of previously reasonable people. It has therefore faced numerous accusations of being a cult that brainwashes people.

In this chapter, I analyse cult accusations surrounding QAnon, using interviews with former members, and qualitative analysis of political journalism and social media. Why does this movement inspire such accusations? What about the current political moment in America has created these dynamics? The examination of these questions is framed with the literature on new religious movements and cult rhetoric to ask why the word 'cult' persists in popular culture while it has been discarded by scholars. Rather than interpreting QAnon as a form of mental poison that determines the behaviour of those exposed to it, I suggest that it is better understood as a bubble. The metaphor of bubbles is common in the media and scholarship on the media, with the effect of being exposed to some messages and content, and not others, described as media bubbles, content bubbles or filter bubbles (Forberg 2022: 292; Eady et al. 2019). While this metaphor is often used as an uncritical descriptor, I argue that there is merit in thinking with bubbles to take seriously the harm of QAnon and similar social phenomena without using the blunt force instrument of the category 'cult'. Bubbles are containers that are simultaneously isolating, fragile and temporary; secure yet insecure (Sloterdijk 2011: 18–19). The ephemeral nature of bubbles resonates with the network of QAnon, in which influencers, videos and posts appear only to disappear, often with little trace left (e.g. Rothschild 2021: 27). While inside the bubble, those involved in QAnon are held in community with each other and the outside world is sealed off. Yet the transience of this community is revealed repeatedly, as the bubble bursts and disappears once again.

The Qult

While QAnon is still a relatively recent phenomenon, with the first Q drops appearing in October 2017, much of the media commentary so far connects it to the category 'cult' (Rothschild 2021: 182–91). For journalist Mike Rothschild it is both a conspiracy theory *and* a cult, although the difference between the two categories is not meaningfully parsed. Cult accusations start early in the Q story, with Paul Furber, the admin who ran the board that Q originally posted on, in 2018 describing the hostile takeover of Q from 4chan onto 8chan as the work of 'a small group of imposters who play their followers like a cult' (Rothschild 2021: 39). Rothschild describes QAnon as 'rapidly growing, enthusiastic, prolific' and vulnerable to 'exploitation' as 'cultic movements dependent on information passed down from top to bottom' are (2021: 73). This does not suffice analytically, because if all groups that grew quickly and were organized in vertical hierarchies were cults, many economic, cultural and educational organizations could be defined as such. However, Rothschild does caution that QAnon is not a group with a single charismatic leader, but rather an online social network with its own ideology.

The emergence of this network from its online haunts into offline spaces was met with further cult accusations. People wearing Q merchandise, holding signs with Q-related slogans such as 'WWG1WWA' (where we go one, we go all), started appearing at Trump rallies (Rothschild 2021: 69). The *Washington Post* called QAnon a 'deranged conspiracy cult' after a Trump rally in Tampa in 2018 (Stanley-Becker 2018). *Vox* called it a cult because it was not based on facts but religious fervour (Coaston 2019). An article in *The Guardian* based on two first-person survivor interviews focused on Australians getting into QAnon during the Covid-19 pandemic, blamed Facebook algorithms, and called it a 'far-right cult' (Badham 2021). In an op-ed in *The Los Angeles Times*, an extremism studies professor called QAnon both a cult and a national security threat, referring to the Rajneeshis and Heaven's Gate as previous examples of the category (Blazakis 2021).

These accusations follow a pattern now familiar in new religious movements (NRM) studies. A cult has weird beliefs, followers are marked out by their slogans and manners of dress, their enthusiasm is suspicious, and the likelihood of violence is high. Moreover, the most extreme and violent examples of NRMs, such as the Rajneeshis and Heaven's Gate, are used as models for the norm (Snow 2023). Moving on from the old arguments of the 'cult scene' about the scholarly validity of the term (Barker 2014), what is clear is that the word itself has not lost any utility for the media. It remains a way of signifying a form of belief that is not only untrue, but dangerous. And perhaps the inability to accurately delineate new (bad) from old (good) religion is indicative of a deeper subtext. Not just strange beliefs, but belief itself is suspicious, indicative of a lack of logic and reason (Rothschild 2021: 85). When commentators ask whether QAnon adherents are clinging to a belief in a just world or simply overextending an evolutionary tendency for apophenia, they express a desire to psychologize belief. They describe the appeal of QAnon as a search for approval, affirmation and the desire to be a part of something, in a community of like-minded people, to be one of the righteous, fighting on the side of good (Rothschild 2021: 100–1). The implicit problem is of people prioritizing their feelings over facts; the desire to be part of a group becomes more important than whether it is true that Democrats eat babies, as is alleged in QAnon. What they are participating in is social group formation.

The process of the formation of QAnon is recent enough that it can be identified through the digital footprint it has left. It has shifted and transformed with the times, incorporating novel theories about Covid-19 and vaccinations, responding to current events. Rothschild (2021: 34–48, 67–83) traces this formation through ascending spheres of influence, from a handful of anonymous posters on the chans, to since-banned subreddits on Reddit, and from there the Qtubers, pasting together their own video amalgams of things they read on the chans and Reddit, spread through the recommender systems of YouTube to a wider, more mainstream audience. Then some of the celebrity spokespeople in right-wing conspiracy media picked up on QAnon, disseminating it further, first the website *Infowars* and its bellicose host and owner Alex Jones, and then comedian and actor Roseanne Barr tweeting about it. The explosion in audience enabled further sites to be set up, the drop aggregators (such as QMap), then #QAnon became a Twitter trend, and it jumped into unregulated private Facebook groups, and from there to more mainstream conservative sites, including Fox News, Breitbart and Gateway Pundit. It received a significant boost from retweets from Donald Trump's Twitter account (Rothschild 2021: 67–8). From there it began to receive widespread attention in the media, especially as marches, rallies and public violence invoking QAnon increased, and there was a significant presence of QAnon-related people in the attack on the Capitol on 6 January 2021. QAnon progressed through a rapid ascendance from the darker, weirder corners of the internet up towards more mainstream, widely accessed sites, like bubbles rising up to the surface.

QAnon's progression through online space has been fast-moving, scorched earth, leaving little trace, moving from the chans to YouTube to social media then banned. The first significant censorship came when r/GreatAwakening was banned on Reddit, and then after 6 January the major social media platforms deplatformed accounts and hashtags associated with QAnon. Posts were scrubbed, videos deleted and a bestselling book on Amazon was then removed from the retail site (Rothschild 2021: 70–2; Bond 2021). The book was called *QAnon: An Invitation to the Great Awakening* by 'WWG1WGA' – a collective of early Q influencers that subsequently fell out and labelled each other grifters. A man livestreamed his police chase on Facebook, claiming that Q was communicating with him via classic rock radio, until he was arrested, and then soon the livestream was taken down and gone (Rothschild 2021: 107–8). Members falling out with each other, dissolving into in-fighting, is a persistent theme in new religious movements and voluntary associations more generally. The fissures among factions drive an ongoing sense of instability, like bubbles popping soon after they form.

QAnon has been called both a cult and a conspiracy theory, or a conspiracy cult. These labels point to a connection between the categories of cult and of conspiracy theory. While established and accepted religions have their nonempirical claims validated as 'belief', cults have conspiracy theories. They thrive on secret (stigmatized, suppressed) knowledge, known only to the few (Robertson 2022: 652). In this regard, QAnon flourished in part due to the injunction to 'do your own research'. The Q-curious were not fed answers, but rather prompted to ask questions, and find out for themselves, even if some answers were still rejected *a priori* (i.e. that Hillary Clinton is not a demon). The process of finding out for themselves fuelled the sheer level of online content produced by Anons, albeit much of it repackaged and repetitive. It allowed those involved to see themselves as having a form of special power, they called themselves 'autists' (Rothschild 2021: 44). They were decoding the hidden clues, following the crumbs, able to see things that others could not, to discern truths that others refused to see. They called themselves awake, unlike 'the sheeple'. This is a typical categorization of reality into those who know and those who do not, common among evangelical Protestants and people involved in new age spirituality (Crockford 2021b: 99). Awakening metaphors are apt descriptions of religious conversions, encapsulating the sense of sheer transformation in consciousness. Not coincidentally, evangelical Protestantism and new age spirituality are the two most common religious overlaps for QAnon (Argentino 2021; Juergensmeyer 2022; Beauchamp 2022; Robertson and Amarasingam 2022). This points to another facet of QAnon; much of it is not original, but a reformulation of preexisting narratives, symbols and beliefs.

Due to its intensity and apocalypticism, QAnon has been compared to a new religious movement (Argentino 2020a, b; LaFrance 2020). Despite the negative tenor of many of its tenets, for those who participate, it can be a source of hope. Anons see themselves as the good guys, fighting for a righteous cause (Beverley 2020: 154). They feel important, as a digital soldier, they are valued and worthwhile. They are saving the world. It can become an obsession, with everything else shut out. Addiction metaphors arise, with QAnon called religion in a Marxist sense, as an opium for the people (Rothschild 2021: 94). There are ritual elements in the decoding practices of 'bakers' who take the drops and bake them until they become something others can digest (Rothschild 2021: 96). The predictions of the Q poster soon attained the status of prophecy among the network of Anons (Robertson and Amarasingam 2022: 200–2; Harding and Martin 2021). Unfulfilled predictions, of arrests and military tribunals, occurred from the start. The first Q drop claimed Hillary Clinton would be arrested in two days and extradition requests had already been processed.[4] In the run up to the 2020 presidential election, the Q drops maintained that Trump would win, but that the Democrats would try to steal the election from him if it looked like he was losing. Such predictions evoke the classic 'when prophecy fails' frame (Festinger, Riecken and Schachter 1956; Jenkins 2013). The constant failures of drops to predict events has not undermined every believer, a dynamic that is by-now well-known in the study of millenarian movements. The mysterious Q figure is readily figured as a prophet because of their primarily textual form; a persona that exists in word only.

Given the resemblances QAnon bears to a new religious movement, it has been responded to by its own version of the anticult movement. Online disinformation and extremism researchers, both professional and amateur, identify QAnon as a 'cult' and call-out its perils and excesses (Conner and MacMurray 2022: 1055). Being critical of QAnon can bring similar levels of online engagement and renown as disseminating QAnon content. Much of the animus is directed towards helping people who have 'lost' relatives to QAnon (e.g. the subreddit r/QAnonCasualties). There is a corresponding revival of the brainwashing concept to explain why people get lost down the 'algorithmic rabbit hole' of QAnon (Uscinski 2022: 551; Conner and MacMurray 2022: 1064). Many aspects of QAnon make it a relevant subject for NRM scholars to study, with characteristics that fit both scholarly definitions of an NRM and popular understandings of 'cult'.

Ex-Anon

The dominant trend in NRM studies to date has been a systematic deconstruction of the category 'cult' and the typological definitions used to substantiate this category (Barker 2010: Tabor and Gallagher 1995; Richardson 2021; Melton 2007). This trend has produced a consensus view that 'cult' is a word for a religious group that you do not like.[5] Catherine Wessinger (2021) has applied this consensus view to QAnon: 'the word "cult" comes with a ready-made explanation that is illogically and pejoratively applied to groups and movements with differing characteristics. People are using the term "cult" to stigmatize groups and movements that they simply do not like.' Wessinger instead describes QAnon as an extension of what she calls the Euro-American Nativist Millennial Movement (see Wessinger 2000), which seeks to wage a second American Revolution, and/or civil war, to maintain the religious and political dominance of white Christians in the United States. Her approach shares explanatory ground with those who identify Christian nationalism as an important animus in QAnon (Armaly, Buckley and Enders 2022; Onishi 2023).

NRM scholars continue to insist that 'cult' is a pejorative term that should be rejected; popular culture and media has clearly not heard them. Distrust of ex-members is part of the scholarly rejection of the term 'cult'. Tabor and Gallagher (1995: 135) argued that 'disgruntled former members' and the anticult movement have dominated the conversation on cults, perpetuating harmful stereotypes. Former members have been cast as biased because of their experiences in groups. Yet at the same time, former members are undeniably those with intimate, working knowledge of what groups are like in practice, and not just the polished front that may be shown to outsiders. For some ex-members, the word 'cult' is an appropriate and helpful description of the harmful experiences they have had.

QAnon has a large online presence, and has received a lot of media coverage, but it does not have wide public support (Enders et al. 2022: 1847). And while QAnon is described as a movement by those who support it, it is not a movement in the organized, party-political sense. It has no chapters or branches, there is no membership list, the leader could be Donald Trump or an anonymous image board poster whose identity can only be guessed. QAnon exists predominantly in messages, posts, videos, books and merchandise online, with some presence at rallies and protests offline, and sporadic acts of stochastic violence. It moves with the floating ephemerality of bubbles rather than the crashing wave of a movement. Studying this fugacious flow presents some problems. Much of the research completed so far involves scraping vast amount of data from the internet and analysing that. This gives a wide-angle view of QAnon at scale, but it only looks at the digital footprint. Contacting current QAnon members is risky because they perceive journalists and academics as traitors and tend to dox those that contact them. For ethical and methodological reasons, I chose to study a small number of former QAnon members who were all women. My approach maintained researcher safety, gave a close, first-hand view of what it was like on an everyday basis to participate in QAnon in line with my ethnographic training, and provided information on women participants, who are often less focused on in the existing research (Bracewell 2021).

Chae-rin[6] lived in Virginia and described herself as a 'recovering Q addict'. Born in Louisiana to a Korean mom and an American dad, she was forty-one years old, and ran her own dog walking and pet sitting business from her home. She already spent much of her time on her computer at home, and so she had plenty of time to spend on QAnon. Two years before we spoke, she got into it through a friend. He said that he had found something, what he called 'all-time top intel', secret information direct from the military: the Q drops. She thought it sounded cool.

Initially her exposure to QAnon came via this same friend, who would send her links via text and talk on the phone, reading things to her that he had read. Then, as she engaged more directly it was always through Facebook, where her network became dominated by QAnon people, who would share things from Telegram, Instagram and the Q drops themselves. Although the people in her network were 'obsessed' with it, they did not seem to have clear ideas what it was about. No one in her online QAnon circles could tell her how long it had been around, they just seemed to be into it because everyone else was into it. Yet people from all over the world were on Facebook posting non-stop about Q and the drops, seeking secret codes. This indicates a strong influence of social norms, the desire to be doing what everyone else seemed to be doing, even if the perception of who constituted 'everyone' was algorithmically circumscribed.

Chae-rin observed that it was when Q stopped posting in December 2020 that people really started making stuff up, all sorts of crazy theories. Some of these Chae-rin subscribed to herself; she believed that JFK Jr. was alive for about a year (see Beverley 2020: 116–20). Among QAnon networks, it is common to allege that famous people fake their deaths. Joe Biden is said to be Jim Carrey in a mask. Q drop 969 stated that 'Actors are acting'.[7] This drop also describes the Parkland school shooting as 'fake' and a 'distraction'. This is all part of the pervasive theme in QAnon that what is reported in the media is a façade, purposefully constructed by the deep state to keep people (or sheeple) asleep – unaware of their activities. It plays on the long-standing claim in conspiracy theories that major events are 'false flags', operations whose true purposes have been disguised or have been entirely faked using 'crisis actors' (Murawska 2013: 331). Chae-rin told me that after Q stopped posting, Anons continued this theme, claiming that the White House was a movie set, a false copy used because the real one had already been destroyed.

The engagement with false flag explanations of current events opened many other 'rabbit holes' for Chae-rin: lizard people live under houses, and the government feeds them children. She feared going out at night, lest she got eaten by lizard people. The Reptilians are a lizard-like race of aliens that was popularized in conspiracy theory lore by David Icke (Robertson 2013). QAnon maintained Icke's claim that members of the global elite, such as the Royal Family, shapeshift into human form to appear normal, but added that they also used adrenochrome to do so. This chemical substance is said to be violently extracted from the adrenal glands of children, and its effects are like a drug that both gets you high and keeps you young (Rothschild 2021: 52–4). Claims of harvesting this chemical compound from children echo antisemitic blood libel myths dating to the twelfth century in England. Reflecting on how she believed these outlandish claims, Chae-rin said that she shouldn't use the word 'insane', but QAnon did turn people mad.

Yet there was something ultimately frustrating about QAnon. Chae-rin described waiting for the plan to happen for years, and nothing happened. What were they waiting for? Anons would enjoin each other to 'trust the plan', and 'keep praying', 'we'll win in the end' and 'stay strong, patriots'. It was a millenarian expectation that was never fulfilled, leaving people suspended in anxious waiting. In QAnon they said, 'those who know don't sleep'; knowing the truth and the plan meant they could not relax or sleep. Chae-rin would stay up all night, looking at QAnon content. It affected her hygiene, and others' too, they did not wash regularly. Q said to do their own research and get the message out there; that was more important. Doing her own online research took precedence over her physical needs.

Chae-rin had another word for it; she called it a 'cult'. The first reason she gave for this assessment was how people became isolated from outside information because the mainstream media could not be trusted. People got rid of their TVs because Q told them not to watch the news. They had no idea what was going on in the world because they were not accessing other media; they only knew about what people in QAnon said. They would state 'Q said so, so it's true' if contradicted. If anyone questioned anything they were immediately attacked by other Anons online. Chae-rin reached a point when she said, 'I don't think we're watching a movie anymore'. And when she stated this online, her thousands of QAnon Facebook friends took screenshots and told others to watch out for her, slandering her. They immediately turned on her. As soon as she questioned the orthodoxy, she got called a traitor and a Nazi.

Chae-rin also identified QAnon as a 'cult' because they were waiting for their leader to return. They still believed Trump was the real president, who would return any day – a belief she compared to the Second Coming. She believed it too, until the end of April 2021 when things were not adding up for her. Trump did not come back on 4 March 2021, as predicted.[8] If he was coming back, he would have already, she reasoned. That was when she began to interpret QAnon as waiting for their messiah to return, that trusting the plan was a way of denying reality. She saw that Joe Biden was president, and she could no longer believe what was claimed in QAnon. If Trump told people to go harm others, they would do it 'in a heartbeat'. She likened him to a cult leader. She thought he held rallies to make money from people, he was not being sincere. But still a lot of people fell into it overnight, in her perception, many people were led astray. The word 'cult' described for Chae-rin her experience of being in a network that isolated her from outside society, that believed in a saviour, Trump, who would soon return to bring the plan to fruition, and that when this orthodoxy was contradicted, viciously expelled the non-believer. The term 'cult' framed her experiences, made them legible and coherent. As a label, it helped her.

Chae-rin's use of the term was likely informed by her own prior experiences, as well as the cultural associations of the word. She grew up in a strict Pentecostal church that, she said, traumatized and 'brainwashed' her. She described herself as someone who believed everything she was told, and that was what made her a perfect candidate to fall for QAnon. She no longer attended church, which she thought was better for her. It was in church that she was told she had to vote for Republican, or she would go to hell, because God is Republican. In the next election she anticipated voting Democratic for the first time. It was clear her religious experiences informed her understanding of QAnon. Jesus had not come back and people still believed that, she told me, and they had been saying that for over a thousand years. QAnon was like a religious belief in her estimation. Q used religious themes and biblical quotes in the drops. She thought it likely that some would continue believing in Q, just as they continued believing in the Second Coming of Jesus. She had wanted it to be true because it was comforting to believe, a fantasy world in which the good guys won against bad guys. People did not want to leave their fantasy world.

Understanding her involvement in QAnon as being in a 'cult' provided a route towards healing from the experience. She told me that she was doing a lot better since she left QAnon, that reality was better. The best thing about being out was that she was not disappointed every single day anymore. In QAnon, every day was a disappointment, just lies upon lies. She deleted her social media accounts and sought mental health treatment, taking care to bathe and sleep every day. Chae-rin's account illustrates the time commitment being part of QAnon involved, the need to stay afloat in a constant flow of information. That flow of content was as isolating and warping to perceptions as living in a remote compound. The social network of QAnon created media and content bubbles that sealed off a minority, like a digital commune. When Chae-rin left the bubble, the word that made sense to her to describe what it was like inside was 'cult'.

Monica[9] lived in New York State, and like Chae-rin, she also first heard about QAnon from an in-person acquaintance. When Q first started posting on 4chan in 2017–18, her ex-partner was 'obsessed' with it. He had been a Trump supporter from the beginning. At first, she found his fervour off putting, but the more he talked about it to her, the more her interest grew. He would send her links, articles, things from 'funky websites that weren't true', and he would post about it on Facebook, he was in many different QAnon-focused Facebook groups. He told her what they meant, about the influencers decoding the drops on YouTube, and she would not watch. She was busy working and did not have the time or inclination to pay attention. Around late 2018 to early 2019, she 'reversed course' and started to watch the people who would break them down on YouTube, well-known Q influencers like Praying Medic, Jordan Sather, BardsFM, that would break down the decodes. It was the child trafficking allegations that made her change her mind; she wanted to do something positive to help children. Also, she was slightly conspiracy minded already, in that she felt the public did not know the full truth about 9/11. Having grown up with the Patriot Act, and the wars in Iraq and Afghanistan, it seemed like there were so many secrets from the government. That sense of mistrust led her down what she described as a 'very dark path'.

During 2019, Monica's life devolved from enjoying her job and time with her children to being completely immersed in QAnon. Then things worsened during 2020 when the Covid-19 pandemic hit. As an admin for a QAnon Telegram channel, she spent sixteen to eighteen hours a day online, staying up all night, required to have her voice chat open on the channel to monitor it. It became physically and emotionally taxing. It was her responsibility to prevent attacks by 'the shills and the trolls' that would come to disrupt the channel.[10] It became taxing on her mental health, as she was not sleeping or eating right. She became depressed and angry; she did not feel like her normal self.

Unlike Chae-rin, Monica never stopped reading news from media outside of QAnon networks. Self-described as naturally curious, she liked to read 'both sides' rather than accepting 'one side'. However, she knew it was the norm for people very committed to QAnon to not read what they called the 'fake news'. Monica read that Trump was earning money for his businesses through charging foreign diplomats, and other allegations of financial malfeasance. When she asked a question about it in the Telegram channel, the other Anons attacked her, saying it was 'fake news propaganda' and calling her a 'traitor'. They immediately shifted her into the category – traitor – used for the enemies of QAnon. Her Telegram account flooded with messages to 'fuck off' and 'go die', just for asking about what Trump was doing. People that 'used to call me friend' turned against her. She told me:

> You feel like you belong somewhere finally, because in the real world you don't fit in with people, you're different, and you finally find people that you fit in with, and they turn around and spend 9, 10 months doing nothing but attacking you, and trying to destroy you.

Since then, she has been doxed, her legal name, street address, and pictures leaked on to the internet. Someone broke into her house. She received death threats. She found that what she had previously experienced as a welcoming community quickly turned against her when she deviated from their norms.

The experience left her feeling violated and traumatized. 'I fell for it', she told me, and 'I wasted two years of my life'. It destroyed her mental health and ruined her friendships. She called herself paranoid while she was in QAnon, stockpiling food and buying guns in anticipation of martial law that would accompany the arrests of the deep state. She identified this behaviour as not being in the right state of mind, as doing things that she would not have done ordinarily. This feeling of behaving abnormally is often associated with the concept of brainwashing, which has been applied to QAnon followers in particular (Introvigne 2022: 1). When people behave in ways that are very different from their typical behaviour, it calls for an explanation. When the behaviour is as extreme as that described by Monica and Chae-rin, and in the literature on QAnon more widely, it elicits comparisons with forms of mind control, even though brainwashing is considered by scholars as at best a metaphor (Barker 1984).

To explain this dramatic change in her thinking and behaviour, Monica drew a parallel with an abusive relationship. The people involved in QAnon used the same sort of tactics that an abusive partner would do to their victim, she told me, such as gaslighting, deflection and victim blaming. She did not see that at first, even though she was a domestic violence survivor. Then when she did see it, she knew that she had to get out. She compared the loneliness and isolation of the Covid-19 lockdowns to when she left a relationship marked by domestic violence. Without anyone to talk to, she felt sucked in, her brain searching for patterns to which conspiracy theories offered an easy answer. She had talked to many other people in the QAnon movement who had been in abusive relationships at one point or another, and she felt it was part of what made them more susceptible to its grand claims and broken promises. Other people in the movement became a new support system, they called themselves a family, and that was a powerful thing to do to vulnerable people. Everyone was going to meet up when it was all over, once 'the storm' had finally come, and have a huge barbecue party. Those were things to look forward to. Connecting with people through the movement was very powerful, and a significant part of why people did not want to leave, even if they did not believe it. They may not have anybody else, maybe everyone in their life already left them because they would not leave QAnon, so they did not have anyone else except that community. However, for herself, she felt she would rather be lonely.

Monica's main motivation for engaging with QAnon initially was that she saw it as a means to protect children. One of the significant appeals of QAnon to women specifically is the call to 'save the children', capitalizing on gendered themes of protection and care (Bracewell 2021). Child abuse and trafficking are held to be the most heinous crimes in American society, seen for example through the laws regulating sex offenders (Wacquant 2009: 209–39). This status speaks to a primary social value: protecting the innocent. The enemies of QAnon are defined as the worst of the worst, guilty of unspeakable crimes, and therefore any action against them is justifiable, even violence and insurrection.

Monica grew up Roman Catholic, although she stopped attending church when she was fifteen years old. She did not have much of a belief in God, and instead rebelled against a form of religion that she felt was too strict. When involved in QAnon, she found herself saving Bible verses and reading them and sharing them, proclaiming 'God wins' and 'God has this'. However, she was not sure if she ever really believed this. When it came to a belief in God, she was ambivalent, describing herself as 'more of a spiritual person'. She believed there is a higher consciousness, and practised yoga and was into crystals. Her description of her religious affiliation places her in the scope of new age spirituality, which overlaps with QAnon (Crockford 2021c). The idea of a man in the sky creating everything in seven days did not sit right with her, but when she was in the movement she still claimed, 'God wins!' Reflecting afterwards, she was not sure whether she ever believed it or if she was just going along with what everyone else was saying. The movement felt so huge, they had to win, and because it was so big, God was on their side, so it did not matter if she believed it, because they all believed it. Monica's ambivalence about God reflects what Chae-rin said about the importance of following along with the norms of the movement, becoming something larger than herself was both fulfilling in itself but also meant she could feel a part of something without subscribing to every aspect.

Like Chae-rin, Monica identified herself as someone who followed what others were doing. And she similarly called QAnon a cult, describing it to me as 'a violent, anti-Semitic cult'. The reasons she gave for this description also echoed Chae-rin's: it isolated people from those around them, it demanded so much time and energy it caused people to neglect their basic needs, it could not brook any dissent, those who questioned the norms of the community were violently excluded and ostracized. This is the perception that two former participants in QAnon had, the image they saw looking through a figurative rear-view mirror at their prior behaviour. Those still within QAnon insist that it is not a cult because they stress the importance of thinking for yourself, not accepting anyone else's opinion but following 'logic, research, and information', and moreover, no one has even met the leader (if the leader is thought of as Q) (Beverley 2020: 37). Current members often have diametrically opposed views on a group or movement to ex-members, particularly on the issue of whether it is a cult or not (Tabor and Gallagher 1995: 136–7). At least part of this divergence can be attributed to how loaded and pejorative the term 'cult' is, few would willingly admit to being in a cult. It is a retrospective evaluation, much as abuse is often only labelled as such after it has occurred. As Monica evaluated her own actions, she only labelled it as a cult once she was out of it, when she was in it, she did not see it that way. Scholars want to discard the word 'cult' because of its imprecision and negative associations, but it continues to be used because people find few other words fit to describe a group or movement, political or religious, that they have left because they experienced it as controlling, isolating and violent.

The storm

Much of the negative stereotyping around the category 'cult' stems from an association with public violence, with horrific events like the mass murder of the Peoples Temple in Jonestown and the Branch Davidians at Waco standing metonymically for the assumed inevitable end of 'cults' (Moore 2018). Much work has been done by NRM scholars to dissociate the category of new religious movements and a propensity for violence (Barker 2010: 202–3). However, some groups do have principles and ideas that support 'cultures of violence' that predispose members to perpetrate violent acts (Juergensmeyer 2017: 12). QAnon's public violence began in June 2018, less than a year after the first drops appeared in 4chan. A veteran named Matthew Wright engaged in a heavily armed standoff with police at the Hoover Dam, demanding full disclosure of the 'OIG report'[11] posted about by Q that was meant to reveal the lies of the deep state. As part of a pattern of counter-narrative, he was dismissed as fake on

8chan, a false flag to discredit the movement (Rothschild 2021: 44). Individual acts of homicide, child abduction and threats of violence have been committed by people who were influenced by QAnon (Amarasingam and Argentino 2020: 40–2; Rothschild 2021: 106–21).

It was the Capitol Siege on 6 January 2021 that brought QAnon's propensity for collective, political violence to the fore (Lee et al. 2022: 4). Many in QAnon saw it as 'the storm' they were waiting for, when Trump would lead the patriots to victory over the deep state. QAnon flags and banners could be seen among the crowds that violently assaulted the seat of American government during the certification of the electoral count, an act of insurrection that was part of a larger attempt to overturn the results of the 2020 presidential election in Donald Trump's favour. One of the most prominent figures in the scenes recorded from that day was Jake Angeli, who became known as the 'QAnon Shaman' because of his vociferous support of QAnon and his self-identification as a shaman (Crockford 2021c).

For those inside the QAnon bubble, the violent scenes were not taken at face value. Chae-rin told me that when the Capitol Siege occurred, she thought it was all fake. Others in the movement told her not to watch it because it was a false flag attack. She did not watch it on the news until after she left QAnon. She did not know that Trump supporters and QAnon had attacked the Capitol because she did not see the footage. Q did not post about it; it was only discussed among Anons on Facebook. Like the incident at the Hoover Dam, all violent events blamed on QAnon were false flags. She read that the Capitol rioters were not really patriots, they were 'bad guys' in costume, disguised to look like movement members, the 'good guys'. They did not know that people were being arrested and tried for participation in the attack. People that lived an hour from her had been arrested and she had no idea until late 2021. She thought it was just a movie, with actors playing their roles. She had no idea it was an insurrection, that they stormed the Capitol, that it was an attack on American democracy, until after she left QAnon.

By contrast, Monica was aware of the Capitol Siege. She knew people personally who went. They wanted her to go with them, but she stayed home. As a single parent, she refused to put herself in dangerous situations. And she felt sure that something bad was going to happen, she had a sinking feeling in her stomach. Previously in Washington, DC, after Trump rallies there were shootings, stabbings, brawls that she had seen reported on YouTube livestreams. And so, when people she knew were preparing for 6 January, she feared they might be hurt. When she watched it livestreamed on YouTube, she could not believe what was happening. She watched Trump's speech on the Ellipse, in which he told his supporters to march down to the Capitol building, and she could not believe it. Monica thought democracy was going to fall that day. 6 January was the biggest turning point for her. People she knew there sent her videos from the scene, who were subsequently reported to the FBI by their own family members. Afterwards, they changed the story, saying it was a peaceful protest and it was antifa[12] that was responsible for the violence. But it did not make any sense to her, why would antifa go in disguise?

Continuing the pattern of counter-narrative, QAnon dismissed 6 January as fake afterwards, even though members had been part of the planning and were recorded taking part on the day (Lee et al. 2022). Jake Angeli was called a crisis actor, another a deep state false flag to discredit the movement. In this pattern of action and denial, the bubble structure of QAnon is revealed. Evident, yet elusive, flying out of reach when it is nearly caught, a movement in which everything solid melts into the air. The distortion seems intended to deny responsibility, but also reality entirely, that everything that is seen on screen is a performance. Even QAnon as a movement itself disappears, with the claim in Q drop 4881[13] that there is no QAnon. Even though it was called that in its initial years, for example in the book *QAnon: An Invitation to the Great Awakening* (WWG1WGA 2019), written collaboratively by a group of early Q influencers.

The shifting explanations for events and the extreme dissociation of members from anything outside of QAnon to the extent that they deny or do not know about such a significant event as the Capitol Siege signal to outsiders that there is something very wrong about QAnon. It stands beyond the narrative of political polarization; it is not just a case of opposition between two parties. QAnon involves the 'brainwashing' of 'dupes' from an outsider perspective, they are so wrong there must be something controlling their minds. The idea of brainwashing draws on the horror at the subversion of agency, that people can be manipulated into violence they would not otherwise countenance.

At the same time, the rhetoric of QAnon seems dangerous because it draws figurative lines between patriots and traitors, and traitors can and should be executed. This is the kind of language that rationalizes and justifies genocides. Parallels can be drawn between the language used in QAnon about a 'secret war' between good and evil and the language of terrorists (Juergensmeyer 2022). Mark Juergensmeyer (2017: 7) describes religious terrorism as public violence justified by religion, perpetrated by pious people with a clearly articulated moral vision for the world but that then promotes and justifies violence. 'Terrorists' are not monsters, but socially well-adjusted people socialized into extreme worldviews and exceptional communities. They see themselves often as armies, making strategic manoeuvres, in a war against enemies that is necessary for their own survival. QAnon has a similar 'transcendent moralism' and 'ritual intensity' that Juergensmeyer (2017: 9) locates in religious violence as well as the idea of a 'cosmic war' played out on the human plane. Is QAnon a form of religious terrorism? The word 'terrorism' denotes that the violence is perceived as unwarranted, if it is believed that it is justified then the violence is called 'war'. QAnon perceives itself as fighting a war; those outside the bubble call that terrorism. The word 'terrorism' echoes 'cult' in several ways: both are used as external labels, often applied by observers and survivors, to name and understand a violent and traumatic experience, driven by normative sentiments regarding the legitimacy of its motivation rather than a descriptive or analytic account of what that experience was. 'Cult' as a category refers to a socially unacceptable religious group or political movement whose actions are seen as unjustified.

Conclusion: Locating QAnon

On 17 October 2020, Q posted drop 4881: 'There is "Q". There are "Anons". There is no Qanon.' Above the text is a link to a tweet posted on the same date from right-wing media commentator Grant Stinchfield that reads:

> The media calls #Q a cult group that believes in Satanic Sex rings, vampires and inter dimensional beings. I searched #QAnons posts and found Zero mention of any of those things. ZERO. The media lies to hurt @realDonaldTrump #FakeNews #qanon.

Following the pattern of counter-narrative, the accusation of being a 'cult' is flipped back on to the media, transmuted into just another lie they spread to destroy QAnon and Trump. Denying it is a 'cult' is part of what QAnon does to make themselves seem less harmful. This drop came in the run up to the 2020 presidential election that Trump contested, leading to the political violence of 6 January, and it has to be viewed in that context, as part of a wider putsch. Scholars need to take into consideration who it benefits to say that there is no such thing as a cult.

Beyond this consideration, 'cult' is a term that has value and meaning for survivors. They joined a community that harmed them, that did not fulfil its promises. Many such promises are largely unachievable (all debts forgiven, eternal youth from advanced alien palliative technology, ascending to another dimension of consciousness and so on). Those that are achievable (such as overthrowing the government) involve behaviour that transgresses personal boundaries, undermining a solid sense of self. When a person tires of their relationship with a group that treats them abusively, and they leave, they may find that the word 'cult' is the one that most closely fits their experience. It signals a shift from believing to not believing, the bursting of their bubble.

For those still involved, they are trying to see a world in which justice, truth, 'the good' are still triumphing, despite all the evidence they see for the opposite. They seek the triumph of good, and they are fighting a moral battle to win. They see themselves as being on the side of righteousness, as saving the innocent. This is a powerful motivator that is not rational, but rather an emotive religious and ethical impetus. Those that label their righteous crusade as a 'cult' are easily sublimated into the amorphous blob of enemies, ever shifting with the terrain of battle.

The word 'cult' is a shapeshifter, semantically morphing with the intentions of whoever uses it. As an analytical term, it resists rigorous definition. If it can be stripped of its subjectivity, what it refers to structurally is a religious or religion-like group that is self-consciously building a new form of society, but that the rest of society defines as socially unacceptable. However, the subjectivity will always remain because language lives in its social contexts, so a 'cult' will also always have the connotation of a group you disagree with, that you think is morally wrong, and if people believe in it, there must be something wrong with them. When calling something a cult, or conspiracy theory, you take a stance on the social acceptability, or lack thereof, of the thing so labelled.

Cult accusations are signs of social conflicts, disagreements over how life should be lived in a society. Social consensus reality relies on a consensus and sometimes that consensus shifts. Something is happening now that makes 'cult' accusations more frequent, popular and meaningful on a wider scale. A social group that wants to overthrow the government is likely to be seen as socially unacceptable by those who do not seek such revolutionary change. QAnon is also not an isolated phenomenon. It is part of wide-scale social divisions between political cleavages in American society. There is a sense of grievance and resentment, of anger against those perceived as elite, an emotion that becomes warped into allegations of child trafficking and murder. QAnon is an online movement, and it is also a social group with its own values, norms and beliefs. They perceive themselves as a movement fighting for truth and justice; outsiders see a cult spreading conspiracy theories.

Notes

1. Q drop 364 archived https://qanon.pub/?q=follow%20the%20crumbs (accessed 4 November 2022).
2. The term 'digital soldier' is used in Q drops 4637 and 4509 https://qanon.pub/?q=digital%20soldier (accessed 4/11/22); Rothschild (2021: 10) posits the origin as a speech by Gen. Michael Flynn praising Donald Trump's online supporters in 2016, and it was subsequently taken up in QAnon, before it was used in a Q drop.
3. A data analysis approach to the Q drops and what they tell us about the identity of the poster can be found in the Q Origins Project, hosted by Bellingcat: https://www.bellingcat.com/news/rest-of-world/2021/05/10/where-in-the-world-is-q-clues-from-image-metadata/ The documentary by Cullen Hoback, *Q: Into the Storm*, made a compelling case that the administrator of 8kun (formerly 8chan), Ronald Watkins, and his father, Jim Watkins, the owner of the site, were behind the posts, at least once they moved away from 4chan. This is also the opinion of former administrator of 8kun/8chan Fredrick Brennan, based on his technical knowledge of how the tripcodes on the image board work (Francescani 2020).
4. Q drop 1 archived https://qanon.pub/?q=HRC%20extrad (accessed 5 November 2022).
5. This has been my own conclusion in earlier work (Crockford 2018: 109).
6. A pseudonym. Phone interview in October 2021, followed up via text messages in 2022.
7. Q drop 969 archived: https://qanon.pub/?q=actors%20are%20acting (accessed 2 November 2022).
8. An idea from sovereign citizen ideology that the 'true' inauguration date is 4 March, see Spocchia (2021).
9. A pseudonym. Zoom interview in April 2022, follow up via direct messages on Twitter.
10. Trolling is a feature of online discourse, defined as 'something inflammatory, off-topic, shocking, or intentionally incorrect with the purpose of creating an argument with others' (Wesch and Digital Ethnography Class of Spring 2009 2009: 94).
11. A reference to an internal Department of Justice report on Hillary Clinton's use of a private email server. It had been released publicly the day before Wright went to the Hoover Dam, proving his intention or awareness of current events vague.
12. Antifa is short for 'anti-fascist action' which is used as a right-wing label for anyone who opposes Trump, especially people who may be protesting against him or in support of BlackLivesMatter or other left-wing causes.
13. Q drop 4881 archived https://qanon.pub/?q=there%20is%20%27q%27 (accessed 4 November 2022).

References

Amarasingam, A. and M.-A. Argentino (2020), 'The QAnon Conspiracy Theory: A Security Threat in the Making?', *CTC Sentinel*, 13 (7): 1–12.

Argentino, M.-A. (2020a), 'The Church of QAnon: Will Conspiracy Theories form the Basis of a New Religious Movement?', *The Conversation*, 18 May. Available at https://theconversation.com/the-church-of-qanon-will-conspiracy-theories-form-the-basis-of-a-new-religious-movement-137859 (accessed 5 November 2022).

Argentino, M.-A. (2020b), 'In the Name Of the Father, Son, and Q: Why It's Important to See QAnon as a "Hyper-Real" Religion', *Religion Dispatches*, 28 May. Available at https://religiondispatches.org/in-the-name-of-the-father-son-and-q-why-its-important-to-see-qanon-as-a-hyper-real-religion/ (accessed 5 November 2022).

Argentino, M.-A. (2021), 'Pastel QAnon', *GNET Insights*, 17 March. Available at https://gnet-research.org/2021/03/17/pastel-qanon/ (accessed 5 November 2022).

Armaly, M. T., D. T. Buckley and A. M. Enders (2022), 'Christian Nationalism and Political Violence: Victimhood, Racial Identity, Conspiracy, and Support for the Capitol Attacks', *Political Behavior*, 44 (2): 937–60.

Badham, V. (2021), 'QAnon: How the Far-right Cult took Australians Down a "Rabbit Hole" of Extremism', *The Guardian*, 13 November. Available at https://www.theguardian.com/us-news/2021/nov/14/qanon-how-the-far-right-cult-took-australians-down-a-rabbit-hole-of-extremism (accessed 5 November 2022).

Badiou, A. (2013), *Being and Event*, trans. O. Feltham. London: Bloomsbury Academic.

Barker, E. (1984), *The Making of a Moonie: Choice or Brainwashing?*. London: Wiley-Blackwell.

Barker, E. (2010), 'The Cult as a Social Problem', in T. Hjelm (ed.), *Religion and Social Problems*, 198–212. New York: Routledge.

Barker, E. (2014), 'The Not-So-New Religious Movements: Changes in "the Cult Scene" over the Past Forty Years', *Temenos*, 50 (2): 235–56.

Beauchamp, J. D. (2022), 'Evangelical Identity and QAnon: Why Christians Are Finding New Mission Fields in Political Conspiracy', *Journal of Religion and Violence*, July.

Beverley, J. A. (2020), *The QAnon Deception: Everything You Need to Know about the World's Most Dangerous Conspiracy Theory*. Concord: EqualTime Books.

Blazakis, J. (2021), 'Op-Ed: Why QAnon's Similarity to Other Cults Makes it a Significant National Security Threat', *Los Angeles Times*, 21 February. Available at https://www.latimes.com/opinion/story/2021-02-21/qanon-cults-capitol-attack-trump-threat (accessed 5 November 2022).

Bond, S. (2021), 'Unwelcome On Facebook and Twitter, QAnon Followers Flock To Fringe Sites', *NPR*, 31 January. Available at https://www.npr.org/2021/01/31/962104747/unwelcome-on-facebook-twitter-qanon-followers-flock-to-fringe-sites (accessed 5 November 2022).

Bracewell, L. (2021), 'Gender, Populism, and the QAnon Conspiracy Movement', *Frontiers in Sociology*, 5 (January): 3–6.

Coaston, J. (2019), 'The Mueller Investigation is over. QAnon, the Conspiracy Theory that Grew Around It, Is Not', *Vox*, 29 March. Available at https://www.vox.com/policy-and-politics/2019/3/29/18286890/qanon-mueller-report-barr-trump-conspiracy-theories (accessed 5 November 2022).

Conner, C. T. and N. MacMurray (2022), 'The Perfect Storm: A Subcultural Analysis of the QAnon Movement', *Critical Sociology*, 48 (6): 1049–71.

Crockford, S. (2018), 'How Do You Know When You're in a Cult? The Continuing Influence of Peoples Temple and Jonestown in Contemporary Minority Religions and Popular Culture', *Nova Religio*, 22 (2): 93–114.

Crockford, S. (2021a), 'Starseeds', in B. E. Zeller (ed.), *Handbook of UFO Religions*, 403–22. Leiden: Brill.

Crockford, S. (2021b), *Ripples of the Universe: Spirituality in Sedona, Arizona*. Chicago: University of Chicago Press.

Crockford, S. (2021c), 'Q Shaman's New Age-Radical Right Blend Hints at the Blurring of Seemingly Disparate Categories', *Religion Dispatches*, 11 January. Available at https://religiondispatches.org/q-shamans-new-age-radical-right-blend-hints-at-the-blurring-of-seemingly-disparate-categories/ (accessed 5 November 2022).

Eady, G., J. Nagler, A. Guess, J. Zilinsky and J. A. Tucker (2019), 'How Many People Live in Political Bubbles on Social Media? Evidence from Linked Survey and Twitter Data', *SAGE Open*, 9 (1): 1–21.

Enders, A. M., J. E. Uscinski, C. A. Klofstad, S. Wuchty, M. I. Seelig, J. R. Funchion, M. N. Murthi, K. Premaratne and J. Stoler (2022), 'Who Supports QAnon? A Case Study in Political Extremism', *Journal of Politics*, 84 (3): 1844–49.

Festinger, L., H. Riecken and S. Schachter (1956), *When Prophecy Fails*. Minneapolis: University of Minnesota Press.

Forberg, P. L. (2022), 'From the Fringe to the Fore: An Algorithmic Ethnography of the Far-Right Conspiracy Theory Group QAnon', *Journal of Contemporary Ethnography*, 51 (3): 291–317.

Francescani, C. (2020), 'The Men behind QAnon', *ABC News*, 22 September. Available at https://abcnews.go.com/Politics/men-qanon/story (accessed 5 November 2022).

Harding, S. and E. Martin (2021), 'Trump Time, Prophetic Time and the Time of the Lost Cause', *Anthropology Now*, 13 (1): 30–36.

Hoseini, M., P. Melo, F. Benevenuto, A. Feldmann and S. Zannettou (2021), 'On the Globalization of the QAnon Conspiracy Theory through Telegram', *ArXiv Preprint*, 2105 (13020).

Introvigne, M. (2022), *Brainwashing: Reality or Myth?*. Cambridge: Cambridge University Press.

Jenkins, T. (2013), *Of Flying Saucers and Social Scientists: A Re-Reading of When Prophecy Fails and of Cognitive Dissonance*. London: Palgrave Macmillan.

Juergensmeyer, M. (2017), *Terror in the Mind of God: The Global Rise of Religious Violence*, 4th edn. Oakland: University of California Press.

Juergensmeyer, M. (2022), 'QAnon as Religious Terrorism', *Journal of Religion and Violence*, July.

LaFrance, A. (2020), 'The Prophecies of Q', *The Atlantic*, 14 May. Available at https://www.theatlantic.com/magazine/archive/2020/06/qanon-nothing-can-stop-what-is-coming/610567/ (accessed 5 November 2022).

Lee, C. S., J. Merizalde, J. D. Colautti, J. An and H. Kwak (2022), 'Storm the Capitol: Linking Offline Political Speech and Online Twitter Extra-Representational Participation on QAnon and the January 6 Insurrection', *Frontiers in Sociology*, 7 (May).

Melton, J. G. (2007), 'Perspective: New New Religions: Revisiting a Concept', *Nova Religio*, 10 (4): 103–12.

Moore, R. (2018), 'Godwin's Law and Jones' Corollary: The Problem of Using Extremes to Make Predictions', *Nova Religio*, 22 (2): 145–54.

Murawska, S. (2013), 'False Flag Operation in Context of Conspiracy Theory as a Myth Which Legitimizes Actions of Ruling Class', *Prace Ethnograficzne*, 41 (4): 329–34.

Onishi, B. (2023), *Preparing for War: The Extremist History of White Christian Nationalism - And What Comes Next*. Abergavenny: Broadleaf Books.

Papasavva, A., M. Aliapoulios, C. Ballard, E. De Cristofaro, G. Stringhini, S. Zannettou and J. Blackburn (2022), 'The Gospel According to Q: Understanding the QAnon Conspiracy from the Perspective of Canonical Information', *Proceedings of the Sixteenth International AAAI Conference on Web and Social Media*. Available at http://arxiv.org/abs/2101.08750 (accessed 5 November 2022).

Rhodes, S. C. (2022), 'Filter Bubbles, Echo Chambers, and Fake News: How Social Media Conditions Individuals to Be Less Critical of Political Misinformation', *Political Communication*, 39 (1): 1–22.

Richardson, J. T. (2021), 'The Myth of the Omnipotent Leader: The Social Construction of a Misleading Account of Leadership in New Religious Movements', *Nova Religio*, 24 (4): 11–25.

Robertson, D. G. (2013), 'David Icke's Reptilian Thesis and the Development of New Age Theodicy', *International Journal for the Study of New Religions*, 4 (1): 27–47.

Robertson, D. G. (2022), 'Crippled Epistemologies: Conspiracy Theories, Religion, and Knowledge', *Social Research*, 89 (3): 651–77.

Robertson, D. G. and A. Amarasingam (2022), 'How Conspiracy Theorists Argue: Epistemic Capital in the QAnon Social Media Sphere', *Popular Communication*, 20 (3): 193–207.

Rothschild, M. (2021), *The Storm Is upon Us: How QAnon Became a Movement, Cult, and Conspiracy Theory of Everything*. New York: Melville House.

Sloterdijk, P. (2011), *Spheres: Volume 1: Bubbles – Microspherology*, trans. W. Hoban. Los Angeles: Semiotext(e).

Snow, D. A. (2023), 'Cults', in D. A. Snow, D. Della Porta, D. McAdam, and B. Klandermans (eds), *The Wiley Blackwell Encyclopedia of Social and Political Movements*, Second Edition, 233–9. New York: John Wiley & Sons.

Spocchia, G. (2021), 'QAnon Merges with White Extremists and Spreads New Conspiracy Trump will be President Again on March 4', *The Independent*, 26 January. Available at https://www.independent.co.uk/news/world/americas/us-election-2020/qanon-trump-march-sovereign-citizen-fbi-b1792830.html (accessed 5 November 2022).

Stanley-Becker, I. (2018), '"We are Q": A Deranged Conspiracy Cult Leaps from the Internet to the Crowd at Trump's "MAGA" Tour', *The Washington Post*, 1 August. Available at https://www.washingtonpost.com/news/morning-mix/wp/2018/08/01/we-are-q-a-deranged-conspiracy-cult-leaps-from-the-internet-to-the-crowd-at-trumps-maga-tour/ (accessed 5 November 2022).

Tabor, J. D. and E. V. Gallagher (1995), *Why Waco?: Cults and the Battle for Religious Freedom in America*. Berkeley: University of California Press.

Uscinski, J. E. (2022), 'Getting QAnon Wrong and Right', *Social Research*, 89 (3): 551–78.

Wacquant, L. J. D. (2009), *Punishing the Poor: The Neoliberal Government of Social Insecurity*. Durham: Duke University Press.

Wesch, M. and Digital Ethnography Class of Spring 2009 (2009), 'Anonymous, Anonymity, and the End(s) of Identity and Groups Online: Lessons from the "First Internet-Based Superconsciousness"', in N. L. Whitehead and M. Wesch (eds), *Human No More: Digital Subjectivities, Unhuman Subjects, and the End of Anthropology*, 89–104. Boulder: University Press of Colorado.

Wessinger, C. (2000), *How the Millennium Comes Violently: From Jonestown to Heaven's Gate*. New York: Seven Bridges Press.

Wessinger, C. (2021), '"Cult" is an Inaccurate, Unhelpful and Dangerous Label for Followers of Trump, QAnon, and 1/6', *Religion Dispatches*, 19 July. Available at https://religiondispatches.org/cult-is-an-inaccurate-unhelpful-and-dangerous-label-for-followers-of-trump-qanon-and-1-6/ (accessed 5 November 2022).

WWG1WGA (2019), *QAnon: An Invitation to the Great Awakening*. Dallas: Relentlessly Creative Books.

Xavier, A. W., R. Amour and the Q Origins Project (2021), 'Where in the World is Q? Clues from Image Metadata', *Bellingcat*, 10 May. Available at https://www.bellingcat.com/news/rest-of-world/2021/05/10/where-in-the-world-is-q-clues-from-image-metadata/ (accessed 5 November 2022).

10

Playing at religion

Understanding contemporary spiritual experiences in popular culture

Vivian Asimos

The study of religion and popular culture can be divided into three primary approaches. The first is how religions are portrayed in popular culture (e.g. Wysocki 2018). These approaches are useful in understanding the creator(s) perspectives on religion more generally or a specific religion. The second is how popular culture is understood and treated by specific religions. This can be in how religions use popular culture affects understandings of contemporary religion (e.g. Pumphrey 2018), or in how religions may accept or reject specific aspects of popular culture (e.g. Vogt 2011). The third approach to the study of religion and popular culture is to see the two as the same: not how popular culture or religion uses the other, but in how popular culture *is* religion.

Part of this approach is the study of hyper-real or invented religions, which use fictional worlds to create a new religion outside of the fiction practised (Davidsen 2012; Possamai 2012; Cusack and Kosnáč 2017). Hyper-real religions are fascinating in the way they are constructed, and the way they are understood by both those adhering to the religion and those viewing the religion from the outside, however this is not where I typically centre my own approach to the study of religion and popular culture, and therefore is not the purview of this particular chapter. Hyper-real religions focus on particular types of fans of popular culture, but do not encompass the vast majority. I do not believe that one has to put Jedi on a census record to feel that *Star Wars* means something significant to them. Another aspect of the popular culture as religion approach is seeing popular culture engagement as a form of implicit religion. Implicit religion is about how religious-like experiences can be found outside of traditional religious circles (Bailey 1998). As I will discuss further in the chapter,

I find this more of an issue of the emic/etic divide, and the insistence of religion being found where others may not see it as an issue worth thinking about.

Rather, my focus has historically been on the nature of myth and mythology (Asimos 2019b, 2021). This has been for several reasons, one being that terminology regarding aspects of religion is found in fans regularly, including uses of words like 'ritual', 'mythology' and 'cult' without actually engaging with the larger concept of 'religion'.

Essentially, there is a neglected area in the literature related to religion and popular culture. There is a grey area in which meaning-making is occurring, but not to so strong an extent as that which is representative in hyper-real religions. In many ways, this will reveal much in the way the average person engages with popular culture. The way I typically approach the study of religion has been to push our definitions. I push our definitions of religion, our definitions of mythology, our definitions of ritual and so on in order to consider the most diverse ways we can understand these aspects. What has been fascinating in this endeavour is that it allows meaningful aspects to be found in new locations, without being clouded by any of my preconceived notions of what something like 'religion' or 'mythology' is.

During fieldwork talking with fans of *The Legend of Zelda* video game series, I chatted with one participant who had a tattoo from the video game series on their arm. The symbol references an in-game mythology of divinely wrought three-triangles known as the Triforce, which will grant someone any wish as long as they have an equal amount of wisdom, power and courage. My participant talked about the Triforce on their arm in a similar matter – they reflected on how when faced with important decisions in their life, they think about approaching the matter with equal amounts of wisdom, power and courage.

My participant represents this grey middle ground who finds intense meaning in popular culture. This participant would never put Hylian[1] on a census record, as a Jedi would who is a member of the hyper-real religion Jediism derived from popular culture. Nor are they indifferent to this piece of pop culture; it clearly means so much to them that they have permanently marked their body with this mythology and continuously refers to it as they move through life.

Other experiences of meaning-making or deeply emotional experiences are present in contemporary experiences of popular culture. The video game *Journey*, for example, allows the player to play out a pilgrimage from the desert to the top of a mountain. One player wrote: 'I've always been an atheist, but i swear I had a spiritual experience from playing this game [*sic*]' (u/Fortunatious 2018). By exploring these experiences of spirituality, as well as the rhetoric of mythology, cult and other aspects of religion, we are able to push our questioning not on where we find what we already think of as religion, but rather to consider what religion *can be*.

Cult rhetoric in popular culture

From television shows like *Buffy the Vampire Slayer* and *The X-Files*, to films such as *The Rocky Horror Picture Show* and *The Evil Dead*, popular culture is often described as 'cultic'. 'Cult' films, 'cult' shows or pieces of popular culture which claim a 'cult' following are all ways the religious language of 'cult' is used in popular culture. However, media scholars seem to disagree on what it is that makes something a 'cult' piece.

Most understandings of the cult media rely heavily on Eco's definition, which states that the cult object 'must be loved' but also needs to 'provide a completely furnished world so that fans can quote characters and episodes as if they were aspects of the fan's private sectarian world, a world about which one can make up quizzes and play trivia games so that the adepts of the sect recognize through each other a shared expertise' (Eco 1985). However, Eco's definition of the cult media object relies on both characteristics of the object and its reception, but does not spend as much time focusing on aspects of the mechanisms which underlie the object, such as the way it was distributed (Gwenllian-Jones and Pearson 2004).

At one point, cultic television and films were associated with small-scale fanbases based particularly on the piece's failure to reach mainstream popularity (Guern 2004). This, however, started to change when ways in which television was distributed began to alter. There became a shift between a centralized network of television to a multi-channel distribution network (Reeves, Rodgers and Epstein 1996). The resultant globalization, as well as television syndication, meant that television programmers shifted from wanting a massive audience to seeking out small 'niche' audiences for their programmes. These are more 'deliberate' cult television shows, as opposed to the accidental ones which simply did not reach mainstream audiences as before, such as *Twin Peaks*, or *the X-Files* (Gwenllian-Jones and Pearson 2004).

A cult piece of pop culture appears, then, to be defined by its fanbase, whether it is one that occurred accidentally or deliberately, but always exclusively by its fervour. As Eco points out, the fans share a similar language and behaviour associated with the media. Cult followings are defined by particularly intense and devoted fanbases, whose participation with pop culture keeps the emotions of it all alive (Deslippe 2023).

The conception of cultic pop culture belies an important facet to popular culture, especially in its relationship to religion: the power of the fan. As I discussed earlier, popular culture invites fans to embrace and connect to the media they love. They tattoo the media on their body, they wear clothes that harken to the piece, or even to specific characters, and they seek out others who also embrace and love the same pieces they do. The original understanding of the 'fan' was as a 'fanatic' – an overly enthused other who stressed their connections to their pop culture of choice to the detriment of their day-to-day life. Contemporary fan studies only see fans as those who are emotionally engaged and invested in popular culture narratives (Gray, Sandvoss and Harrington 2007: 10). Fans are a clear indication of how contemporary audiences engage with contemporary narratives – with emotional investment which has the potential to directly affect the audience on a deep emotional level.

Often, popular culture audiences are described as passive – they allow the narratives to happen to them but do little to push back or critically consider the narrative itself. This is echoed more explicitly in discourse around digital popular culture, most notably in the conception of when an image or video has gone 'viral' – a term connoting disease, something passing through audiences; viral happens to them without thought, not something they create for themselves. Michel de Certeau's view of readership, however, shifts the notion of the passive audience. He describes readers as people who 'poach' in their environment (1984), a concept which was picked up by Henry Jenkins. Jenkins sees the same concept in what he called 'textual poachers', fans who comb through the media like texts, and take elements from these mediums to bring out new elements and ideas through their personal creativity (Jenkins 1992). These outputs are in the form of written stories, called fanfiction; in the form of hand-crafted costume, called cosplay; and in the development of personal essays posted on blogs or in a visual form on YouTube.

Fans do refer to their pieces as cultic, but this phrasing should not be mistakenly applied to the piece of media itself. Rather, it can only exist within the context of people and the fans themselves – it requires a certain level of emotional engagement, of concern and care, and of the formation of a community which sees connection – and sometimes safety – in the relationships formed.

Other religious language is not uncommon to find in popular culture and the way fans talk about their interests. Fans may refer to their 'rituals' of engagement, or discuss and theorize about the 'mythology' or 'mythos' of a series. In some cases, you get individuals like the reddit user cited at the beginning of this chapter, who referred to playing a video game as a 'spiritual' experience. These individuals would probably fall under the idea of the 'cultic' audience – the audience that sees deep meaning and connection to their media of choice and hold onto that with intensity. This does not mean, however, that these individuals would ascribe this as their functional religion. Religious language is often used as a marker of meaning, rather than as a one-to-one understanding of religious intention in pop culture.

Pop culture as meaning-making

In the beginning of this chapter, I reflected on meeting a fan of *The Legend of Zelda* series who had a mark from the mythology of the world tattooed on their arm. They had told me about their guidance in life through the tattoo on their arm. This guidance relied on this individual having a close relationship with both the mythology of the game world and the games themselves. My *Zelda* participant is by far not the only person who has developed a relationship of meaning-making of pop culture.

An emotional connection to meaningful stories makes up the backbone of what makes a consumer interested in spending time in the fictional world. Michel de Certeau described consumers as active 'poachers' (de Certeau 1984), but a poacher must be interested in their environment and the sources of their prey. The consumerist poacher doesn't just consume without discretion – they actively seek what gives them meaning.

Joseph Laycock explained this in the description of the history of the development of *Masters of the Universe*. Mattel had an action figure of a surfer they wanted to sell, and they tried many different avenues to sell it without success. They hired someone to come in and help them develop a better story for the figure, and the character completely changed from the surfer figure to He-Man – the mythical prince and hero figure. Suddenly, the same figure began to sell tremendously well (Laycock 2010). What Laycock shows us is that myth – meaningful narratives people can emotionally connect to – is what helps to sell rather than an indiscriminate use of advertising. Essentially, even children need detailed and interesting stories.

Cosplay – a portmanteau of 'costume' and 'play' – is when individuals dress as a character from a piece of pop culture. During research with cosplayers, I talked extensively with many of them about their deep emotional connections to pop culture narratives. When discussing their choices of character with a cosplayer, one participant, Rachel (2022), expressed their connection to their fiction of choice:

> Like, when I did Moana, I was like . . . I was just really just really pleased to see like a person that I look like. I mean, I've cut all my hair off now. Like, back then I had, like, the big Moana curly hair. You know, I'm mixed race. I'm not Polynesian. But it was nice to see, like, somebody who physically looks like me represented on screen. And I think when I was watching it, I was like . . . she was just really cool. And then as I was going through, and I was making it, and I was like: No, her story, like, really, really, like, touched me. And I was like: Oh, this is this is . . . yeah, this is something bigger than even I was aware of. So, I think on the surface level, I picked characters because I'm like, You look really cool. But if I psychoanalyze myself, even for a second, I'm like, I think these are just characters that I resonate with on some degree, emotionally.

Rachel explained their connection to story on a deep emotional level, one which started as a simple interest before developing to a deeper level. The character Moana from Disney's film was not just an aesthetic choice, but one built on personal connection of racial differences with those around them and an emotional connection to the story Moana plays out on screen.

Similarly, cosplayer Sam explored their choice in character coming from a reflection of personal trauma and grief. Sam (2022) explained a deep connection to one of their characters, Tohru Honda from *Fruits Basket*:

> I felt so moved to become her because all the things she had been through in her life. She had lost her mom, I had lost my mom . . . like, all these things that happen. I was like, I wish that I could still go out there with a smile on my face at that point in my life. And so I did that, and I did everything I could to be like her when I was in cosplay.

Like Rachel, Sam connected to her character on a deeper emotional level, one that reflected shared experience and shared understanding. Tohru is not just a character that is similar to Sam, but is a character which handled some of the same experiences in a more optimistic way, which Sam was desperate to emulate during an intense period of grief.

Both Rachel and Sam demonstrate how individuals in a fandom are drawn to their pieces of pop culture for intense personal reasons, which extends beyond simple entertainment. The push from simply enjoying something to being a fan is one predicated on the development of these emotional connections. These fans have a deep emotional connection to their fandom that also includes aspects of language, action – a cultic connection, based on our idea of cultic pop culture. It requires the individual to see their piece of fandom as an important piece of personal mythology – an important factor in individual meaning formation.

For many people like Rachel and Sam, their intense interest in pop culture is something beyond simple enjoyment. Their personal connection to be seen as inherently *religious*. This is not, however, an advocation of implicit religion. The term 'implicit religion' infers a position of being religious even when the participants themselves may not acknowledge it as such (Bailey 1998). Essentially what would be happening here in the use of implicit religion would be an over-reliance on the academic's worldview, to the detriment of truly listening to that of the participant. Not only does the language of the academic's viewpoint get overshone but so, too, does the academic's own personal definition of religion. If my personal definition of religion is inherently different than that of my participant, the discussion is no longer a discourse between these various views, but becomes, instead, an overriding of my own over that of my participant.

Instead, something really interesting happens when we focus on the words and experiences of fans rather than on personal academic understandings: we see the world through a different set of eyes. The piece of pop culture becomes nuanced, as does the fan themselves. It is not just that there are overly enthused and crazed others who sacrifice themselves for the sake of their pop culture of choice, or people who are indifferent. There are levels of interest and engagement, a variety of experiences and multiple different ways of connecting to pop culture in a variety of ways. Giving up the academic perspective for the sake of seeking an understanding unveils a complex wave of different viewpoints that can truly illuminate some interesting facets to the study of religion.

In order to truly get at the heart of this, we should first consider, or reconsider, notions of definitions.

Pushing definitional boundaries

When beginning the study of religion as an undergraduate student, I found the trouble of definitions more troublesome than interesting. People seemed to have a variety of different understandings of what religion could be. While this is definitely true of the academic study of religion, it is also true of individuals outside of academia. When academics added to the complexity by heaping on their own definitions, it became tricky. A definition based on substantive features, such as 'existence of gods' (Tylor 2010), for example, could be ousted as not useful because it does not apply to something firmly understood as 'religion'. However, often these discourses of which definitions are applicable and which are not are often based on preconceived notions of what religion is as it is already understood by the scholar. For example, Tylor's need for an existence of gods could be argued as incorrect due to it being non-applicable to Buddhism – but this requires the academic to already consider Buddhism a religion, which is not necessarily a given.

I started to see the fun in definitions when I began my PhD. I found it interesting to stretch definitions and see how far I could push them. My personal definition of choice was always 'mythology'. I found that my definition of mythology seemed quite stretched and broad for academics. Instead of focusing on aspects such as conceptions of 'sacredness', I instead focused on the idea of myth as something meaningful. A myth, for my research, is a narrative (or something akin to a narrative) which an individual or community uses to understand themselves and the world around them (Asimos 2019b, 2021).

While some academics may see this definition as quite broad, my participants have found it both useful and obvious. In an email chain for a podcast appearance, I was told by the hosts how this 'made a lot of sense' and that it paired with how they viewed things. In chats with a cosplayer I was told how their pop culture fandoms are basically like mythology now, before I even brought up the subject.

Essentially pushing a definition to one step below a breaking point, enjoying the flexibility of definitions, has two primary effects: (1) shifting the academic view of the term beyond simply looking at other academic definitions and (2) allowing new applications of familiar terms.

The first effect – shifting the academic view of the term – is related to the understanding of what a term may mean outside of academic considerations of it. As I mentioned previously, the shifting understanding of myth to be stretched and understood differently actually fit more with participants' views of storytelling than other approaches. The flexibility presented in playing with definitions allows the researcher to get closer to the raw emotions and connections held by the community being studied.

Definitions can be used, therefore, as research tools, rather than hard and fast rules the researcher should live within no matter what. I previously stated my definition of myth as meaningful narratives an individual may use to understand themselves. This definition I hold may drastically change if I began researching a new community who had different views and understandings of stories. This is not to say that my previous definition would suddenly be wrong – only that the definition I used in the first environment fit that particular community's view of myths and mythology, which may not be how another social grouping sees the same thing. Keeping our definitions flexible allows researchers to see the world through others' eyes – which should be our goal. In other words, our definitions of choice should reflect those we are talking about, rather than ourselves.

The second effect of flexibility in our definitions allows for new applications of familiar terms. By using words in new ways, we shift our preconceived notions. As researchers, we have many biases of our own – not just from our personal background, but also from our position *as academics*. We carry with us the definitions and understandings of the academics who have come before us, and often rely heavily on these conceptions as we move through our career and life. Our definitions of religion are reliant on other definitions of religion, and we stick fiercely to these, often to the detriment of where others – non-academics – may see religion. The flexibility of definitions forces us, as academics, to live outside our preset comfort zones.

In the discussion earlier on cult rhetoric, I discussed the importance of the cultic audience in the definition of what makes something either a 'cult film' or 'cult tv show'. The cult following are the primary adherents, the deeply involved lovers who find reverence, love and connection in the popular culture narrative. The phrasing of the 'cult' reference relates to the conceptions of religion, particularly small religious groups that others outside the community may not understand.

The use of the word 'cult' is done partly in jest, but also reveals the feelings of the community involved. There is a truth to the jest – otherwise, a different word may have been chosen instead. Mythology, religion, cult – these are all words fans of pop culture use to understand the worlds of connection they create with fiction and with others who love the fiction as well.

During research at CoxCon, a fan convention for YouTuber Jesse Cox, I talked to several individuals who expressed intense connection to the community of fans, rather than just the content. One mentioned how easy it was to talk to new people at the convention, despite having social anxiety, because 'you know who you're talking to has something in common with you. You share the same value' (Asimos 2019a). It may seem odd to assume one has the same innate values as a stranger simply because you enjoy the same YouTube channel, but there is a lot to this for the communities which band together in fandom. They tend to be from the same niche audience groups that producers seek to create their deliberate 'cult' network of fans. Fans share the same language, and find meaning in the same narratives. This means that there is something deeply connecting them together. They are a cultic network, one which understands themselves in others through language, action and an inherently understood levels of shared values.

This is all to say that popular culture can unite people. It gives the cultic fanbase a community of like-minded togetherness. It provides a shared language and shared experience. They express their rituals and discuss their connections to the mythology. They sometimes brand this mythology on their skin. The true issue with approaching discussions of this with the idea of implicit religion is that I would, in my mind, already have a tried and true definition of religion in mind, which I would readily apply to these community groups of fans. The difficulty with most approaches would be the same – a preset conception of what is religion and what is not. Which is the piece of pop culture and which is the religion in order to directly compare.

But let us, for example, stretch a definition of religion, push it so that it is not a comparison between one and another in like. Nor is it a replacement of one. But it is, instead, a greater understanding of the emotional connections and inherent relationships that exist between people and fiction – a reciprocal relationship of bonding and care. Suddenly, it is not that I – the academic – transform these individuals' conceptions of themselves and what they are doing. Rather, it is them – the participants, the fans, the cultic audience – who transform my conception of them and of what they are doing. It causes us to question not only what way cult is being used in these forms, but also what a cultic religion has the possibility of being.

The true impact of a study of religion and popular culture, of diving into the world of cultic appreciation, deep rooted community bases and connections to mythic fiction, is the alteration of definitions of religion. It does not transform what religion is – not on the substantial or functional aspects of other definitions. Rather, it transforms our academic understanding of where religion can be found, of what religion may look like and what religion *can actually be*.

'New' religion is all around, not because it is new. And not because it takes the form of recognized churches with established doctrines. Not because the texts are either written or not. But because individuals engage with aspects of meaning in new and interesting ways constantly. They are always creating meaning, connecting to those stories of meaning, and then poaching them to recreate with their individual creativity something inherently new and interesting from that. If we let go of what we conventionally consider religion, we may be able to see these individual acts of creativity and interest happening all around us in the form of cultic networks of television shows, YouTube channels and films.

Note

1 Hylian refers to the human race in *The Legend of Zelda* lore.

References

Asimos, V. (2019a), 'Navigating Through Space Butterflies: CoxCon 2017 and Fieldwork Presentation of Contemporary Movements', *Fieldwork in Religion*, 14 (2): 181–94.

Asimos, V. (2019b), 'Video Games as Contemporary Mythology', *Implicit Religion*, 21 (1): 92–109.

Asimos, V. (2021), *Digital Mythology and the Internet's Monster*. London: Bloomsbury.

Bailey, E. (1998), *Implicit Religion: An Introduction*. London: Middlesex University Press.

Certeau, M. de (1984), *The Practice of Everyday Life*. 1: ... 2. print. Berkeley: University of California Press.

Cusack, C. M. and P. Kosnác, eds (2017), *Fiction, Invention, and Hyper-Reality: From Popular Culture to Religion*. New York: Routledge.

Davidsen, M. A. (2012), 'The Spiritual Milieu Based on J.R.R Tolkien's Literary Mythology', in A. Possamai (ed.), *Handbook of Hyper-Real Religions*, 185–204. Leiden: Brill.

Deslippe, P. (2023), 'Past the Pejorative: Understanding the Word "Cult" Through Its Use in American Newspapers during the Nineties', *Implicit Religion*, 24 (2): 195–217.

Eco, U. (1985), '"Casablanca": Cult Movies and Intertextual Collage', *SubStance*, 14 (2): 3. https://doi.org/10.2307/3685047

Gray, J., C. Sandvoss and C. L. Harrington (2007), 'Introduction: Why Study Fans?', in J. Gray, C. Sandvoss and C. L. Harrington (eds), *Fandom: Identities and Communities in a Mediated World*, 1–16, New York: New York University Press.

Guern, P. Le (2004), 'Toward a Constructivist Approach to Media Cult', in S. Gwenllian-Jones and R. E. Pearson (eds), R. Crangle (trans.), *Cult Television*, 3–25. Minneapolis: University of Minnesota Press.

Gwenllian-Jones, S. and R. E. Pearson (2004), 'Introduction', in S. Gwenllian-Jones and R. E. Pearson (eds), *Cult Television*, ix–xx. Minneapolis: University of Minnesota Press.

Jenkins, H. (1992), *Textual Poachers: Television Fans & Participatory Culture*. New York: Routledge.

Laycock, J. (2010), 'Myth Sells: Mattel's Commission of The Masters of the Universe Bible', *The Journal of Religion and Popular Culture*, 22 (2): 4. https://doi.org/10.3138/jrpc.22.2.004

Possamai, A., ed. (2012), *Handbook of Hyper-Real Religions*. Leiden and Boston: Brill.

Pumphrey, N. B. (2019), *Superman and the Bible: How the Idea of Superheroes Affects the Reading of Scripture*. Jefferson: McFarland & Company, Inc., Publishers.

Rachel (2022), Cosplay Interview. Personal interview.

Reeves, J. L., M. C. Rodgers and M. Epstein (1996), 'Rewriting Popularity: The Cult Files', in D. Lavery, A. Hague and M. Cartwright (eds), *Deny All Knowledge: Reading the X- Files*, 22–35. London: Faber.

Sam (2022), Cosplay Interview. Personal interview.

Tylor, E. B. (2010), *Primitive Culture: Researches into the Development of Mythology, Philosophy, Religion, Art, and Custom*. Cambridge Library Collection Anthropology. Cambridge: Cambridge University Press.

u/Fortunatious. (2018), 'I Finally Sat down and Played Journey. I've Always Been an Atheist, but I Swear I Had a Spiritual Experience from Playing This Game, and i Wept after the End. Anyone Else Have an Experience like This with Journey or Any Other Game?', *Reddit*. Available at https://www.reddit.com/r/gaming/comments/93433o/i_finally_sat_down_and_played_journey_ive_always/ (accessed 15 April 2023).

Vogt, B. (2011), *The Church and New Media: Blogging Converts, Online Activists, and Bishops Who Tweet*. Huntington: Our Sunday Visitor.

Wysocki, J. (2018), 'Critique with Limits – The Construction of American Religion in BioShock: Infinite', *Religions*, 9 (5): 150. https://doi.org/10.3390/rel9050150

11

Attempting to educate journalists about the role of cult essentialism in the Branch Davidians–federal agents conflict

Catherine Wessinger

Since the twentieth century, the word 'cult' has been the term that people have applied (in the English-speaking world) to religions they do not like and fear (Wessinger 2012, 2017; Richardson 1993). Use of the word 'cult' implies that certain religious groups are qualitatively different from other religions of the world, when that is not the case, except perhaps in size. The diverse religious groups and movements that have been labelled 'cults' have little in common with each other except that some members of the public do not like them. A major problem caused by the contemporary meaning assigned to the term 'cult', which originally meant 'worship', is that it promotes 'cult essentialism', defined by sociologist John R. Hall as the point of view that 'cultists' and the 'cult leader' are totally to blame when there has been a violent situation involving members (Hall with Schuyler and Trinh 2000: 16). 'Essentialism' when applied to a religion is the assumption that the religion has some sort of unchanging essence, which is never the case (Prothero 2020: 9–11, 13–14). Religions always change over time and members of small, unconventional religions involved in conflicts are usually caught up in *interactive situations* in which members choose their actions in response to actions of their opponents (Wessinger 2000; Richardson 2010; Hall with Schuyler and Trinh 2000; Moore 2009).

The cult essentialist outlook is an inaccurate stereotype in which people, including law enforcement agents and journalists, assume that all groups that have been labelled 'cults' are the same. It is assumed that 'cults' all have an 'omnipotent leader', the followers are 'passive, brainwashed followers' (Richardson 2021), and 'cults' result in murder and mass suicide (Gibbs 1993; Kantrowitz 1993a, b). These assumptions prevent law enforcement agents and journalists from undertaking careful investigations into a case involving religious believers in which deaths, or other illegal actions, have occurred. As shown by new religions scholar Massimo Introvigne in his reports in *Bitter Winter: A Magazine on Religious Liberty and Human Rights*, when a government labels a religious group with a word that has the equivalent negative connotation as the English term 'cult', and news organizations cooperate in perpetuating that labelling of a group, it becomes justification for government agents persecuting and even killing members (Introvigne 2018, 2022).

The cult essentialist stereotype associated with the word 'cult', or other words such as *secte* in Europe, or *xie jiao* in the People's Republic of China, conveys a simplistic explanation for consumers of news media and documentaries. When a religious group is labelled a 'cult' in the news media and by law enforcement agents, it has the effect of dehumanizing the members, including children, so law enforcement agents feel justified in taking aggressive actions against the group, even while members of the public are looking on through the lenses of news media. However, again, violent episodes involving members of unconventional religions are typically interactive. The quality of the interactions between believers and agents and agencies in mainstream society determines whether there will be a peaceful or violent outcome (Wessinger 2000; Richardson 2010).

During and after the 1993 Branch Davidians–federal agents conflict at Mount Carmel Center outside Waco, Texas, law enforcement agents and government officials promoted the cult essentialist perspective of the Branch Davidians to journalists, so they would publish 'cult' news stories that members of the public would understand as justifying the unnecessary violent actions of federal agents against the community (Wessinger 2006: 159–62). Most journalists covering the events at Mount Carmel Center in 1993 attended press briefings by FBI agents and reported what FBI officials said about the Branch Davidians, instead of doing their own investigative reporting. The initial exception among journalists was Dick J. Reavis, who immediately began conducting his own investigation and published the first journalistic book on the case, *The Ashes of Waco* (1995). Lee Hancock, a reporter with the *Dallas Morning News*, initially wrote stories using the word 'cult' and reflecting the cult essentialist perspective. As the years went by and she continued covering the case through the 1994 criminal trial of some of the Branch Davidian survivors and the 2000 wrongful death civil trial brought by survivors and relatives of deceased Branch Davidians against the government, in response to educational efforts by scholars giving interviews, Hancock abandoned describing the Branch Davidians with the pejorative term 'cult' in favour of doing in-depth investigative reporting that revealed significant facts (Wessinger 2006: 159–62).

In the twenty-first century, the word 'cult' and its associated cult essentialism are rampant in documentaries that have aired about the Branch Davidians and other unconventional religious groups. Even if the word 'cult' is not used in the documentary, the cult essentialist perspective remains prominent in the depictions of the Branch Davidians and their prophet and Endtime Christ, David Koresh (1959–1993). In 2017 producers with mainstream news programmes contacted me for background information for documentaries that would air about the time of the twenty-fifth anniversary of the fire at Mount Carmel Center, which was the culmination of the FBI tank (Combat Engineering Vehicle) and tear gas assault of the residence on 19 April 1993. Twenty-two children (including two trauma-born infants), seven teenagers and forty-seven adults died in the fire (Wessinger 2016). I provided each producer or director who contacted me with pdfs of internal FBI documents, which are found in the Lee Hancock Collection, now at the Southwestern Writers Collection in the archive of Texas State University. I explained to each director or producer the significance of these documents. These FBI documents show that FBI officials knew about the Branch Davidians' apocalyptic theology of martyrdom. Yet FBI officials decided to order the implementation of the tank and gas assault anyway.

The information contained in the FBI documents provided to producers and directors was not covered in the television documentaries that aired in late 2017 and in 2018. The majority of these documentaries promoted the cult essentialist perspective about the Branch Davidians–federal agents conflict, which sociologist Stuart A. Wright has called 'drive-by journalism' (2019: 118). Even the comparably good documentaries did not attempt to treat the internal FBI documents.

We are left to speculate on why the information that FBI officials were briefed on the Branch Davidians' apocalyptic theology of martyrdom, as shown by the FBI's documents, was not reported in the 2017–18 documentaries. It could be that American mainstream news corporations did not want to offend officials in the US government, including the FBI, who are major sources of information for news stories. It also could be that what is revealed in memos and reports is not visually interesting enough to be included in a documentary. This was confirmed for me by journalist, author and producer Jeff Guinn, who told me that the 'mantra' of documentary makers is 'Keeping eyes on the screen' (2023). Or, perhaps, the cult essentialist perspective is such an attractive draw to viewers, there is reluctance to complicate the narrative by introducing documents that indicate that FBI officials planned and implemented a dangerous tank and CS gas assault against a community, containing small children and pregnant women, whose adults believed they would be martyred in an assault by government agents as the prelude to being resurrected and then carrying out judgement on humanity before the Endtime Christ's kingdom is established in the Holy Land.

The Branch Davidians–federal agents conflict

The Branch Davidians–federal agents conflict began on the morning of Sunday, 28 February 1993, with an attempted 'dynamic entry' of the Mount Carmel Center residence by seventy-six agents with the Bureau of Alcohol, Tobacco, and Firearms (ATF). The resulting shootout caused the deaths of six Branch Davidians and four ATF agents (Wessinger 2000: 57). ATF agents alleged that the Branch Davidians were converting legally purchased semiautomatic AR-15 rifles to automatic M-16 rifles, without applying for the required federal licence and paying the fee (Wessinger 2016). ATF agents who visited Koresh's licensed gun dealer had turned down Koresh's invitation, offered by telephone, for ATF agents to come to Mount Carmel openly to inspect his weapons (Henry McMahon testimony in House of Representatives 1995: 1:162–3). The affidavit written to obtain a judge's approval for the search warrant and arrest warrant for Koresh resorted to 'cult' rhetoric and allegations that Koresh was having sex with underage girls, although child sex abuse charges do not come under the ATF's jurisdiction. Koresh was having sex with underage girls and other women who were considered to be his wives by community members. The allegations of child abuse had been investigated in 1992 by a Texas Child Protective Services social worker, and the case had been closed for lack of evidence (Tabor and Gallagher 1995: 100–3).

FBI agents arrived on 1 March 1993, and presided over most of the 51-day siege. FBI agents on site included the commander and operators in the FBI's Hostage Rescue Team (HRT, the tactical team), a series of three FBI negotiation coordinators who supervised negotiations carried out primarily by police officers from Austin, Texas (Shirley 2021) and a number of FBI special agents in charge from other states who arrived to assist Jeffrey Jamar, the special agent in charge in Texas who was serving as the on-scene commander (Noesner 2010: 148–76). FBI agents on the ground in Waco were supervised by FBI officials in the Strategic Information and Operations Center (SIOC) command centre in the Hoover Building in Washington, DC. Decisions of FBI agents were supposedly supervised by Janet Reno, who was sworn in as attorney general on 12 March 1993. Reno reported to President Bill Clinton, who had begun his first term of office on 20 January 1993 (Wessinger 2017).

Due to negotiations, a total of twenty-one children were sent out of the residence and a total of fourteen adults were taken into custody (Wessinger 2016). However, every time adults came out, HRT operators applied punishments against the remaining Branch Davidians (Tabor n.d.; Wessinger 2000; Wright 2003; Noesner 2010: 148–76). The punishments ranged from turning the building's electricity off, to shining bright spotlights during the nights, blasting high-decibel sounds towards the Branch Davidians throughout the days and nights, and Combat Engineering Vehicles (CEVs) crushing and removing vehicles belonging to Branch Davidians. After the high-decibel sounds started on 24 March, adults decided to stop coming out and they did not send additional children out. Gary Noesner, the first FBI negotiation coordinator, complained to Jamar about the high-decibel sounds and other punishments that were undermining negotiations. Noesner was replaced on 25 March (Noesner 2010: 127).

In April, Koresh and his right-hand man Steve Schneider told negotiators that they would come out after Passover week (5–13 April) concluded. They were waiting to see if they would be martyred during Passover as Koresh had predicted. On 14 April, Koresh sent out a letter stating that God had given him permission to write down his interpretation of the Seven Seals of the book of Revelation. Koresh's letter stated that after his Seven Seals manuscript was given to historians and Bible scholars J. Phillip Arnold and James D. Tabor, he would come out to be taken into custody. Arnold and Tabor had communicated with Koresh via a radio discussion on 1 April. Significantly, also on 14 April, Koresh sent out his signed contract to retain his defence attorney. Schneider sent out his signed contract to retain his attorney the following day (Wessinger 2017: 221; Wessinger 2016). Unfortunately, the significance of Koresh's exit plan was downplayed on 15 April in a conference call with the deputy attorney general in Washington, in which FBI negotiator Byron Sage (1947–2022), from Austin, Texas, said that the negotiations were at 'an impasse' (Wessinger 2017: 225; U.S. Department of Justice 1993: 270–2; Testimony of Byron Sage, in House of Representatives, 3:345). It appears unlikely that Attorney General Reno was told about Koresh's exit plan, or that he had signed a contract to retain the services of a defence attorney (Wessinger 2017: 225–6).

On 12–17 April, FBI officials and some military officers were having meetings with Reno in Washington to persuade her to approve a plan to insert CS gas into the residence (Wessinger 2017: 223–7). She approved the plan on 17 April, after being shown a memo written by a behavioural psychologist saying that he thought the negotiations had been irrevocably damaged, and that Koresh was probably continuing to abuse the children, although there was no evidence that Koresh was doing so (Wessinger 2017: 226–7). Memos from FBI profilers who had warned that an assault would likely result in deaths of children and adults were either not shown to Reno or buried in a binder full of other documents (Wessinger 2017: 207–8, 220, 223, 226–7).

Towards the end of the siege, HRT operators ramped up aggressive actions by throwing flash-bang (percussion) grenades at Branch Davidians when they came outside, and hitting the building with a CEV (Wessinger 2017: 220–1). Nevertheless, Koresh told negotiators on 16 April at 2.35 am that he had completed composing his commentary on the First Seal. He and other Branch Davidians began asking for supplies to use with a battery-operated word processor so they could type up the manuscript. The word processor supplies were delivered at 7.40 pm on 18 April. Schneider told negotiators they would send out the chapter on the First Seal after it was typed (Wessinger 2017: 221–2).

On 19 April, at 6.00 am, HRT operators began firing ferret rounds into the building to release CS gas. Other HRT operators driving CEVs sprayed CS into the building using the vehicles' booms. The CEVs dismantled parts of the wooden building, which contained straw (for insulation) and kerosene (for lanterns). The adults inside the residence put on gas masks, but did not have gas masks for small children. Children from babies to age thirteen, along with their mothers, including two pregnant women who gave birth during the assault, took shelter in a concrete room, a former vault with an open doorway, located directly underneath the central tower of the building.

During the assault, a surveillance device picked up audio from 9.35 am to 9.52 am Central Standard Time, of Schneider in the foyer telling two men (Pablo Cohen and Graeme Craddock) to go outside and indicate to FBI agents that the telephone line to negotiators, lying on the ground, had been severed by a CEV running over it. Schneider said that they wanted to tell negotiators that Koresh's commentary (on the First Seal) had been typed up the night before. This audio from the surveillance device could be heard by officials in SIOC who made notes on it in a log. The severed telephone line was not replaced (Wessinger 2017: 232–3). At 10.00 am Central Standard Time (11.00 am Eastern Standard Time in Washington), Reno left SIOC, where she was watching the assault on closed circuit television, to travel to Baltimore to give a speech, thereby abandoning supervision of the CEV and gas assault (Wessinger 2017: 233–4).

At 11.31 am Central Standard Time, a CEV began driving through the front of the building three times to spray CS gas towards the open doorway of the former vault at 11.49 am (FBI 1993i). I contend that the gassing of the young children and their mothers was a major turning point in the assault. This CEV then moved to the front corner room on the second floor on the southeast side of the building where it inserted its boom into a window and sprayed CS. Flames were seen in the window at 12.07 pm Central Standard Time. A government aircraft flying overhead recorded fires erupting in at least three areas of the building on FLIR (Forward Looking InfraRed) tape (Wessinger 2017: 234–6). The fires quickly became a conflagration that consumed the building. A total of seventy-six people of all ages died in the fire. Nine people escaped the fire, some with severe burns (Wessinger 2016).

Afterwards, a number of journalists with the print news media realized that they had permitted FBI agents in press briefings to mislead them about the Branch Davidians (Rawls 1993). For about a decade, a number of American newspaper reporters were open to scholars' explanations that 'cult' is a pejorative word and should not be used in carefully researched articles. This openness to not using the word 'cult' faded in the print media over the years and younger reporters with no knowledge of the Branch Davidian case were hired (Wessinger 2006: 171). Religion scholars made less headway in educating documentary makers, and the cult stereotype continued to be promoted in television fictional shows and movies.

Reactions of religious studies scholars to the Mount Carmel Center deaths

American and international religious studies scholars and sociologists of religions were appalled at the actions taken by FBI agents against the Branch Davidian community on 19 April 1993. The scholars understood that this was the incorrect approach to interacting with an apocalyptic group whose members believed that they would be martyred and would subsequently be resurrected as part of the Endtime events. Religious studies scholars thought that FBI agents needed to be educated about the significance of religious beliefs in order to prevent loss of life in a future conflict between FBI agents and members of a religious community. Both religious studies scholars and sociologists of religion made a number of efforts to reach out to FBI agents.

I was asked to compile a list of 'Scholars of Religion: PhDs and PhD Candidates in History of Religions, Sociology, Communications, Political Science', who were available to serve as consultants to the FBI in relevant cases. This list was delivered in May 1997. Dr Barbara DeConcini, director of the more than 8,000-member American Academy of Religion (AAR), had been calling the FBI since 1993 to make them aware of the AAR as a source of scholars who could serve as consultants when needed. She arranged for a meeting on 5 June 1998, in Washington, DC, in the Hoover Building, with FBI agents with the Critical Incident Response Group. I was privileged to accompany Dr DeConcini and Dr Eugene V. Gallagher to that meeting. AAR staff subsequently set up private meetings between FBI agents and scholars at the annual meeting in November 1998. In June 1999, Massimo Introvigne's CESNUR (Center for Studies on New Religions) and the FBI Critical Incident Response Group cosponsored a seminar on 'Law Enforcement and Religious Violence' in Fredericksburg, Virginia, in which religion scholars, FBI agents and members of the New York Police Department attended. In November 1999, in conjunction with the AAR annual meeting in Boston, Dr Richard Landes, director of the Center for Millennial Studies at Boston University, arranged for a private session in which FBI agents and religion scholars discussed a recent FBI report titled 'Project Megiddo' on apocalyptic groups in the run-up to the year 2000, with religion scholars giving feedback. Arranged private meetings between FBI agents and selected religion scholars have continued at AAR annual meetings.

Scholars involved in these AAR meetings soon learned that since FBI agents retire at a comparatively young age, it appeared that there was no institutional memory of the mistakes made with the Branch Davidians and what may have been learned by agents.

Revelations in FBI documents in the Lee Hancock collection

On 26 September 2003, I conducted a telephone interview with Lee Hancock, investigative reporter with the *Dallas Morning News*. She had written informative news stories reporting on how FBI negotiators protested the aggressive tactics of the HRT against the Branch Davidians that undermined the negotiations (Hancock 1999b); how FBI behavioural scientist Pete Smerick had co-authored memos warning that sending in tanks would result in the deaths of children in the residence and would prompt Koresh and the adults to adopt a 'bunker mentality' and choose to die rather than surrender (Hancock 1999b); how when adults came out the remaining Branch Davidians were punished by FBI agents by cutting off electricity, crushing Branch Davidians' vehicles with CEVs and blasting high-decibel sounds (Hancock 1999b). Hancock wrote news stories on how, despite FBI congressional testimony to the contrary, an HRT operator had fired a 'pyrotechnic device' releasing CS gas on the morning of 19 April 1993 (Hancock 1999a); and how FBI officials were aware that a tactical assault on the Branch Davidians would likely result in deaths (Wessinger 2006: 159–61).

In my telephone interview with Hancock, she said that she saw herself as advocating for the 'other than the easy, pat explanation of what happened'. She aimed to investigate and describe in detail what happened in the conflict without depicting one side or the other as being solely responsible for the deaths. She said that sometimes in news stories 'people need to be informed that there are no good guys and bad guys, that there are no easy answers' (Wessinger 2006: 161). She acknowledged that 'the government screwed up, and . . . lied, and . . . misrepresented some things, absolutely, and they should be held to a higher standard' (Wessinger 2006: 162).

Hancock told me that she had been reporting on this case for ten years, she was no longer going to report on it, and she offered to send me all the materials she had collected. I gladly accepted the offer. When I opened the boxes, to my surprise, I saw that they contained reports from Texas Rangers, internal FBI memos on interviews with people who knew Branch Davidians, including Koresh, negotiation memos, reports, various logs, collected interviews with FBI agents, depositions, a large expanding folder labelled 'Reno Briefing File', a compiled 594-pages FBI Major Event Log with entries dating from 28 February 1993 to 4 May 1993 (with only two entries for 19 April 1993), in addition to a separate 19 April 1993 log, and pleadings and transcripts from the 2000 trial of the wrongful death lawsuits brought by Branch Davidian survivors and the relatives of deceased Branch Davidians, among many other materials. I was particularly interested to find a document titled 'Suicide Addendum 4/18/19', which appeared to be a final FBI assessment of the likelihood of group suicide by the Branch Davidians in response to an assault by FBI agents, dated the day before the CEV and gas assault. The boxes also contained a series of memos written by profilers Pete Smerick and Mark Young, which advised that the HRT should pull back and not take aggressive actions against the Branch Davidians, or otherwise, there would be deaths, including children. I took the materials to my university's archive, and they were stored in eight acid-free boxes in the Monroe Library at Loyola University New Orleans, and a general list of their contents was made. I made an initial report on the Hancock Collection in 2009 in a special issue of *Nova Religio* (Wessinger 2009b), in which scholars Kenneth

G. C. Newport, Stuart A. Wright and myself considered the Branch Davidians–FBI agents conflict to try to determine who bore the greatest responsibility for the deaths on 19 April 1993 (Newport 2009; Wessinger 2009a; Wright 2009).

In 2009, at the 19 April memorial in Waco, I met Joel Minor, then an archivist at the Wittliff Collections archive at Texas State University in San Marcos, Texas. I was impressed with his work on the Dick Reavis Collection, which had been donated to the Southwestern Writers Collection in the Wittliff Collections, so I recommended to Lee Hancock that her materials be moved to Texas State University, where they were added to the Southwestern Writers Collection (Southwestern Writers Collection n.d.). Before the Hancock materials left my university's archive, I went through the entire collection and had selected documents scanned into pdf files.

When I went through the entire Hancock Collection in 2009, I found three documents that can be associated with the 'Suicide Addendum 4/18/93' making a total of four typed documents that summarize the findings of FBI agents' interviews with people who knew the Branch Davidians, including interviews with past and current Branch Davidians. There are two documents reporting the findings of interviews about the significance of Passover to the Branch Davidians titled 'Passover Summary' dated 1 April 1993, and 'Passover Addendum' dated 18 April 1993. These two documents reveal that FBI agents were told that Koresh's interpretations of biblical prophecies about the group's martyrdom by government agents indicated that Koresh and the Branch Davidians thought this event would occur during Passover. However, if it did not happen during the dates for Passover, there was the possibility of a subsequent 'Second Passover' (FBI 1993b; Wessinger 2017: 228). A document titled 'Suicide References' dated 27 March 1993, and a follow-up document titled 'Suicide Addendum' dated 18 April 1993, indicate that agents assessed Koresh and the Branch Davidians for the possibility of group suicide. People who knew Koresh reported that they did not believe he was suicidal, but they thought he might orchestrate a 'suicide by cop' scenario to make his interpretations of biblical prophecies come true (FBI 1993c, d). The 'Suicide Addendum' included a one-paragraph summary of a report written by FBI negotiation coordinator Clint Van Zandt and Dr Joseph Krofcheck, 9 dated April 1993, which concluded that Koresh was 'fully capable of creating circumstances that could take the lives of all his followers and as many of the authorities as possible' (FBI 1993d: 2).

The copy of the FBI Major Event Log in the Hancock Collection is redacted. Some names and telephone numbers are blacked out, but nevertheless many names and telephone numbers are left visible. Additionally, the pages containing entries for all of 8 and 9 March and half of 10 March (page 181 to page 248) are missing in the Major Event Log in the Hancock Collection (FBI 1993e; Wessinger 2017: 216). However, the entire unredacted FBI Major Event Log is in the online 'FBI Vault' of archival materials for the Branch Davidian case (FBI 1993f). This scan of the Major Event Log includes the separate 19 April 1993 log. This complete Major Event Log indicates that from 8 March through 10 March 1993, numerous people contacted FBI agents offering their services as mediators, which FBI negotiators call 'third-party intermediaries'. People offering to serve as intermediaries include a Harvard psychiatrist who said he had experience with 'cult victims' (10 March, 15.45), relatives of Branch Davidians inside the residence and 'cult deprogrammer' Rick Ross (8 March, 13.50). The entry for 10 March 1993 (23.10) indicates that Steve Schneider asked for a mediator to facilitate negotiations. A man named James Vincent, who had studied Koresh's teachings with Branch Davidians Steve and Judy Schneider and Mike and Kathy Schroeder, called to say that if a theologian could discuss the Bible's prophecies with Koresh, Koresh would probably listen (8 March, 15.15). Vincent offered to shed light on the Branch Davidians' biblical mindset. The action taken for this entry on the log reads, 'No Lead', indicating that he was not contacted. The entry on 8 March 1993 (16.00) reports that J. Phillip Arnold, PhD, Reunion Institute, Houston stopped by 'to offer his assistance interpreting Revelations [*sic*] and the 7 seals. Not believed to be a quack – legit'. Action taken reads: 'None'. A 'Dr Haynes' called to recommend that the negotiators 'identify persons with theological expertise' to consult (9 March, 9.00). On 9 March 1993 (15.00), a neighbour of the Branch Davidians offered to serve as mediator.

A shocking revelation on the 19 April 1993 log in the Hancock Collection is the entry indicating that early that morning at 1.25 am, a medical doctor, a paediatric burn specialist at the Galveston Burn Center, called to offer his assistance (if needed). There is a handwritten question mark next to this entry, which I presume was put there by Lee Hancock (FBI 1993g).

Overall, the information contained in the internal FBI documents in the Lee Hancock Collection, in addition to content of recorded negotiations with Branch Davidians and conversations among the Branch Davidians picked up by surveillance devices, indicate that FBI officials were well informed that the Branch Davidian adults believed in Koresh's apocalyptic interpretations of Bible passages that members of the community would be martyred in an assault, and would probably die in a fire (Wessinger 2009a, 2017).

Therefore, questions remain about the attitude of FBI agents towards the Branch Davidians. Knowing the Branch Davidians' expectations that they would die in a government assault and resulting fire, the building was made of wood and contained straw and kerosene, the residence contained gun powder and grenades, and there was a propane tank located outside directly behind the central tower, why did FBI officials plan and execute the CEV and CS gas assault on 19 April 1993? This seems to me to be an important question that producers and directors would want to address in documentaries. Although I have given pdfs of these internal FBI documents to numerous producers and directors who have consulted with me since 2009, and I have discussed the materials' significance with them, at the time of this writing in November 2022, no documentary has reported on these FBI documents and attempted to answer this question.

Andy Segal, director, *Waco*: Faith, Fear and Fire (2011)

The first producer to whom I gave documents in the Hancock Collection was Andy Segal, Senior Producer at CNN, with whom I had multiple communications in 2010 by telephone and email. I sent him the Major Event Log, the 19 April 1993 log, memos written by profilers Pete Smerick and Mark Young, the two 'Suicide' documents, and the two 'Passover' documents. The documentary, *Waco: Faith, Fear and Fire*, aired on Sunday, 17 April 2011.

It is a good documentary that carefully follows the chronology of the events from the ATF assault on 28 February 1993, to the FBI CEV and gas assault on 19 April 1993. I know that Segal used the Major Event Log, because when he gave me a tour of the CNN studios in Atlanta in November 2010, I saw the pages printed out and stacked on a chair in his office. In *Waco: Faith, Fear and Fire*, Lee Hancock is interviewed on the perspectives of law enforcement agents. Dick Reavis describes the perspectives of the Branch Davidians and also the American citizens who were alarmed by what federal agents did to the Branch Davidians. Former Branch Davidian Kathy Jones states that she left Mount Carmel before the events in 1993 because she did not want to become one of Koresh's wives. Branch Davidian survivors Clive Doyle (1941–2022) and Sheila Martin are sensitively interviewed by reporter Drew Griffin. Koresh and people inside the residence, including the children, are humanized by showing clips from videos recorded during the siege (see Branch Davidians 1993).

The documentary contains excerpts from a lengthy interview with retired FBI negotiator Gary Noesner. Noesner states that the efforts of the negotiators were undermined by the actions of the HRT operators. He believes that greater patience on the part of FBI agents would have resulted in more people coming out and sending more children out (Segal 2011, Part 2: 10:48).

Waco: Faith, Fear and Fire mentions only one of the internal FBI documents in the Hancock Collection. The 5 March 1993 memo written by profilers Pete Smerick and Mark C. Young is quoted as stating that Koresh has 'characteristics associated with psychopaths', and that his followers have 'low self-esteem, are unable to act or think for themselves, and are easily manipulated' (Segal 2011: Part 1, 18:46; Smerick-Young 1993). The portion of the Smerick-Young memo cited in the documentary reinforces the cult essentialist view that a 'cult leader' has total control over followers who are 'passive, brainwashed followers' (Richardson 2021). The documentary does not mention that this same 5 March 1993 memo advises that the HRT should deescalate tactical actions to demonstrate to the Branch Davidians that Koresh's predictions of martyrdom were incorrect. The two FBI 'Passover' documents and the two 'Suicide' documents are not explicitly discussed in the documentary, but scenes of the dead at Jonestown in 1978 are shown early in the documentary, and it is stated that FBI agents were evaluating the Branch Davidians for the possibility for committing mass suicide/murder.

2017–18 documentaries

In 2016 and 2017, I was consulted by producers and directors for a number of documentaries that were being made to air close to the time of the twenty-fifth anniversary of the fire. I provided the key materials contained in the Lee Hancock Collection to all of them. None of the resulting documentaries mentioned these internal FBI documents.

Waco mini-series

As early as 2015 I had a long telephone discussion on 12 June 2015, with John Erick Dowdle and Drew Dowdle, about a multi-episode dramatization that they were writing and would direct. When they called me, the first thing one of them said was that they aimed to 'humanize the people'. The six-part mini-series *Waco* aired on the Paramount Channel beginning on 24 January 2018, and in 2020 it was made available on Netflix, where it attracted many viewers. It is a good dramatization – and most dramatizations are very bad. The ATF raid scenes appear to be realistic. Actor Taylor Kitsch did an excellent job playing David Koresh, humanizing him while not excusing his sexual relations with underage girls. The character of FBI negotiation coordinator Gary Noesner, played by Michael Shannon, articulates the concerns that the real Noesner continues to have about how the negotiations were undermined by the actions of the HRT operators. The scenes of the 19 April 1993 gas and CEV assault are moving, but too fictionalized. The former vault with the open doorway is depicted as having an actual vault door, and for dramatic effect, a scene depicts the mothers and children being locked inside. This fictionalized final episode of the series depicts Rachel Jones Howell Koresh (1969–93), David Koresh's legal wife, struggling to get out of the vault and save her three children while begging the HRT commander to help them. In order to have this fictionalized scene of interaction between Rachel and the HRT commander, the CEV is shown knocking down the walls of the vault – but none of this happened. Of the internal FBI documents that I provided to the Dowdle brothers, for their purposes in a dramatization of the events, only the logs providing the sequence of the events in the FBI siege would have been relevant to their project.

CBS News, *48 Hours: The Secrets of Waco*

In 2016 I had telephone interviews with a development producer for CBS *48 Hours*. When she came to see me at my university, I gave her a flash drive containing the selected internal FBI documents from the Hancock Collection, and I explained to her their significance. The *48 Hours* episode titled *The Secrets of Waco* aired on 29 December 2017. Out of the 2017–18 documentaries, the CBS *48 Hours* documentary is one of the weakest. It contains factual errors, misleading statements and an overt cult essentialist perspective. Interviews with neighbours and former Branch Davidians report information that was indeed concerning about the group: target practice in the field behind the Mount Carmel residence; Koresh having sex with underage girls and taking other women as his wives; mistreatment of former Branch Davidian Grace Adams (1960–2021) by keeping her confined to a cabin at Mount Carmel after she had a mental breakdown (see Adams and Alpha 2018); and the delivery of grenade casings. Much is made of the accumulation of weapons in United Parcel Service deliveries, but they were legal purchases. It is alleged that after the fire forty-eight fully automatic weapons were discovered in the ashes (37.46).

At the beginning of *The Secrets of Waco*, Lee Hancock narrates, 'Waco was a tale of a religious fringe group that decided to fight back against the federal government and murdered federal law enforcement and, at the end of the siege, burned themselves up rather than come out' (27–42). This statement sets the tone for the rest of the documentary. Sensationalized subtitles in all caps are inserted into the beginning of the documentary when David Koresh is being discussed: A SELF-PROCLAIMED PROPHET; ACCUSED OF UNHOLY ACTS; PREACHING ARMAGEDDON. The Branch Davidians are called a 'cult' twice in the documentary (5.08, 15.02), and the spectre of 'brainwashing' is elicited when it is stated that 'Koresh had dozens of followers sitting spellbound for hours listening to his end-of-the-world sermons of doom' (10.00). Retired ATF agent Bill Buford, who planned the attempted 'dynamic entry', and who was badly wounded when he attempted to enter the residence through a second-floor window during the 28 February 1993 raid, states that after the element of surprise was lost, '[t]he raid should not have gone forward, absolutely not' (29.03).

Retired FBI negotiator Byron Sage is interviewed in *The Secrets of Waco*. He attempts to put all of the blame for the deaths on the Branch Davidians. When asked about the FBI's use of tanks and CS gas in a building with children inside, he replies, 'We believed that those parents . . . would grab those kids and get them out' (35.02). Of the nine Branch Davidians who escaped the fire, Sage comments, 'Not one of them brought a child' (37.10). Sage blames Clive Doyle, who for twenty-eight years gave interviews to articulate a Branch Davidian survivor's perspective of the events, for setting the fire. *48 Hours* correspondent Peter Van Sant states that on 19 April 1993, 'Doyle took the time to rescue a dog leaving his eighteen-year-old daughter [Shari Doyle] behind' (38:00). Doyle responds, 'I didn't know exactly where she was'. This is an accurate statement, because Doyle was on the first floor in the building's chapel, but Shari was on the second floor. Van Sant tells Doyle that, after the fire started, he should have run through the 'compound' looking for his daughter, but Doyle's consistent account has been that the heat of the fire overhead pushed him down to the floor and then he stumbled out of a hole made by a CEV in an outside wall, right before the flames engulfed the people behind him (Doyle with Wessinger and Wittmer 2012: 150–4). Doyle responds to Van Sant, 'I kick myself that I didn't rescue somebody, or helped somebody, my daughter or somebody else, but you're so traumatized, you're in pain, that you don't think straight' (38.18).

The documentary asserts that 'secretly recorded FBI audiotapes prove that the Branch Davidians ignited the fatal fire' (38.44). These are tapes of voices discussing pouring fuel, but they have not been released to the public for study. I have not heard such discussions on surveillance device audiotapes recorded on 19 April 1993 found in the Mark Swett Collection in the Texas Collection Archive at Baylor University. Branch Davidian survivor Graeme Craddock testified that someone in the chapel was pouring fuel, but he has never revealed the identity of that person (Craddock 1999). In the documentary, Byron Sage accuses Clive Doyle of spreading fuel because his uncovered hands were burned when he plunged out through the hole in the wall as the building was being consumed by fire. Sage asserts that doctors said that Doyle's hands 'were permeated with diesel fuel' (39.02). However, the text statements scrolled after the end of the documentary state that Clive Doyle was acquitted of all charges in the 1994 criminal trial and no surviving Branch Davidian was accused of setting the fire (42.39). This text further states that all of the eleven Branch Davidians who were defendants in the 1994 criminal trial were acquitted of charges of conspiracy to murder federal agents, and nine of them were convicted on lesser charges (42.34).

In *The Secrets of Waco*, Van Sant and Sage are permitted to make unproven allegations against Clive Doyle, but the producers and CBS News protect themselves from being sued for libel by stating the facts of the outcome of the criminal trial in the scrolled text at the end. When Van Sant asks Doyle, 'Is the reason you could not get your daughter because you were spreading fuel?' Doyle replies, 'That's what the FBI would like is to blame me' (39.16). In this documentary, Lee Hancock takes a stand on which party bears the majority of the blame for the deaths: 'Absolutely, David Koresh' (39.36). No scholars are interviewed in this documentary and there is no discussion of the FBI materials from the Lee Hancock Collection.

Reelz Cable Network, *Murder Made Me Famous*

I was contacted by a writer/director with AMS Pictures who was making a documentary to be aired on Reelz Cable Network. This is the instance where I feel that the nature of the documentary was most misrepresented to me. The writer/director told me that Reelz Cable Network produces documentaries to educate young people, so I agreed to the interview. In fact, Reelz airs sensationalized stories presented as documentaries. Reelz is available to satellite television subscribers, so I have never watched it. The writer/director came to my university on 18 May 2017, and interviewed me at length in a studio on campus. She asked intelligent questions and I gave her the internal FBI documents in my possession and discussed them. I made recommendations for other people to interview. After this 'documentary' aired on 25 November 2017, I learned that she had been making a segment in a Reelz series named *Murder Made Me Famous*. Needless to say, if I had known the name of the series, I would not have cooperated. The trailer for the 'documentary' indicates that this episode was very sensationalized, capitalizing on the 'cult' stereotype. The Branch Davidians are described as 'the polygamous cult led by David Koresh' and the residence is termed a 'compound'. The statements of 'facts' in the trailer are completely erroneous. It conflates the 28 February 1993 raid by ATF agents and the FBI CEV and gas assault on 19 April 1993: 'Did the ATF fire the first shot and ignite the whole compound?' (Smith 2017b). The dramatized scenes are cheesy. I am not shown in the trailer, and I hope my interview was left out of this purported 'documentary'.

ABC, *Truth and Lies: Waco*

I met an ABC News *20/20* producer at the 19 April 2017 memorial in the Mount Carmel chapel constructed in 2000. She was there with a camera team filming. Later she called me for a consultation and I sent her the usual internal FBI documents. *Truth and Lies: Waco* (Pearson 2018: 1.21.35 mins.) aired on ABC on 11 October 2018. The documentary is of interest to researchers for interviews with a variety of people who participated in the events at Mount Carmel Center in 1993. The documentary is not marred by badly done reenactments, although I believe that recordings of David Koresh's voice were distorted to make him sound deranged and dangerous, or at least, ominous. The documentary's cinematography includes panoramic and aerial views of the lush beauty of the east Texas countryside in the spring, and evocative blurred shots of a young man walking across a field with a Bible in his hand and stopping to read it.

This documentary does not directly call the Branch Davidians a 'cult', but television news reports aired at the beginning and throughout the documentary repeatedly call them a 'religious cult' and a 'cult group'. Besides principals who were interviewed, two reporters are shown making statements about the case and the people involved throughout the documentary: Mary Garofalo, identified as a journalist for *A Current Affair* [U.S.], and Terry Moran, an ABC correspondent. At the beginning of the documentary, Garofalo states, 'David Koresh was a monster. He was a highly unstable, self-proclaimed messiah who used the Bible, he used scriptures, as a weapon' (1.51). At 2.17 minutes, a male voice, probably that of David Bunds, the brother of Koresh's former wife Robyn Bunds, is heard saying: 'He was an embodiment of evil. He was the complete absolute dictator of every facet of everyone's life'. (All the members of the Bunds family – the parents, David Bunds and his wife, and Robyn Bunds with her son by Koresh – left the group on their own initiative.)

The documentary shows clips of an earlier interview with Bonnie Haldeman, David Koresh's mother, who was stabbed to death by her mentally ill sister in 2009 (Nailling 2018). Bonnie Haldeman gave birth to her son Vernon Howell (David Koresh) when she was fourteen (Haldeman 2007). After she is shown in the documentary stating that she believes that 'God was working on David' in his childhood to prepare him for 'the work he had for him later on' (4.08), Garofalo then purports to know the mind of Koresh's mother, alleging that Haldeman was proud that her son 'made something of himself... even if it was infamous' (4.29). Since I interviewed Bonnie Haldeman at length and edited her autobiography, I would characterize her motivation differently. She loved her son and his children. She wished that David had made different choices, but she knew she had no control over her adult son's actions. She had a realistic view of her son. She did not see him as a Christ (personal conversation). When requested to do so, Bonnie Haldeman always spoke to reporters to humanize her son and grandchildren.

The people interviewed in *Truth and Lies: Waco* include three of David Koresh's former wives, Dana Okimoto, Robyn Bunds and, lastly, Kiri Jewell. It is difficult to watch the former wives discuss Koresh's sexual relations with underage girls. Some of the women were of legal age of consent in Texas when he first had sex with them. Robyn Bunds states that she became one of Koresh's wives when she was seventeen, and that is the legal age of consent in Texas. Other young wives were fourteen, which in 1993 was the age a girl could marry with parental permission. However, Michele Jones, the sister of Koresh's legal wife, Rachel Jones Howell Koresh, was twelve when he had sex with her (Thibodeau with Whiteson 1999: 104–5), and Kiri Jewell was ten when her mother left her in a motel room with Koresh (18.19; Kiri Jewell testimony in House of Representatives 1995: 1:147–57). In *Truth and Lies: Waco*, Kiri Jewell expresses the most insight into Koresh:

> He used his doctrine to fill a hole in himself. He talked about what he feared from society, his looks, he couldn't get women. To try to fill those gaps in his life, he created this new prophecy that would do that. (14.27)

Robyn Bunds explains the reason Koresh took all the single and also married women as his wives. 'It was for a purpose. He said he was God and that he carried God's seed, and you could have God's child, and then in the end you kind of fall in love with him, because he was very lovable at times' (17.26).

In his media review published in 2019, sociologist Stuart A. Wright criticizes *Truth and Lies: Waco* for not asking the hard questions about the motivations for the actions of the ATF and FBI agents, and instead focusing on the 'scandalous practices of the group' (Wright 2019: 110–11). This is an accurate assessment. The documentary does not mention that in 1994 a social worker with Texas Child Protective Services investigated the group for possible child abuse, and had to close the case for lack of evidence (Joyce Sparks testimony in House of Representatives 1995: 1:575–9).

Other former Branch Davidians interviewed in *Truth and Lies: Waco* were David Bunds, and Joann Vaega, who was six in 1993 and whose parents died in the fire. Branch Davidian survivors interviewed are Kathryn Schroeder, Clive Doyle, Sheila Martin and David Thibodeau. Kathryn Schroeder, who testified for the prosecution in the 1994 criminal trial of eleven Branch Davidian survivors, has ongoingly demonstrated her commitment to telling the truth while maintaining her belief in David Koresh (1.21.01). She gave me a lengthy interview in 2019, which includes her description of the group's plan on 2 March 1993, for a group suicide after drawing gunfire from FBI agents, which was not carried out when Koresh said God had told him to wait (Schroeder 2019). In *Truth and Lies: Waco*, Schroeder states, 'Nobody planned on coming out alive. We were all going to die. There was not going to be a "giving up" situation' (44.54). Doyle, Martin and Thibodeau describe what they saw and heard during the ATF raid. Doyle and Thibodeau describe their experiences during the FBI CEV and gas assault and the fire. Clive Doyle gives his account of his experiences in the fire and how he escaped, which is also in his autobiography (Doyle with Wessinger and Wittmer 2012: 150–4). It is good to have a video recording of his account of barely escaping the fire. Sheila Martin expresses her Branch Davidian spirituality that gives her the strength to carry on after the deaths of her husband and her four older children in the fire, and the subsequent death of her fifth child. About the FBI HRT operators outside their door during the siege, Thibodeau states, 'We'd become ever more distrustful [of the FBI agents], obviously, of their actions. What they say and what they do are two different things' (1.02:07). 'It seemed to me like everything that they did was a dare. It's like, "Okay, come on, we want you to shoot"' (1.02:20).

Retired FBI agents interviewed in *Truth and Lies: Waco* are Bob Ricks, former special agent in charge in Oklahoma City who conducted many of the press briefings in Waco in 1993; Gregg McCrary, a former profiler; Jeff Allovio, former HRT sniper; Byron Sage; Gary Noesner; and Danny Coulson. While Sage blames Koresh for the deaths at Mount Carmel, Noesner indicates that in 1993 he understood that it was an interactive situation, and that the actions of the HRT operators were undermining the negotiations. He makes a point that is made in the mini-series *Waco* by the Noesner character: 'The paradox of power is the harder you push the more likely you are to get resistance' (59.44).

In *Truth and Lies: Waco*, Coulson is identified simply as 'FBI Hostage Rescue Team', which is misleading. He was the founder of the Hostage Rescue Team. He commanded the HRT during a siege of an extreme right-wing Christian community called the Covenant, the Sword, and the Arm of the Lord (CSA) in 1985. On that occasion, Coulson permitted the chief negotiator, Clint Van Zandt, who was also sent to be negotiation coordinator at Waco (Noesner 2010: 127–8), to implement innovative negotiation tactics, which succeeded in the peaceful resolution of the siege (Coulson 1999: 209–31). In 1993, Coulson was deputy assistant director of the FBI. The Major Event Log indicates that he spent time during the WACMUR case in the SIOC in the Hoover Building in Washington, DC, where officials were supervising the FBI teams and their commanders in Waco. Surprisingly, during the WACMUR siege, on 20 March, Coulson gave permission to the on-scene commander (Jamar) to take aggressive actions against the Branch Davidians, with the two men agreeing 'that we seem to get more productive results when we put pressure on the compound'. The log further states that they 'both agree that more pressure is needed' (FBI 1993e: 20 March 1993, 21:16; Wessinger 2017: 215). This statement put into the log was inaccurate. On 19 March, two Branch Davidian men had come out. The aggressive HRT actions were put on hold until after 21 March, when seven adults came out, and on 23 March, the last person came out. On 24 March, high-decibel sounds began to be blasted at the Branch Davidians in the residence, and bright spotlights were shown all night. From 25 to 28 March, CEVs destroyed vehicles and go-carts, with similar aggressive actions by the HRT continuing throughout the siege (Wessinger 2000: 74–5). In *Truth and Lies: Waco*, Coulson makes a statement about the events at Mount Carmel Center that reflects an awareness of the FBI behavioural scientists' conclusion that Koresh was capable of orchestrating a 'suicide by cop' scenario: 'It's all a part of the apocalyptic theory that gives them salvation. They are going to try to make you kill them' (45.14). Therefore, Coulson's statement towards the end of the documentary, 'I don't think people really understood how evil he was. He led his people into death. Sometimes, no matter your best efforts, you're not going to win, you're not going to beat them' (1.19:26), obfuscates the fact that he knew from his experience as HRT commander in the CSA case how good negotiations coupled with a low-key tactical presence can result in suspects surrendering to FBI agents without bloodshed.

After the chronological treatment of the events at Mount Carmel Center in 1993, *Truth and Lies: Waco* shifts to showing 1990s footage of the young Alex Jones, host of Infowars.com, at Mount Carmel and giving his views of what happened there, and current interviews with Alex Jones, and his former cameraman Mike Hanson, who has collected memorabilia about the Branch Davidians–federal agents conflict. Jones organized sympathizers to build a chapel on the site of the residence that burned at Mount Carmel, which was completed in 2000. The implication in the documentary appears to be that only conspiracy theorists are critical of what federal agents did to the Branch Davidians. Additionally, in 1993 the young Alex Jones had not yet morphed into the extreme conspiracy theorist, alleging that school shootings were not real and making money from selling supplements on his show, and who used his show to urge people to go to Washington, DC, on 6 January 2021 and participate in the insurrection (CNN 2022; Sullivan 2022).

Truth and Lies: Waco asserts that a new group of Branch Davidians lives at Mount Carmel Center. However, the current owner of the Mount Carmel property, who never followed David Koresh, has very few followers. The people shown in the documentary as filling the chapel for a service were there for the 19 April 2017 memorial led by Clive Doyle, which I attended.

As in previous documentaries and in news articles (Bryce 1999), retired FBI agent Byron Sage put all the blame for the deaths on Koresh and the adult Branch Davidians. At the end of *Truth and Lies: Waco*, other retired law enforcement agents also put all blame on Koresh. Although clips from the interview with Gary Noesner are shown throughout the documentary, at the end, no statement from Noesner is included about whom he regards as having responsibility for the deaths. On 18 April 2013, I participated in a symposium at Baylor University in Waco titled 'Reflecting on an American Tragedy: The Branch Davidians 20 Years After', organized by religions scholar J. Gordon Melton, in which Noesner gave a presentation. After my presentation, Sheila Martin and Clive Doyle were invited up front to answer questions from the audience. After the end of the symposium, I saw Noesner and Doyle deep in conversation. I walked up in time to hear Noesner apologize to Doyle for the deaths. He stated that if he had been permitted to remain as negotiation coordinator throughout the siege, he believes he could have gotten more people out, perhaps all of them (Wessinger 2013a).

Other than perhaps using the Major Event Log for the chronology of events in 1993, none of the other internal FBI documents that I provided to the producer and director were utilized in ABC's *Truth and Lies: Waco* (Pearson 2018).

HLN, *How It Really Happened with Hill Harper: Waco, Part 2: End of Days*

In 2017 I was contacted by producers with the series *How It Really Happened with Hill Harper* on HLN, which is owned by CNN Global. A producer came to New Orleans and interviewed me on 12 December 2017. I gave these producers a lot of information, including the internal FBI documents that I obtained from the Hancock Collection. Good questions were asked in the interview. Two one-hour segments aired in April 2018. The Part 1 segment on the ATF assault and shootout is titled 'Waco: God, Guns and the Government'. I will not focus on the Part 1 segment, because the congressional report (House of Representatives 1996) and the retired ATF agents have all agreed that the raid should have never been carried out after the element of surprise was lost. The Part 2 segment on the conflict between Branch Davidians and FBI agents is titled *End of Days* (42 mins.) (HLN 2018). Here I cite the DVD that the producers kindly donated to my university's library. I assign this documentary to my students.

End of Days contains thoughtful interviews with people involved in the case, including Branch Davidian survivors, retired FBI agents Gary Noesner and Byron Sage, journalist Dick Reavis, Koresh's attorney Dick DeGuerin, retired ATF agents, historian Dr J. Phillip Arnold, and Mark Potok of Southern Poverty Law Center. During the siege, Potok was present at the area in the countryside called Satellite City, three miles away from Mount Carmel Center, where all the news reporters and camera persons were located. Towards the end of the documentary, Potok does a good job connecting the Waco events to outrage on the radical right in America and how on 19 April 1995, Timothy McVeigh (1968–2001) carried out the Oklahoma City bombing of a federal office building, killing 168 people, including children, as revenge for what was done to the Branch Davidians (40.11ff.). Former national correspondent for CNN Dan Ronan was also present at Satellite City and is interviewed to provide filler explanations and narrative. Ronan's demeanour is serious, his statements are factual, and he does not sensationalize as did journalist Mary Garofalo in ABC *Truth and Lies: Waco*. Brief clips from my interview are included in the HLN documentary.

How It Really Happened with Hill Harper: Waco, Part 2, End of Days aired on 11 November 2018. It is a tightly constructed documentary that highlights the tragedy of the unnecessarily aggressive actions taken against the Branch Davidians by the FBI's HRT, thereby preventing a negotiated resolution. Gary Noesner narrates a good bit of the first part as he describes the disconnect between the negotiators and the HRT, particularly in the persons of Dick Rogers, commander of the HRT, and Jeffrey Jamar, the special agent in charge from San Antonio who served as on-scene commander. Noesner describes the anger of Jamar and Rogers even after seven people came out on 21 March due to negotiations, saying they were not enough (16.23). He describes tactics carried out by the HRT operators, such as following up a conciliatory gesture by the negotiators, such as sending in milk for the children, with the HRT turning off the building's electricity so there was no way for the Branch Davidians to keep perishable food cold. Noesner describes this as an 'agitation technique' that has been proven not to work (15.39). Dr J. Phillip Arnold is given the opportunity to describe how he drove to Waco to try to explain the Branch Davidians' theology to FBI agents, how he and Dr James D. Tabor directed a radio broadcast to Koresh and the Branch Davidians interpreting Bible passages as indicating that they could come out and be taken into custody. Koresh's attorney Dick DeGuerin explains how, after he went inside the residence several times, on 14 April he brought out Koresh's letter describing his plan to come out after he composed his commentary on the Seven Seals. DeGuerin reports that before he left Waco on 14 April, the FBI told him, 'We've got all the time in the world' (25.25).

Sage explains that the on-scene commander, Jeffrey Jamar, had agreed to give Koresh two weeks to write the manuscript, since Koresh had estimated he needed two days to compose his commentary on each of the Seven Seals. Negotiation audiotape is played in which Steve Schneider tells a negotiator on 16 April that Koresh had completed his commentary on the First Seal (27.06). Sage stresses that Koresh never sent out any evidence he had written the commentary on the First Seal (27.20), but Sage does not reveal that the Branch Davidians were asking for supplies to use with a battery-operated word processor (FBI 1993e: 16 April, 14.59, 15.01, 15.04). Noesner states that the FBI was looking bad politically, because the agency did not appear to have control of the situation involving the Branch Davidians, which was dragging out and costing a lot of money (27.44). There is discussion of the briefing that Attorney General Janet Reno was given when she was told that Koresh either at the current time or in the future would be abusing children, in order to get her to approve the CEV and CS gas plan (27.56ff.). DeGuerin states that he thinks that Reno 'had the wool pulled over her eyes' by FBI officials who knew how to 'push her buttons' (28.24). Clive Doyle recounts his experiences inside the building just before the fire started overhead and the heat pushed him to the floor, and it was the screaming of men behind him that impelled him to jump through a hole made in the wall by a CEV (32.28; 35.07ff.; 35.50). Again, it is good that Doyle's account, repeated many times, is preserved in a documentary, since he is now deceased.

Sage explains that he would move heaven and earth to get his family members and grandchildren out of a room into which CS gas is inserted (32.38). Doyle reports that CS on the skin burns like battery acid (32.53). Sage describes how, after the fire burned the entire building down,

> [t]he on-scene commander comes up to me, put his hand on my shoulder, and he said, 'Well, looks like negotiations are over. You've got the crime scene'. And he left. And I was dumbfounded. (36.17)

Sage also describes how he was traumatized when he looked inside the concrete room, the former vault, in which young children and their mothers died (37.40). Sage states, 'If David would have sent out proof of his progress as he had promised, I don't think we would have ever moved forward [with the CEV and gas assault]. We never received anything [from David]' (38.36).

A video clip is shown of the on-scene commander, Special Agent in Charge Jeffrey Jamar, speaking at a press conference and stating, 'We had absolute certain intelligence that the First Seal wasn't even started yet' (38.46). Of course, the Major Event Log shows that the word processing supplies were sent inside on the evening of 18 April at 7.40 pm (Wessinger 2017: 222). In *End of Days*, Dr J. Phillip Arnold and Dick Reavis report that Ruth Riddle escaped the fire with a computer disk in her pocket on which was saved the typed document containing Koresh's commentary on the First Seal (38.52; 38.59). No mention is made of Steve Schneider, Pablo Cohen and Graeme Craddock attempting to get a working telephone line to negotiators on the morning of 19 April, during the assault, so FBI agents could be told of the progress that had been made in typing up Koresh's commentary on the First Seal (Wessinger 2017: 232–3).

Instead of airing unfounded allegations about Clive Doyle starting the fire, in *End of Days*, Doyle is permitted to express his feelings about the death of his eighteen-year-old daughter, Shari Doyle, in the fire. 'I learned that my daughter hadn't made it. It tears you up inside thinking of the pain and horror and fear and everything else she probably went through' (36.53).

The conclusion of *End of Days* is more constructive than retired federal law enforcement agents asserting how evil Koresh was, as in *Truth and Lies: Waco*. Potok states that he sees the Waco case as 'the beginning of the end of these aggressive siege tactics [by federal agents]' (39.18). DeGuerin stresses that the tank and gas assault was a terrible decision because there were innocent children and women inside who had nothing to do with any crime (39.28). DeGuerin states that, yes, Koresh was partly to blame because he did not come out, but in defence of Koresh and the other Branch Davidians, the residence was their home, and they had no reason to give up their home (39.51). Noesner states that 'Waco reinforced for me what I've believed for a long time: We really need to listen to other people' (39.37). In his final remarks, the host of the show, Hill Harper, states that changes were made in the FBI after the Waco case, and that now the FBI's policy with barricaded subjects is 'infinite patience' (41.16ff.). This was demonstrated in the 81-day low-key siege of the Montana Freemen in 1996 (Wessinger 2000: 158–217), in which Noesner was the negotiation coordinator (Noesner 2010: 148–76), and in the approach to the occupation in January 2016 of the Malheur National Wildlife Refuge in Oregon by Ammon Bundy and his supporters. This siege was so low-key that the people who were occupying the wildlife refuge were permitted to come and go, until arrests were made (Perez and Yan 2016).

I think that the producers and perhaps the director of *End of Days* read my *Nova Religio* article on what surveillance device audiotapes reveal (Wessinger 2009a), and my chapter in the edited book *FBI and Religion*, in which I discuss the internal FBI documents that show that FBI decision-makers would have been briefed on the Branch Davidians' apocalyptic theology of martyrdom (Wessinger 2017). However, *End of Days* does not go so far as to consider the implications of internal FBI documents such as the 'Passover' reports and the 'Suicide' reports in the Hancock Collection.

18 April 2018 interpretation by Lee Hancock in the *Dallas Morning News*

On 18 April 2018, the *Dallas Morning News* published an article by Lee Hancock titled 'How the Branch Davidians Set the Fires for a Self-fulfilling Prophecy', not as an opinion-editorial, but under 'News – Crime' (Hancock 2018). The second sentence in the article excuses FBI agents for not paying attention to audio from surveillance devices in which Branch Davidians discussed the prospect of dying in a prophesied fire. 'FBI agents monitored 444 intercepted conversations over 47 days but couldn't always understand what was being said.' I had no problem hearing those discussions on audiotapes, obtained from the Texas Collection archive at Baylor University, in the Mark Swett Collection, with ordinary headphones (Wessinger 2009a). Hancock's essay recounts a conversation on 13 April 1993, about trusting God when a tank hits you or when you burn. This was Branch Davidian Scott Sonobe summarizing a talk that Koresh had given to the group (Wessinger 2009a: 37). Hancock's article states that on 14 April 1993, Koresh sent out a letter out via his attorney saying he would write his 'decoded message of the Seven Seals'. She writes that although FBI agents 'sent in ribbons and typewriter batteries, FBI officials say Koresh refused to show them proof he was writing anything'. This statement covers up the fact that the word processor supplies were not sent into the residence until late on the evening of 18 April. It also omits that during the FBI CEV and gas assault on 19 April, from 9.10 am to 9.52 am, Branch Davidian men (Pablo Cohen and Graeme Craddock) supervised by Steve Schneider signalled to FBI agents that the telephone line to negotiators had been severed when a CEV ran over it, and they wanted it fixed. On the recorded surveillance device audiotape, Schneider can be heard saying they wanted to inform FBI agents about the progress that had been made the night before in typing up the first chapter of the manuscript (Wessinger 2017: 38-9). I have put the audio of the two sides of the surveillance device audiotape containing these conversations on my YouTube channel (FBI 1993h: Parts 1 and 2).

Hancock reports a conversation between Koresh and Schneider, recorded by a surveillance device on 17 April 1993, in which they discuss everyone dying in an FBI assault. I plan to see if I can locate this audiotape in the Mark Swett Collection.

Hancock's article discusses Branch Davidians' conversations on 18 April about dying in a fire to fulfil prophecy, which I discuss in my *Nova Religio* article (Wessinger 2009a: 38-9). However, the Hancock article does not mention that this discussion among some Branch Davidians occurred immediately after a negotiation audiotape and a surveillance device audiotape both recorded an argument that Koresh had with a negotiator named Henry after Koresh realized that a raid was imminent. Koresh demanded, '*what do you men really want?*' and he warned that the FBI agents were putting him (and God) into a corner and putting the lives of his wives, children, his friends and himself in danger (Tabor 1995; audiotape transcribed in Wessinger 2000: 105-12; Wessinger 2009a: 37-8). The Branch Davidians' conversations about prophecy being fulfilled by their deaths in a fire were very clearly heard in surveillance device audio after this argument, which ended with the audiotape cut off, and should have alerted FBI decision-makers that the Branch Davidians expected to die in a fire.

The Hancock article repeats the FBI allegation that around 5.59 am on 19 April 1993, after Sage called into the building to tell the Branch Davidians that CEVs would gas the building, that 'Someone throws the Davidians' phone outside'. However, in 1995, Graeme Craddock testified to a congressional committee that the telephone was sitting in its usual location in the foyer when he went there to try to fix the line to negotiators. Craddock additionally testified that even if the telephone had been thrown outside, there were other telephones that he could have connected to the line, if it had been working (Wessinger 2017: 233; Graeme Craddock testimony in Hearings before the Committee on the Judiciary 1995: 171–2). Hancock's article also reports that an FBI log records that at 6.29 am that 'FBI commanders report that a CEV accidentally cut the Davidians' telephone line'.

The Hancock article discusses surveillance audiotapes that FBI agents have alleged as recording Branch Davidians discussing pouring fuel, beginning as early as 6.09 am. I did not find such audiotapes in the Swett Collection, so again, I put no credence in them until I can hear them myself. Hancock's article reports that the Branch Davidians wanted their telephone line to negotiators fixed (this is also in Wessinger 2009a). She reports that at 9.30 am the HRT commander (Rogers) and the on-site commander (Jamar) decided to send a tank into the building to gas the vault at the bottom of the central tower; this was not actually done until two hours later. She discusses other conversations about lighting fires picked up by surveillance devices about 11.25 am. I have not heard these tapes – the FBI should make them available to researchers. She reports that at 11.49 am, an HRT operator radioed about the vault being gassed, saying that is 'where many hostiles [are] located' (see FBI 1993i). Of course, the 'hostiles' were mothers, young children and two pregnant women who at some point miscarried their babies.

Hancock reports that at 12.06 pm, 'An HRT member reports seeing a Davidian moving his hands as if pouring something and flames appearing'. Doyle in his autobiography reports that in the criminal trial, upon cross-examination, the HRT operator's report of seeing a man making a sweeping motion with his hands occurred earlier in the morning inside the foyer, after a tank had crashed through the door, not at 12.06 pm (Doyle with Wessinger and Wittmer 2012: 169). Hancock reports that at 12.07 pm, an aircraft circling overhead filming with a far-infrared camera recorded on heat-sensitive FLIR videotape a fire starting on the second floor, quickly followed by fire in the kitchen and then the chapel. This is generally correct, although experts put the fires as being in the cafeteria, the southeast front corner bedroom on the second floor, the stage in the chapel on the first floor and later the catwalk going over the chapel on the second floor (Wetherington 2000; Wickström 2000). Hancock's article mentions that a woman who jumped out of the building from the second floor had a computer disk containing Koresh's 'partial manuscript'. Hancock, based on FBI agents' accounts, asserts that the woman (Ruth Riddle) attempted to run back into the burning building, but was prevented from doing so by HRT operators. Doyle reports that Ruth Riddle told him that her ankle was broken and she fell back towards the burning building when she attempted to walk. Photos taken by FBI agents appear to corroborate this account (Doyle with Wessinger and Wittmer 2012: 154; Wessinger 2013b).

Hancock's article makes an allegation that has been made before by Byron Sage, that there was fuel on the shoes of the people who escaped the fire. Hancock's article does not mention that during the siege a tank had knocked over and removed fuel storage containers located outside the building, and the survivors coming out from the east side of the building had to walk through that fuel-soaked area. Clearly referring to Sage's allegations about Clive Doyle, Hancock writes that 'one emerges with hands on fire and lighter fluid saturating his coat sleeves'. This allegation ignores Doyle's account that primarily his hands were not covered by clothing when he escaped the fire, and that during the siege that he had poured kerosene into lanterns. Additionally, the government pressed no charges against Doyle for lighting the fire, because there was no evidence that he had done so (Doyle with Wessinger and Wittmer 2012: 152, 166). Hancock's bio at the end of the article states: 'She is working on a history of the siege and its aftermath.'

This article by Hancock misrepresented facts so inaccurately and without contextualization, I was motivated to subscribe to the *Dallas Morning News* to leave two comments pointing out the article's errors, and to argue that the fire occurred within an interactive context in which FBI agents' actions were as important as the Branch Davidians' actions. I pointed out that the subheading for 18 April was missing in the article, and the 18 April subheading was added. In my first comment, I concluded: 'There are many errors and mischaracterizations of facts in this narrative that are aimed at obscuring the interactions the FBI agents had with the Branch Davidians that led to the deaths on April 19, 1993' (Wessinger 2018).

Reunion Institute documentary: *The Waco Branch Davidian Tragedy: What Have We Learned?* (2020)

In response to the inadequate documentaries in which commentary provided by scholars was edited and shortened, in 2019 four scholars of the Branch Davidians–federal agents conflict – J. Phillip Arnold, James D. Tabor, Catherine

Wessinger and Stuart A. Wright – met in a Houston studio and were filmed discussing what we have learned from our research since 1993. In planning for our filmed discussion, helpful input was provided by Dr Erin Prophet. This film titled *The Waco Branch Davidian Tragedy: What Have We Learned?* (2020: 2.52.59 mins.), produced by J. Phillip Arnold, and directed by Minji Lee, copyright Reunion Institute, was published on my YouTube channel on 9 April 2021 (Lee 2020a), where the video has received 2,100 views as of 6 January 2024. With Dr Arnold's permission, I cut out the shorter sections of the movie and made them into separate videos, which were also uploaded to my YouTube channel. These segments have also received numerous views. The same video with a different title, *The 1993 Waco Branch Davidian Tragedy Revisited: What Really Happened?* (Lee 2020b: 2.52.59 mins.), was uploaded to James D. Tabor's YouTube channel on 12 July 2021, where it had received 45,000 views as of 6 January 2024.

In the film, J. Phillip Arnold describes how in 1993 he drove to Waco from Houston to attempt to advise the FBI agents about David Koresh's apocalyptic teachings, and was rebuffed by Special Agent in Charge Bob Ricks, who told him that no one can understand what Koresh is saying. Arnold and James D. Tabor describe how, after they heard from a journalist that the FBI was planning to carry out an assault against the Mount Carmel residence, they contacted Ron Engelman of the Ron Engelman talk show on KBGS-Dallas radio, and obtained permission to discuss interpretations of the Bible's apocalyptic prophecies on 1 April 1993 on his show. Branch Davidians inside the residence heard the show, and later an audiotape of their radio discussion was sent inside so Koresh could listen to it. In their discussion, Arnold and Tabor argued that the 'waiting period' described in the Fifth Seal in Revelation could be a long period of time before the rest of the Branch Davidian community would be martyred, and that in the meantime, Koresh could come out and write down his message while in jail. Stuart A. Wright discusses how the FBI negotiation protocols were sabotaged by actions of the HRT. I discuss what I learned from reading selected internal FBI documents in the Hancock Collection, listening to negotiation and surveillance device audiotapes, and interviewing Branch Davidian survivors. One of the many topics discussed by the scholars in the film are the problems caused by use of the word 'cult', including dehumanization of believers, prompting or justifying unnecessarily aggressive actions by law enforcement agents and cult essentialism that inhibits careful research and understanding of religious movements.

Conclusion

Documentaries continue to be made on 'cults', because they attract viewers and therefore advertisers. Independent documentary makers construct their products to sell to large television entertainment outlets. Documentary producers and directors who work for large news media corporations are paid to make such documentaries. It is about making money, even if the same topic is treated over and over again in documentaries, with diverse results in terms of quality. Writers, producers and directors have varying commitments to making well-researched, accurate documentaries. Many probably are required to impose a sensationalized 'cult' frame on the subject matter by the television outlet or publisher paying for the final product (see remarks by Doyle 2019). In 2023, we can expect a flood of 'Waco' documentaries and books for the thirtieth anniversary of the Branch Davidians–federal agents conflict.

This survey of the documentaries and dramatizations that aired in 2017–18 about the Waco case, whose directors or producers contacted me for input and to whom I gave key internal FBI documents found in the Lee Hancock Collection, demonstrates that none of them – even the good documentaries – utilized all of the FBI documents that I provided. At the most, people writing some of the documentaries and the *Waco* mini-series dramatization utilized the Major Event Log and the 19 April 1993 log. No use was made of the memos by FBI behavioural scientists, and the 'Passover' and 'Suicide' summary documents, which indicate that FBI decision-makers would have been aware of the Branch Davidians' belief in an apocalyptic theology of martyrdom when the 19 April 1993 tank and CS gas assault on the Branch Davidians was carried out.

In their 1988 book, *Manufacturing Consent: The Political Economy of the Mass Media*, Edward S. Herman and Noam Chomsky elucidate five 'filters' utilized to determine what is reported in news media. The first filter is the concentrated ownership of news media into profit-oriented mass-media firms. The third filter is 'the reliance of the media on information provided by government, business, and "experts" funded and approved by these primary sources and agents of power' (Herman and Chomsky 1988: 2; see also Richardson 1995). In other words, employees of major news corporations such as ABC, CBS, CNN and CNN's subsidiary HLN will want to avoid alienating officials in government agencies who are important sources of information on news stories.

An example of this concern not to alienate law enforcement authorities is depicted in *Waco: The Rules of Engagement* (Gazecki 1997), which remains the best documentary on the Branch Davidians–federal agents conflict so far. *Waco:*

The Rules of Engagement was the first documentary to discuss the question of whether or not the far-infrared video (FLIR) recorded from an airplane circling over Mount Carmel Center during the FBI assault on 19 April 1993 shows federal agents behind the building emerging from a CEV and directing gunfire towards the Branch Davidians. FLIR expert Dr Edward F. Allard is shown pointing out rapid flashes of light visible in the FLIR video that he states are automatic gunfire from two individuals directed towards people in the building (1.58.37; 2.20.00ff). *Waco: The Rules of Engagement* reports that Infraspection Institute was asked to analyze the Waco FLIR videotapes for CBS *60 Minutes* (2.00.37), and Infraspection's report judged that the FLIR tapes showed rapid gunfire being directed towards the building. A second letter from Infraspection Institute stated, 'due to the potentially sensitive nature of this material and the resulting negative repercussions to Infraspection, we are choosing to decline any further comment surrounding this taped incident and our subsequent professional opinion regarding its viewing' (2.01.05). Infraspection Institute's analysis also indicated that people were visible on the FLIR tapes 'entering, exiting or being run over by an armored vehicle' (2.01.29).

The Final Report produced by Special Counsel John C. Danforth in 2000 states that the flashes of light in question on the FLIR tapes are 'reflections or "glint" coming from debris scattered in and around the complex'. This conclusion is based on an experimental 'reenactment' conducted by a United Kingdom FLIR analysis company in 2000 at Fort Hood, Texas (Danforth 2000: 18). However, the Danforth Final Report does not mention the preliminary report in March 2000 made by FLIR expert Carlos Ghigliotti (1957–2000), who had been hired by the House of Representatives Reform Committee to analyze the Waco FLIR tapes. His report indicates that there was a gunfight between Branch Davidians in the gymnasium and two agents behind the building on 19 April 1993, who then subsequently fired into other areas of the building. Ghigliotti was not able to complete his report because he died on 28 April 2000, at age forty-two, of a heart attack. Before he died, he faxed a copy of his preliminary report to attorney David Hardy, who published it as an appendix in his book (Hardy with Kimball 2001: Appendix I: 337–42; Lei 2000). None of the documentaries that aired in 2017–18 discussed the question of the evidence on the FLIR videotapes. There is scope for a future documentary to take a close look at the FLIR videotapes with input from a new generation of FLIR experts.

A number of the 'Waco' documentaries forthcoming in 2023 are not being produced by mainstream news organizations that would wish to maintain friendly relations with federal law enforcement agencies, so we will see whether or not these documentaries explore the hard questions about the interactions of FBI agents with the Branch Davidians, including why the CEV and CS gas assault was carried out although Koresh was in the process of implementing his exit plan, and FBI officials knew about the Branch Davidians' apocalyptic theology of martyrdom. Will the authors of some of the forthcoming documentaries and books be willing to delve into the FBI behavioural scientists' analysis of Koresh and the Branch Davidians, the 'Passover' and 'Suicide' summary documents, and what the Reno Briefing File may indicate about how she was misled into approving the tank and gas assault plan?

Herman and Chomsky's first filter, 'the size, concentrated ownership, owner wealth, and profit orientation of the dominant mass-media firms' remains relevant (Herman and Chomsky 1988: 2). After decades of sociologists and religious studies scholars attempting to educate journalists about the detrimental effects of labelling a group a 'cult' (Wright 1997) or otherwise depicting a group in terms of cult essentialism, success has been achieved in only some instances. Cult essentialism provides journalists and media consumers with easy answers to complex cases. The sensationalized 'cult' narrative attracts viewers and readers, and hence makes money.

This survey of some of the 2017–18 documentaries on the 1993 'Waco' case demonstrates that a documentary can perpetuate the essentialized 'cult' narrative about the Branch Davidians, although it does not explicitly apply the term 'cult'. I am aware that some writers, producers and directors are aiming to produce intelligent, well-researched treatments in 2023. We will see if the documentaries, dramatizations and books forthcoming in 2023 for the thirtieth anniversary of the conflict between Branch Davidians and federal agents will humanize the people, or if they will continue to perpetuate cult essentialism.

References

ABC News Primetime: The Children of Waco (2003), [TV Programme], ABC, 17 April. Available at https://abcnews.go.com/US/video/april-17-2003-children-waco-52031297.

Adams, G. J. and P. Alpha (2018), *Hearken O Daughter: Three Sisters from New Zealand Travel to Waco, Only Two Return*. n.p.: Book Baby.

Bryce, R. (1999), 'Agent Sage: Still Defending the FBI', *Austin Chronicle*, 12 November. Available at https://www.austinchronicle.com/news/1999-11-12/74651/.

CBS News 48 Hours: Secrets of Waco (2017), [TV programme], CBS, 29 December. Available at https://www.cbsnews.com/video/secrets-of-waco-7/#x.

CNN Special Report: Megaphone for Conspiracy, the Alex Jones Story (2022), [TV programme], CNN, 27 February.

Committee on the Judiciary, United States Senate (1995), *The Aftermath of Waco: Changes in Federal Law Enforcement*, 104–824. Washington, DC: U. S. Government Printing Office.

Coulson, D. O. (1999), *No Heroes: Inside the FBI's Secret Counter-Terror Force*. New York: Pocket Books.

Craddock, G. (1999), 'Oral and Videotaped Deposition, 28 October: 201-05; and on 29 October: 2:254, 259–64, 405', in *Isabel G. Andrade, et al v. Phillip J. Cojnacki, et al*, United States District Court for the Western District of Texas, Waco Division, No. W-96-CA-139.

Danforth, J. C. (2000), 'Final Report to the Deputy Attorney General Concerning the 1993 Confrontation at the Mt. Carmel Complex, Waco, Texas'.

Doyle, C. (2019), 'Interview by Catherine Wessinger on his Experiences with the Media, 8 August'. Part 1, available at https://www.youtube.com/watch?v=jEP6c3OJHqo&t=139s; Part 2, available at https://www.youtube.com/watch?v=T3fFAn7006o (accessed 21 April 2023).

Doyle, C., C. Wessinger and M. D. Wittmer (2012), *A Journey to Waco: Autobiography of a Branch Davidian*. Lanham: Rowman & Littlefield.

FBI (1993a), 'Passover Summary', 1 April. Document in the Lee Hancock Collection, Southwestern Writers Collection, Texas State University.

FBI (1993b), 'Passover Addendum', 18 April. Document in the Lee Hancock Collection, Southwestern Writers Collection, Texas State University.

FBI (1993c), 'Suicide References', 27 March. Document in the Lee Hancock Collection, Southwestern Writers Collection, Texas State University.

FBI (1993d), 'Suicide Addendum', 18 April. Document in the Lee Hancock Collection, Southwestern Writers Collection, Texas State University.

FBI (1993e), 'WACMUR Major Event Log, Redacted'. Document in the Lee Hancock Collection, Southwestern Writers Collection, Texas State University.

FBI (1993f), 'WACMUR Major Event Log, Unredacted'. *FBI Records: The Vault: WACO/Branch Davidian Compound*. Available at https://vault.fbi.gov/waco-branch-davidian-compound/ (accessed 21 April 2023).

FBI (1993g), 'WACMUR Log, 19 April 1993'. Document in the Lee Hancock Collection, Southwestern Writers Collection, Texas State University.

FBI (1993h), 'Bug Tape Audio of Branch Davidians' Conversation as They Attempt to Fix Severed Phone Line to FBI Negotiators', 19 April. Part 1, available at https://www.youtube.com/watch?v=ZTOvuVUsBrQ&t=706s; Part 2, available at https://www.youtube.com/watch?v=NG940yRWTfY&t=1352s (accessed 21 April 2023).

FBI (1993i), 'FLIR Video of Tank Driving Inside Building to Gas Branch Davidian Mothers and Children', 19 April. Available at https://www.youtube.com/watch?v=ddXU2FHdkXk&t=1s (accessed 27 April 2023).

Gibbs, N. (1993), 'The Branch Davidians: Oh, My God, They're Killing Themselves! FBI Agent Bob Ricks', *Time*, 3 May: 1–10. Available at https://content.time.com/time/subscriber/article/0,33009,978360-10,00.html (accessed 21 April 2023).

Guinn, Jeff (2023), Email message to Catherine Wessinger, 26 February.

Haldeman, B. (2007), *Memories of the Branch Davidians: The Autobiography of David Koresh's Mother*, ed. C. Wessinger. Waco: Baylor University Press.

Hall, J. R. (2017), *Gone from the Promised Land: Jonestown in American Cultural History*, 2nd edn. New York: Routledge.

Hall, J. R., P. D. Schuyler and S. Trinh (2000), *Apocalypse Observed: Religious Movements and Violence in North America, Europe, and Japan*. New York: Routledge.

Hancock, L. (1999a), '2 Pyrotechnic Devices Fired at Davidians, Ex-official Says', *Dallas Morning News*, 24 August.

Hancock, L. (1999b), 'FBI Missteps Doomed Siege Talks, Memos Say', *Dallas Morning News*, 30 December.

Hancock, L. (2018), 'How the Branch Davidians Set the Fires for a Self-fulfilling Prophecy of their Doomsday', *Dallas Morning News*, 18 April.

Hannaford, A. (2018), '"Waco" through the Eyes of a Former Branch Davidian: For Clive Doyle, the New Mini-series "Waco" Isn't Just TV Drama – It's Personal', *Texas Monthly*, 24 January. Available at https://www.texasmonthly.com/the-culture/watching-waco-branch-davidians/ (accessed 21 April 2023).

Hardy, D. T. and R. Kimball (2001), *This Is Not an Assault: Penetrating the Web of Official Lies Regarding the Waco Incident*. n.p.: Xlibris Corporation.

Herman, E. S. and N. Chomsky (1988), *Manufacturing Consent: The Political Economy of the Mass Media*. New York: Pantheon Books.

House of Representatives (1995), *Activities of Federal Law Enforcement Agents toward the Branch Davidians*, 3 parts. Washington, DC: U. S. Government Printing Office.

House of Representatives (1996), *Investigation into the Activities of Federal Law Enforcement Agencies Toward the Branch Davidians*, Report 104-749. Washington, DC: U. S. Government Printing Office.

How It Really Happened with Hill Harper: Waco, Part 2, End of Days (2018), [TV programme], HLN, 11 November.

Inside Mount Carmel – Waco, TX, Parts *1–12* (1993), with Branch Davidians. Part 1, available at https://www.youtube.com/watch?v=5tXS-lEPclA (accessed 21 April 2023).

Introvigne, M. (2018), 'If Your Religion Is a Xie Jiao, You Go to Jail – But What Is a Xie Jiao?' *Bitter Winter*, 9 August. Available at https://bitterwinter.org/what-is-a-xie-jiao/ (accessed 21 April 2023).

Introvigne, M. (2022), 'Silantyev, Amelina: Ukrainian "Cults" Have Killed 500 Children in Russia', *Bitter Winter*, 4 November. Available at https://bitterwinter.org/silantyev-amelina-ukrainian-cults-have-killed-500-children-in-russia/.

Kantrowitz, B. (1993a), 'The Messiah of Waco', *Newsweek*, 14 March. Available at https://www.newsweek.com/messiah-waco-191160 (accessed 21 April 2023).

Kantrowitz, B. (1993b), 'Day of Judgment', *Newsweek*, 2 May. Available at https://www.newsweek.com/day-judgement-193530 (accessed 21 April 2023).

Lei, R. (2000), 'The Man Who Knew Too Much', *Washington Post*, 28 May. Available at https://www.washingtonpost.com/archive/lifestyle/2000/05/28/the-man-who-knew-too-much/68c85b3a-913d-4e62-9806-ffecbdb53556/ (accessed 21 April 2023).

Moore, C. (1995), *The Davidian Massacre: Disturbing Questions about Waco Which Must Be Answered*. Franklin and Springfield: Legacy Communications and Gun Owners Foundation.

Moore, R. (2009), *Understanding Jonestown and Peoples Temple*. Westport: Praeger.

Murder Made Me Famous: David Koresh (2017a), [TV programme], Dir. Y. Smith, Reelz Cable Network, 25 November.

Murder Made Me Famous: David Koresh (2017b), [TV trailer], Dir. Y. Smith, Reelz Cable Network, 22 November. Available at https://www.facebook.com/ReelzChannel/videos/10156045869214379/ (accessed 21 April 2023).

Nailling, K. (2018), 'Another Competency Hearing Set for Murder Defendant', *Athens Daily Review*, 13 August. Available at https://www.athensreview.com/news/another-competency-hearing-set-for-murder-defendant/article_4739951e-9f38-11e8-8b0c-d3e32293f485.html (accessed 21 April 2023).

Newport, K. G. C. (2009), '"A Baptism by Fire": The Branch Davidians and Apocalyptic Self-Destruction', *Nova Religio*, 13 (2): 61–94.

Noesner, G. (2010), *Stalling for Time: My Life as an FBI Hostage Negotiator*. New York: Random House.

Perez, E. and H. Yan (2016), 'Ammon Bundy, Other Protestors Arrested in Oregon; LaVoy Finicum Killed', CNN, 27 January. Available at https://www.cnn.com/2016/01/26/us/oregon-wildlife-refuge-siege-arrests (accessed 21 April 2023).

Prothero, S. (2020), *Religion Matters: An Introduction to the World's Religions*. New York: W. W. Norton & Company.

Rawls, W. (1993), 'Debacle at Waco: Print and Broadcast, National and Local, Journalism Displayed Its Unseemly Side', *Nieman Reports*, Summer: 12–15.

Reavis, D. J. (1995), *The Ashes of Waco: An Investigation*. New York: Simon & Schuster.

Richardson, J. T. (1993), 'Definitions of Cult: From Sociological-Technical to Popular-Negative', *Review of Religious Research*, 34 (4): 348–56.

Richardson, J. T. (1995), 'Manufacturing Consent about Koresh: A Structural Analysis of the Role of the Media in the Waco Tragedy', in S. A. Wright (ed.), *Armageddon in Waco: Critical Perspectives of the Branch Davidian Conflict*, 153–76. Chicago: University of Chicago Press.

Richardson, J. T. (2010), 'Minority Religions and the Context of Violence: A Conflict/Interactionist Perspective', *Terrorism and Political Violence*, 13 (1): 103–33.

Richardson, J. T. (2021), 'The Myth of the Omnipotent Leader: The Social Construction of a Misleading Account of Leadership in New Religious Movements', *Nova Religio*, 24 (4): 11–25.

Schroeder, K. (2019), Interview with C. Wessinger, 12 May. Part 10, available at https://www.youtube.com/watch?v=pnl4hgbEdxA&t=9s (accessed 21 April 2023).

Shirley, R. (2021), Interview with C. Wessinger, 11 November, Part 1. Available at https://youtu.be/7Eg4rrvmsXs?si=lU_xeZqCchEBseYZ ; Part 2. Available at https://youtu.be/ryGy3XIyofw?si=RRUBPI4TWe2wZGf6 (accessed 7 January 2024).

Smerick, P. and M. C. Young (1993), 'FBI Memo: Negotiation Strategy Considerations, 5 March'. Document in the Lee Hancock Collection, Southwestern Writers Collection, Texas State University.

Southwestern Writers Collection (n.d.), 'A Guide to the Lee Hancock Collection, 1975–2004', The Wittliff Collections at the Alkek Library, Texas State University-San Marcos. Available at https://gato-docs.its.txst.edu/jcr:e4904dd5-096c-4167-b7eb-9d1131c59452/Hancock_Lee_099.pdf (accessed 21 April 2023).

Sullivan, B. (2022), 'Alex Jones Has Been Ordered to Pay $1 Billion over His Sandy Hook Lies. Will He?', *National Public Radio*, 14 October. Available at https://www.npr.org/2022/10/13/1128860654/alex-jones-sandy-hook-families-money-trial (accessed 21 April 2023).

Tabor, J. D. (n.d.), 'Chronological Interpretive Log/Major Events', *World Religions and Spirituality Project*. Available at https://wrldrels.org/wp-content/uploads/2021/12/Tabor-Chronological-Interpretive-Log-Major-Events-white-background-USE-THIS-VERSION.pdf (accessed 21 April 2023).

Tabor, J. D. (1995), 'The Last Recorded Words of David Koresh, April 16 and 18, 1993', Audiotape produced and narrated by J. D. Tabor based on FBI negotiation tapes. Available at https://www.youtube.com/watch?v=2Xs78xrPo9E (accessed 21 April 2023).

Tabor, J. D. and E. V. Gallagher (1995), *Why Waco? Cults and the Battle for Religious Freedom in America*. Berkeley: University of California Press.

The 1993 Waco Branch Davidian Tragedy Revisited: What Really Happened? (2020), [Film], Dir. M. Lee. USA: Reunion Institute. Available at https://www.youtube.com/watch?v=s5qw0WlB-aw (accessed 21 April 2023).

Thibodeau, D. and L. Whiteson (1999), *A Place Called Waco: A Survivor's Story*. New York: Public Affairs.

Truth and Lies: Waco (2018), [TV programme], Dir. M. Pearson, ABC News, 11 October. Available at https://vimeo.com/264143037 (accessed 21 April 2023).

United States Department of Justice (1993), *Report to the Deputy Attorney General on the Events at Waco, Texas, February 28 to April 19, 1993*, redacted version. Washington, DC: U.S. Department of Justice.

Waco: Faith, Fear, and Fire (2011), [TV programme], Dir. A. Segal, CNN, 17 April. Part 1, available at https://vimeo.com/23810150; Part 2, available at https://vimeo.com/23833269 (accessed 21 April 2023).

Waco: The Rules of Engagement (1997), [Film], Dir. W. Gazecki. USA: Somford Entertainment. Available at https://vimeo.com/511837429 (accessed 21 April 2023).

The Waco Branch Davidian Tragedy: What Have We Learned? (2020), [Film], Dir. M Lee. USA: Reunion Institute. Available at https://www.youtube.com/watch?v=9ASYZbOPpXQ (accessed 21 April 2023).

Wessinger, C. (2000), *How the Millennium Comes Violently: From Jonestown to Heaven's Gate*. New York: Seven Bridges Press.

Wessinger, C. (2006), 'The Branch Davidians and Religion Reporting – A Ten-Year Retrospective', in K. G. C. Newport and C. Gribben (eds), *Expecting the End: Millennialism in Social and Historical Context*, 147–72. Waco: Baylor University Press.

Wessinger, C. (2009a), 'Deaths in the Fire at the Branch Davidians' Mount Carmel: Who Bears Responsibility?', *Nova Religio*, 13 (2): 25–60.

Wessinger, C. (2009b), 'The Lee Hancock Collection: Federal and State Materials on the Branch Davidian Case', *Nova Religio*, 13 (2): 114–25.

Wessinger, C. (2012), '"Cults" in America: Discourse and Outcomes', in S. J. Stein (ed.), *Religions in America,* vol 3: *1945 to Present*, 511–31. New York: Cambridge University Press.

Wessinger, C. (2013a), Email message to David G. Bromley reporting what Gary Noesner said to Clive Doyle on 18 April 2013.

Wessinger, C., comp. (2013b), 'Assault on the Branch Davidian Community: A Photographic Retrospective', 30 June, in Branch Davidian Archives, *World Religions and Spirituality Project*. Available at https://wrldrels.org/wp-content/uploads/2016/02/Assault-on-the-Branch-Davidian-Community-A-Photographic-Retrospective.pdf (accessed 21 April 2023).

Wessinger, C. (2016), 'Branch Davidians (1981–2006)', *World Religions and Spirituality Project*, 10 October. Available at https://wrldrels.org/2016/02/25/branch-davidians-2/ (accessed 21 April 2023).

Wessinger, C. (2017), 'The FBI's "Cult War" against the Branch Davidians', in S. A. Johnson and S. Weitzman (eds), *The FBI and Religion: Faith and National Security before and after 9/11*, 203–331. Oakland: University of California Press.

Wessinger, C. (2018), Word document containing two comments that were posted online in response to article by Lee Hancock, 'How the Branch Davidians Set the Fires for a Self-fulfilling Prophecy of their Doomsday', *Dallas Morning News*, 18 April. The comments on this article are no longer visible on the *Dallas Morning News* webpage.

Wetherington, W. (2000), 'Final Report Concerning the Fire at the Branch Davidian Complex, Waco, Texas, April 19, 1993', in Special Counsel J. C. Danforth, *Final Report to the Deputy Attorney General Concerning the 1993 Confrontation at the Mt. Carmel Complex, Waco, Texas*, 1–23.

White, P. (2022), 'John Leguizamo, David Costabile & J. Smith-Cameron among Cast in Paramount+'s "Waco" Sequel Series', *Deadline*, 25 April. Available at https://deadline

.com/2022/04/john-leguizamo-david-costabile-j-smith-cameron-waco-1235008417/ (accessed 21 April 2023).

Wickström, U. (2000), 'Fire Analysis of the Events at Waco, Texas, 19 April 1993', in Special Counsel J. C. Danforth, *Final Report to the Deputy Attorney General Concerning the 1993 Confrontation at the Mt. Carmel Complex, Waco, Texas*, 1–17.

Wright, S. A. (1997), 'Media Coverage of Unconventional Religions: Any "Good News" for Minority Faiths?', Special Issue: Mass Media and Unconventional Religion, *Review of Religious Research*, 39 (2): 101–15.

Wright, S. A. (2003), 'A Decade after Waco: Reassessing Crisis Negotiations at Mount Carmel in Light of New Government Disclosures', *Nova Religio*, 7 (2): 101–10.

Wright, S. A. (2009), 'Revisiting the Branch Davidian Mass Suicide Debate', *Nova Religio*, 13 (2): 4–24.

Wright, S. A. (2019), 'Media Review: Waco after Twenty-five Years: Media Reconstructions of the Federal Siege of the Branch Davidians', *Nova Religio*, 22 (3): 108–20.

Afterword

Responses and conclusions

W. Michael Ashcraft

Introduction

The cult wars were fought by American, Canadian and British scholars of new religious movements (hereafter NRMs) from the 1970s through the 1990s. Elsewhere I present a detailed account of the arguments separating scholars from one another in those wars (Ashcraft 2018). Scholars of NRMs divided along partisan lines over the value of using the term 'cult'. They did not literally commit acts of violence on scholars across the divide, but they published articles and books excoriating one another and at conferences would shout at one another in panels and sessions. In this volume, Roderick P. Dubrow-Marshall reflects the cult critic position (also called the anticult and cultic studies), finding the term 'cult' to be analytically useful. Other contributors take the opposite stand, a position that cult critics have called cult apologist. Cult critics believe cult apologists are too soft on cults, failing to note aspects of cults that are harmful. These cult apologists, on the other hand, see themselves as providing a rational, unbiased approach to cults, and criticize the cult critics' agenda as partisan and flawed. These scholars would prefer that no label be applied to them at all, seeing themselves as simply academics who produce standard historical and social scientific scholarship.

The cult wars were primarily fought among scholars. Meanwhile the term 'cult' has become popular in general usage in North American and other first-world societies. In spite of misgivings by academics, media and government easily reach for 'cult' when describing or justifying whatever idea, group or practice they find disreputable. Susannah Crockford (this volume) points out that ex-members, especially, do not hesitate to apply the term 'cult' to whatever abusive groups and situations they have exited. Douglas E. Cowan (this volume) finds that university students who take his classes have obtained most of their information about cults from popular culture. The use of 'cult' beyond the academy is so promiscuous that hardly anyone pauses to raise any questions about the utility of this term at the popular level.

What's a scholar to do? Read this volume! It contains alternative, middle-ground uses for 'cult' that avoid the binary status of the old cult wars.

Chapter summaries

In this section I provide brief summaries of all of the chapters in this volume. They are listed in the order that they appear in the table of contents.

In their introductory chapter, the editors, Aled Thomas and Edward Graham-Hyde, note that the term 'cult' has become part of both public debate and contemporary culture: 'appearing in popular culture entertainment, news stories, journalist exposés, and (more recently) within hybrids of political, religious, and conspiracy narratives'. They point out that the term 'cult' lacks the scholarly rigour required to be useful as an analytical term, but greater awareness of the term's usage in larger culture is needed among NRM scholars. The editors conducted a survey with more than 2,000 respondents and found that people tend to associate negative values to terms like 'cult' and 'brainwashing'. The term 'new religious movement' was regarded more favourably, but was not as common in everyday usage as 'cult'. The phrase 'minority religion' would probably be a better candidate for a neutral term.

The editors also note that many disciplines now take ideas about trauma and disaffiliation more seriously than in the past, and scholars who study NRMs need to catch up. Heretofore, NRM scholars distrusted the testimonies of ex-members of NRMs. Many of these ex-members claimed to have been abused and traumatized while involved with NRMs, and that tainted the objectivity of whatever information ex-members provided. But in separating ex-members' stories from the scholarly process, valuable perspective is lost. What the 'insider' to a group or tradition has to say can be just as important as what 'outsiders' report. The editors recommend that NRM scholars pursue field work more avidly and expansively than they have up to now, entering the public arena so that they are interacting with many types of individuals: ex-members, current members, pundits, influencers, reporters and many others.

Suzanne Newcombe and Sarah Harvey write for an important British organization founded during the height of the cult wars: the Information Network Focus on Religious Movements (Inform). Eileen Barker began Inform to provide reliable information about NRMs for people whose loved ones had joined NRMs and for others who had various interests in NRMs. In this pre-internet era it was not always easy to learn about NRMs. Newcombe and Harvey continue the policy at Inform that Barker established: maintain objectivity in discussing and portraying various NRMs, especially those that the public would call cults, like the Moonies (or Unification Church) and Hare Krishnas. To maintain that objectivity, Inform staff tend to avoid the term 'cult'. They see how loaded the term is, and rather than wade through the pros and cons of the debate about the utility of cult with people that come to them for information, they try to steer the conversation towards more specific descriptions of beliefs and behaviours which are associated with a particular group.

George D. Chryssides provides a brief history of the terms 'cult', 'countercult' and 'anticult'. Early detractors of religions that academics would later call NRMs in nineteenth-century Great Britain and the United States took theological positions from within Christian traditions. These countercultists saw groups like Theosophy, Seventh-day Adventism, the Jehovah's Witnesses and Christian Science as veering away from orthodox Christianity into heresy. From then until now, countercultists opposed NRMs that they called cults for theological reasons. Beginning in the 1960s, however, friends and families of young adults who joined NRMs organized themselves to oppose them, calling them cults. Hence their movement's name: anticult. Anticult individuals opposed NRMs because of the latter's social structure – abusive leaders and gullible followers – and its requirement that members sever all relationships except those that united them in their NRM. Unlike countercultists, anticultists didn't object to a group's theology. They opposed abusive behaviour within a NRM's boundaries.

Chryssides warns that criticizing NRMs is tricky because those criticisms often rely heavily on the testimonies of ex-members. Someone who leaves a NRM may have complex motives for depicting their lives in NRMs as traumatic. Their accounts should be compared to perceptions of the NRM held by current members and professionals like academics and journalists.

William Sims Bainbridge recalls the way that he and Rodney Stark used cult in thinking about their joint magnum opus, *A Theory of Religion* (1987). They saw religion as a problem-solving process, involving axioms and theorems that described human action. People, they argued, act out of desire (or need) for rewards. If someone cannot get what they want, they settle for compensators, and the most general of these are supernatural, or religion. Cults are those religious groups that reward socially valued behaviour and punish behaviour not socially desirable. Stark and Bainbridge assumed that religion was a way of determining social action. Because they had generalized cult as religion that compensates for lack of satisfaction by other means, they avoided the controversy regarding the usage of the term 'cult' but in so doing also failed to address the problems in relying on 'cult' as a term of analysis. (Bainbridge and Stark 1979, 1980).

Douglas E. Cowan tells about a learning tool that he uses with his students called the 'Dangerous Cult Exercise'. He asks his students to imagine that they are various kinds of specialists called before a parliamentary committee to answer these three questions: How do they define a dangerous cult? What obligations do they have to larger society? What do they recommend; that is, what do they think should be done by governments to address dangerous cults? After dealing with various answers to these questions, the students eventually must confront the important question: How do we know what we know about cults? Cowan finds that students usually get their information from popular culture: movies, television shows, novels, social media. And invariably, NRMs are portrayed in popular culture as 'dangerous cults'. Peaceful NRMs, that simply exist day-to-day, never run afoul of law enforcement, pay taxes and do not use violence, are not all that interesting. Consumers of popular culture want juicy stories of sex, drama and betrayal. And so NRMs are almost always presented as distorted versions of themselves. But we don't see this because of mechanisms from social psychology like the availability heuristic (the quicker we learn about something the more likely we are to believe it to be true) and source dissociation (we tend to forget where we learned things).

Dubrow-Marshall's chapter describes the term 'cult' from a cult critic's position. Borrowing from West and Langone (West and Langone 1986), he defines a cult as any social group that insists that members adhere to some belief or practice that benefits the group's leader or leaders to the detriment of others, such as members' families and friends. For Dubrow-Marshall, cults aren't necessarily religious. The mark of a group being authentically cultic is the abuse practised within the group and in relation to extra-group entities. For this reason, Dubrow-Marshall rejects comparisons between NRMs and cults. He also sees the value of using the term 'cult' as a therapeutic move. As ex-members exit cult life, they need assurance that their perceptions of cults are accurate, enabling them to transition to a healthier, more integrated life. The term 'cult' can be useful in helping people understand what they sacrificed to join and remain in cults and face the challenge of leaving cults.

Donald A. Westbrook's contribution to this volume is a study of La Luz del Mundo, the Light of the World (LLDM). It is the second largest religious group in Mexico next to the Roman Catholic Church and have thousands of adherents in the United States. The group's current leader, Naasón Joaquín García, is serving a prison sentence for sexual abuse of minors. Westbrook notes that this church has been called a cult, but he finds that label unhelpful. It does not include emic perspectives, that is, the viewpoints of church members, especially regarding their jailed leader. If an observer concludes that the LLDM is a cult, with no further inquiry past that conclusion, then the nuanced, complex and rich beliefs and practices of LLDM members are dismissed out of hand. Westbrook notes that previous researchers failed to account for the group's consistent support of their leader, in spite of the accusations against him. It's because in their theological worldview the leader, or apostle, gives them direct access to God. Also, the LLDM sees itself as restored primitive Christianity. Understandably, from their perspective, neither 'cult' nor 'NRM' quite capture the church. But the appellation 'NRM' is preferable to 'cult', which as Westbrook notes, renders the LLDM as 'Othered and dismissed'.

In Bethan Juliet Oake's chapter, the term 'cult' becomes a label for both the target of presumed authorities' ire, and the authorities themselves. In other words, those who portray others as evil are themselves behaving like the very cults that they condemn. The context for this interesting turn is the Satanic Cult Conspiracy (SCC), a self-appointed coterie of supposed experts on Satanists. The Satanic Panic, which reached its height in the 1980s, was only the latest iteration of a repeating paradigm: Satan is evil, his minions are humans who worship him and these persons must be sought and stopped. At other times in Western history, similar castigation fell on witches, the poor and various other vulnerable members of society. Society's leaders – in government and the church – believed it was their right – indeed, their duty – to pass judgement on supposedly evil individuals and groups. Oake finds an irony in this otherwise straightforward morality play: the good guys who claim to know so much about evil are in fact behaving much like the evil people they condemn. Oake says that cults are typically those that exhibit 'harmful' behaviour, subversion to the 'mainstream', community isolation, presence of 'charismatic leaders' and 'coercion'. These same criteria describe the SCC theorists! Oake's study demonstrates the fluidity of cult and anticult definitions. If one can turn into the other, who are the good guys and who are the bad guys? No clear delineation is discernible.

In her chapter, Susannah Crockford studies the ways that the label 'cult' can be applied to QAnon, a recent set of conspiracy theories and movements that rely heavily on the internet. Crockford argues that individuals who are drawn to QAnon live inside a metaphorical bubble – that is, a mindset that accepts only information derived from supposedly reliable sources, a mindset that vehemently rejects information that might contradict the messages from within the bubble. Crockford replaces 'cult' with 'bubble' as a term of analysis. 'Cult' is a blunt instrument in the hands of those who disagree with whatever movement or organization they find offensive, and it resists rigorous definition. On the other hand, bubbles are, both literally and metaphorically, fragile and ephemeral. The idea of a bubble works very well with QAnon, itself an ephemeral online identity.

Vivian Asimos's contribution to this volume is a discussion of people who spend much of their lives immersed in video games. She argues that scholars approach such individuals with too many preconceived notions of what religion is. Instead, like any good ethnographer, Asimos shows that gamers report having meaningful, spiritual experiences in their gaming life that religious studies scholars would do well to attend to. However, unlike gamers in hyper-real religions, for instance, Asimos's gamers would not take their identification with gaming to the point of putting their gamer name on a census record, something the hard-core hyper-real religionist would do.

In her chapter, Catherine Wessinger adopts a term coined by sociologist John R. Hall, 'cult essentialism', which she applies to the views of opponents of NRMs. Hall and Wessinger claim that cult critics are essentialists, that is, they see cults as monolithic and almost always solely culpable in situations involving violence. What follows is a detailed account of the Waco tragedy of 1993, when federal agents assaulted Mount Carmel Center, a complex of buildings containing many Branch Davidians led by David Koresh and located several miles outside of Waco, Texas. When she was consulted by writers, directors and producers of documentaries, Wessinger gave each of them internal FBI documents that complicate the question of which side – FBI agents or the Branch Davidians – contributed the most to the 19 April 1993 destruction of Mount Carmel Center. None of the documentaries presented information indicating that FBI decision-makers were informed about the apocalyptic theology of martyrdom taught by Koresh. In these documentaries interviewees and clips from 1993 news reports used the term 'cult', conveying a clear message about the Branch Davidians. Wessinger's point throughout the chapter is that the conflict between the Branch Davidians and federal agents occurred in an interactive context, and that reporters and media outlets were major players in the interactions by depicting the Branch Davidians as 'cultists'. The cult essentialist view removes any responsibility from federal agents and others whose actions contributed to the deaths at Mount Carmel Center. Depicting members of a group as 'cultists' dehumanizes them, and diminishes concern for innocents in the group. Wessinger concludes that 'cult' documentaries about the Branch Davidians will continue to air, because their simplistic narratives of the tragedy at Mount Carmel Center attract viewers and advertisers, and thereby make money.

Strategies in cult rhetoric

Several authors in this collection recommend that the term 'cult' simply be dropped from the vocabulary of NRM scholars. Newcombe and Harvey find this to be prudent, given the fact that Inform staff relate to all kinds of people in the public arena. Their priority is providing service to those in need of reliable information, and use of the contentious term 'cult' merely complicates their mission.

Other authors reject the term 'cult' based on their findings in their research on specific groups. Westbrook argues that using 'cult' misses important emic aspects of the church he studied, Light of the World. When he interacted with members of the church, he discovered their rich inner lives, and rich ritual system, that would have been lost if the term 'cult' was used too much. Crockford rejects the term 'cult' in her work on QAnon conspiracists. She prefers a more flexible and accurate term: 'bubble'. She found that QAnon activists, who literally spend untold hours as online participants, fashion metaphorical bubbles of ideas and meaning that reassure them that their worldview is correct. Wessinger argues that people involved in the Waco tragedy made decisions about how they would interact with one another. The idea that the Branch Davidians were a cult stymied more accurate and fine-grained analysis of that NRM and their behaviour. Asimos, although she does not address the dilemma of 'cult' usage directly, does criticize scholars for using the term 'religion' in a way that's similar to how scholars may use (and misuse) the term 'cult'. Like Westbrook, she discovered spiritual experience among the gamers whom she got to know that academic definitions of religion fail to explore. She recommended that scholars find new ways to define religion based on the remarkable testimonies of her subjects. Presumably this might also include redefining 'cult' in ways that scholarship has neglected before now.

Mention of Asimos's critique of religion scholars reminds us that the problem of insiders and outsiders, so important in other areas of religious studies, is also important in discussions about the use of the term 'cult' (see McCutcheon 1999). Chryssides says that it can be risky to include testimonies from ex-members in scholarship. Ex-members can potentially be biased in their assessment of cults, especially if these individuals were mistreated, persecuted, abused and/

or traumatized while living in cult locations where cult beliefs were endlessly affirmed.

Yet Asimos and, to a lesser extent, Westbrook support just the opposite strategy: to respect the testimonies of insider sources by placing them front and centre in one's analysis. The insider/outsider problem is perennial. How much credence do we give to those who claim to have had important experiences while involved with a cult or other religious group, experiences that might have either a positive or negative impact (or both) on the experiencer? Recent scholarship in religious studies incorporate voices of the interviewed and observed alongside the voice or voices of the academic experts. Are religion scholars who continue to insist that care be taken in how testimonies of insiders be used simply behind the times, having failed to turn with others in the postmodern turn?

A definitive answer to these questions is beyond the scope of this chapter, but what we can say for certain is that the definition of cult will be drastically affected depending on what theoretical position one takes. Older scholarship, rooted as it was in a rationalistic, objective position for the scholar, will persist in scepticism about the value of ex-member testimony. The latter would be regarded as too subjective, too tinged with emotionalism. But a younger cohort of scholars, such as Asimos and Westbrook, find members of religious groups, and by extension ex-members also, to be reliable sources of information and insight.

Bainbridge recalls that in his 1978 book *Satan's Power* he defined 'cult' very broadly as 'a culturally innovative cohesive group oriented to supernatural concerns'. Although generalizing the term avoided tricky debates about definition, it left the term 'supernatural' undefined, which Bainbridge admitted. He may have been echoing earlier scholarship in the sociology of religion, which legitimized the term 'cult' by including it in typologies of the time period. J. Milton Yinger (1957), for example, divided religious groups into six categories, based on size of the group and its relationship to larger society. The cult was the smallest and least impactful of types. As I note elsewhere, it 'was relatively small and had no organization, but did have a charismatic leader, and its members were mainly concerned with their own mystical experiences' (Ashcraft 2018: 22). Yinger was writing in 1957, several years before the counterculture, but it's easy to see how his definition might have been useful at a later date for anticultists.

Among other strategies in this volume is an intriguing one by Oake, whose study of Satanic Panic results in a surprising discovery: those claiming to reveal evil cults behave like the very people they condemn. That is, the term 'cult' becomes adhesive: throw it at Satanists and it sticks, then throw it at the supposed experts of Satanism and it sticks there too! Oake's point is instructive, especially for anyone who believes they know enough about some evil individual or group to criticize such individuals and groups without getting their own hands dirty.

Finally, Cowan demonstrates how reliant we are on definitions of cult in popular culture. Most people do not recognize how much popular culture distorts NRMs because of learning mechanisms that affect our perceptions of things we know little about. Cowan names four such mechanisms, drawn from social psychology. Cowan shows, then, that wrong-headed definitions of cults exist quite comfortably in the circus arena of popular culture.

Conclusion

In summary, several contributors to this volume recommend discarding the term 'cult' for study purposes, and their recommendation is based on various reasons, especially the one-size-fits-all nature of cult as a term of analysis. We see as well that the insider/outsider problem impacts how cult is defined. If insider testimony is to be used, the term 'cult' is most likely going to need to be dropped. Some scholars define the term 'cult' in broad terms, but this may reflect an earlier period in the history of sociology of religion. Oake found that the term 'cult' can be used to define both critics of cults and the cults themselves. This makes the definition of cult supple, not a conclusion mainstream scholars of NRMs would normally reach. And Cowan shows that we may be beguiled by popular culture's uses of the term 'cult', requiring some help from social psychologists.

Finally, let us consider Dubrow-Marshall's chapter. In this book, he is an academic cult critic amidst a slate of scholars who have little to no use for the term 'cult'. But cult critic viewpoints are firmly established in a few university-level programmes like the one at the University of Salford where Dubrow-Marshall teaches, as well as the University of Alberta where another prominent cult critic, Stephen A. Kent, is in the sociology department. More significantly, cult critics have an organization, the International Cultic Studies Association (ICSA), that hosts annual international conferences and provides resources such as published materials and contact information on individuals whose therapeutic and academic work relies on definitions of cult that several contributors to this volume reject.

Is it likely that people on both sides of the divide will find common ground? Here to give the last word is Eileen Barker, founder of Inform, who has for many years attended ICSA conferences, where she has presented papers and networked with conference participants. She recognizes that both sides need one another, and must find ways to reach agreement. If cult rhetoric someday enjoys support from all who deal with cults, it will be because Barker's pioneering efforts have borne fruit.

References

Ashcraft, W. M. (2018), *A Historical Introduction to the Study of New Religious Movements*. London: Routledge.

Bainbridge, W. S. and R. Stark (1979), 'Of Churches, Sects, and Cults: Preliminary Concepts for a Theory of Religious Movements', *Journal for the Scientific Study of Religion*, 18: 117–31.

Bainbridge, W. S. and R. Stark (1980), 'Client and Audience Cults in America', *Sociological Analysis*, 41: 199–214.

McCutcheon, R. T., ed. (1999), *The Insider/Outsider Problem in the Study of Religion: A Reader*. London: Cassell.

Stark, R. and W. S. Bainbridge (1987), *A Theory of Religion*. New York: Toronto/Lang.

West, L. and M. Langone (1986), 'Cultism: A Conference for Scholars and Policy Makers. Report of Wingspread Conference', *Cultic Studies Journal*, 3 (1): 117–34.

Yinger, J. M. (1957), *Religion, Society, and the Individual: An Introduction to the Sociology of Religion*. New York: The Macmillan Co.

Index

4chan   135, 136, 154, 156, 165, 168, 173

abuse   9, 11, 14, 16, 22–4, 27, 32–4, 51–6, 96, 98–108, 115, 124, 129, 131, 133–6, 138, 140, 141, 145, 146, 166–8, 193, 195, 208, 212, 229–33, 235
anthropology   64, 65, 107
Anti-Christ   137, 138
anticult   10, 16, 17, 26, 36, 40, 41, 46, 48, 50, 53, 56, 59, 79, 82, 103, 115, 117, 119, 124, 126, 132–4, 140, 143, 146–9, 160, 161, 229, 231, 233, 236
antifa   170, 173
apocalypse   87, 192, 196, 197, 200, 209, 214, 218, 219, 221, 234
apostate   10, 14, 49, 57, 58
apostle   115–26, 233
Armageddon   204
assault   32, 96, 136, 169, 192, 193, 195, 196, 198, 200, 201, 203, 206, 208, 211, 213, 215, 218–21, 234

Barker, Eileen   21, 22, 25–8, 30–2, 34–6, 92, 102, 103, 148, 157, 160, 166, 168, 230, 231, 237, 238
belief/s   7, 8, 16, 22–4, 26–8, 31, 32, 34, 44, 46, 60, 62, 63, 65, 69, 80, 87, 88, 91, 100, 102–5, 144, 146, 147, 157, 159, 163, 164, 167, 172, 196, 208, 219, 231–3, 236
bias   10, 12, 49, 90, 91, 161, 186, 235
Bible   40, 42, 43, 54, 61, 72, 116, 126, 164, 167, 194, 199, 200, 206, 211, 212, 218
Biden, Joe   162, 163
binaries   4, 8, 12, 28, 230
brainwashing   3, 5–7, 15–17, 22, 24, 25, 31, 35, 46–9, 51, 56, 80, 85, 88, 89, 92, 99, 105, 120, 124, 134, 155, 160, 164, 166, 170, 190, 202, 204, 230
Branch Davidians   28, 79, 168, 190–206, 208–12, 214–21, 234, 235

Buddhism   30, 41, 47, 49, 51, 65, 185
Bureau of Alcohol, Tobacco, and Firearms (ATF)   193, 201, 202, 204, 206, 208, 211

Capitol Siege   17, 140, 158, 169, 170
categories   4, 8, 10, 13, 16, 18, 28, 31, 48, 54–6, 82, 96, 131, 139, 147, 156, 157, 159, 160, 165, 168, 171, 236
census   178, 179, 234
Center for Studies on New Religions (CESNUR)   116, 117, 124, 125, 127, 197
charisma   3, 27, 69, 97, 140, 143, 144, 157, 233, 236
Children of God   23, 51, 79
Chomsky, Noam   219, 221
Christ   41–7, 54, 63, 122, 125, 192, 207
Christian Science   42, 44, 65, 66, 73, 231
Christianity   6, 16, 30, 33, 34, 41–7, 54, 55, 60, 61, 65, 66, 71, 73, 80, 116, 117, 119, 132, 134, 138, 139, 141, 142, 209, 231, 233
Church of Jesus Christ of Latter-Day Saints   30, 42, 46, 79, 83, 84, 86, 87, 89, 91, 117, 126, 127
Church of Scientology, *see* Scientology
Clinton, Hillary   136, 141, 154, 159, 173
coercion   24, 34, 55, 96–9, 103–8, 140, 145, 146, 233
cognition   90, 91, 100, 123, 175
Columbia Broadcasting System (CBS)   203, 205, 219, 220
community   9, 10, 12, 13, 17, 22–4, 30, 32, 33, 47, 50, 51, 55, 62, 66, 69, 83, 97, 99, 105, 106, 125, 132, 134, 136, 139, 140, 143, 145, 147, 148, 156, 157, 166–8, 171, 181, 185–7, 191, 193, 196, 200, 209, 218, 233
conflict   41, 123, 126, 190–3, 196, 198, 199, 210, 211, 217, 219, 221, 234

conservative   60, 80, 83, 137, 145, 148, 158
conspiracy   4, 8, 17, 131–3, 135–49, 152–4, 156–9, 162, 165, 166, 172, 174–7, 205, 210, 222, 230, 233, 235
cosplay   181–3, 185
countercult   41–6, 50, 51, 80, 93, 115, 126, 231
Covid-19   7, 8, 72, 116, 118, 123, 138, 157, 158, 165, 166
criminal   23, 32–4, 87, 104, 105, 133, 154, 191, 205, 208, 216
cult
  accusations   17, 154–7, 172
  apologism   9, 10, 13, 52, 56, 229
  essentialism   17, 190–2, 202, 203, 218, 221, 234
  leader   59, 85, 87, 88, 143, 164, 190, 202
  milieu   141, 142, 150, 151
  rhetoric   1, 3, 4, 8, 9, 14–19, 21, 24, 44, 46, 56, 115, 149, 156, 180, 186, 193, 235, 238
  studies   33, 36, 54, 57, 82, 100, 101, 108–13, 229, 237, 238
  wars   8, 9, 17, 21, 37, 103, 104, 150, 151, 229, 230

dangerous   7, 23–5, 28, 79–87, 89, 91, 92, 139, 140, 155, 157, 169, 170, 193, 206, 232
demonology   135, 138
deprogramming   26, 80, 89, 92, 143, 200
devotion   7, 68, 69, 91, 97, 98, 106, 121, 181
discourse   3, 4, 8–10, 13, 16, 17, 26, 29, 32, 34–6, 82, 89, 131, 132, 136, 139, 142, 144, 146–8, 154, 181, 184, 185
discrimination   15, 29–31, 40, 41, 117, 123–6, 148
doctrine   40, 41, 43–6, 97, 104, 187, 207
drugs   137, 163
Durkheim, Émile   61, 120

ecclesiology   44, 55, 126
economic   11, 12, 60, 119, 156
Eddy, Mary Baker   65, 66, 73
education   4, 17, 21, 27, 48, 50, 55, 60, 68, 103, 106, 138, 156, 191, 196

emic   107, 117, 179, 233, 235
emotion   13, 31, 55, 63, 67, 120–2, 140, 165, 172, 179, 181–3, 185, 187, 236
entertainment   4, 11, 183, 219, 230
environment   25, 26, 33, 47, 62, 105, 123, 181, 182, 185
esotericism   55, 137
ethics   4, 69, 96, 161, 172
ethnography   22, 62, 66, 155, 161, 173, 234
etic   117, 179
Europe   40, 45, 47, 61, 104, 191
ex-members   4, 9–14, 47–52, 161, 168, 229–32, 235, 236
exploitation   33, 54–6, 98, 119, 134, 146, 156
extremism   47, 102, 105, 106, 155, 157, 160

facebook   11, 68, 127, 154, 155, 157, 158, 162, 163, 165, 169
faith   29, 30, 34, 41–7, 54, 55, 59, 63, 69, 70, 72, 73, 80, 83, 88, 104, 116, 119, 121, 123, 125, 144, 201, 202
family   22, 24, 26, 30, 34, 36, 47, 53, 64–6, 81, 82, 84, 88, 89, 97–100, 105, 106, 108, 124, 131, 133, 134, 139, 143, 166, 170, 206, 213, 231, 232
Federal Bureau of Investigation (FBI)   87, 151, 170, 191–206, 208–21, 234
fieldwork   11, 12, 16, 116, 118, 120, 154, 179
first-generation   27, 50
framework   10, 16, 21, 34, 91, 98, 134, 146
Free Zone Scientology, *see* Scientology
fundamentalism   41, 42, 91, 133, 137, 145

game   16, 63, 179, 180, 182, 234
  gamers   234, 235
gaslighting   34, 166
gender   35, 61, 120, 139, 167
globalization   126, 180
god   40–3, 45, 54, 60–3, 65, 69–72, 90, 105, 122, 125, 134, 141, 164, 167, 184, 185, 194, 207, 208, 211, 214, 215, 233

goddess   62, 72
government   7–9, 24, 25, 27–30, 34, 36, 60, 62, 82, 83, 96, 101, 104, 105, 134, 145, 154, 162, 165, 169, 172, 191–3, 196, 198, 199, 201, 203, 211, 217, 219, 229, 232, 233

Hare Krishna, *see* International Society for Krishna Consciousness (ISKCON)
health   4, 8, 15, 24, 55, 68, 97, 99–101, 105, 106, 123, 164–6
Heaven's Gate   79, 157
heresy   24, 42, 44–6, 51, 64, 65, 231
Hinduism   30, 41
Hubbard, L. Ron   13, 55, 60, 65, 66
hyper-real religion   178, 179, 234

Icke, David   144, 162
identity   14, 16, 47, 66, 71, 99, 100, 103, 143, 155, 161, 173, 205, 234
ideology   14, 24, 31, 34, 35, 62, 72, 97, 101–3, 105–8, 133, 136, 140, 142, 143, 148, 149, 154, 155, 157, 173
indoctrination   46, 99, 137
Information Network Focus on Religious Movements (Inform)   8, 14–17, 21–36, 230, 231, 235, 237
insider   9–12, 106, 117, 154, 230, 235–7
institutional   12, 13, 30, 33, 34, 53, 60, 64, 65, 69, 72, 117, 154, 197
International Cultic Studies Association (ICSA)   54, 55, 100, 101, 237
International Society for Krishna Consciousness (ISKCON)   47, 79, 108, 111, 231
internet   11, 28, 48, 50, 135, 158, 161, 166, 233
intolerance, *see* discrimination
Islam   30, 41, 61

Japan   36, 49, 66, 155
Jediism   178, 179
Jehovah's Witnesses   50–3, 79, 104, 231
Jones, Alex   144, 158, 210
Jonestown, *see* Peoples Temple
journalism   3, 4, 17, 21, 25, 49, 119, 135, 139, 155, 156, 161, 190–2, 196, 206, 211, 218, 221, 230, 231
justice   107, 108, 155, 172, 173, 194

Koresh, David   87, 192–5, 197–216, 218, 221, 234

La Luz del Mundo (LLDM)   115–20, 122–7, 232, 233
law   21, 24, 28, 43, 49, 55, 56, 83, 87, 89, 96, 97, 105, 106, 108, 134, 138, 166, 190, 191, 197, 201, 203, 210, 211, 213, 218–20, 232
legal   21, 28–30, 33, 34, 54, 55, 65, 68, 80, 86, 87, 96, 104, 116, 124–6, 139, 166, 193, 203, 207
legitimacy   28–31, 54, 126, 134, 171, 236
LGBT   139, 147
liminality   115, 123, 126
linguistics   35, 60
lived religion   7, 11

magic   61, 63–5, 71, 72
media   4, 7, 8, 11, 17, 24, 28, 30, 33, 35, 36, 51–3, 64, 86, 91, 101, 102, 115, 127, 131, 133–7, 146, 154–8, 161–5, 171, 180–2, 191, 196, 207, 219, 221, 229, 232, 234
mental health   55, 99, 100, 164–6
messiah   41, 46, 102, 155, 163, 206
methodology   11, 12, 16–18, 21, 22, 72, 117, 161
Mexico   115, 118–20, 122, 125–7, 232
millenarian   45, 155, 160, 163
mind control, *see* brainwashing
minority religion   3–5, 7–9, 13–15, 17, 21–3, 26–9, 31, 32, 34, 35, 102–4, 108, 230
money   46, 49, 51, 164, 165, 210, 212, 219, 221, 235
Moonies, *see* Unification Church
moral panics   4, 24, 131, 134, 135, 138, 142, 146, 148
Mormonism, *see* Church of Jesus Christ of Latter-Day Saints
Mount Carmel   39, 40, 191–3, 196, 201, 203, 206, 208–11, 218, 220, 234, 235
murder   24, 47, 87–9, 140–2, 168, 172, 190, 202, 203, 205
Muslim, *see* Islam
myth   131, 132, 136, 138, 142, 163, 179, 182, 185–7
  mythology   64, 134, 141, 179, 181, 182, 184–7

Netflix 86, 202
New Kadampa Tradition 47
new religious movements 3, 7, 9–12, 14–18, 27, 29, 40, 41, 44, 46–52, 54–6, 79–90, 92, 102, 115–19, 123, 126, 132, 133, 146, 147, 156–8, 160, 161, 168, 229–35, 237
news 4, 11, 81, 91, 127, 134, 139, 140, 148, 158, 163, 165, 169, 191, 192, 196–8, 203, 205, 206, 210, 211, 214, 217, 219, 220, 230, 234
NXIVM 96, 98

objectivity 11, 25, 27, 49, 86, 230, 231
Occult 68, 76, 132, 133, 137, 138, 145, 147
organizations 8, 12, 13, 22–4, 27, 30–2, 34, 35, 45–53, 55, 60, 65, 67, 84, 88, 96, 99, 101–3, 105, 106, 108, 110, 116, 117, 123, 156, 191, 220, 230, 234, 236, 237
outsiders 9, 12, 13, 115, 117, 134, 143, 148, 149, 161, 170, 172, 230, 235–7

Paganism 24, 62, 83
pandemic, see Covid-19
parliament 24, 80, 232
Parsons, Talcott 64–6, 70
participants 3, 14, 107, 161, 168, 184, 185, 187, 235, 237
pastor 47, 54, 118–20, 122, 124
pejorative 3, 4, 6, 7, 16, 43, 56, 96, 101, 103, 117, 139, 146, 161, 168, 191, 196
Pentecostalism 16, 116, 117, 120, 122, 123, 126, 164
Peoples Temple 47, 168, 202, 226
pilgrimage 118, 120, 179
Pizzagate 135, 136, 140
police 21, 23, 32, 53, 84, 85, 87, 89, 124, 127, 131, 137, 140–2, 158, 168, 193, 197
politics 3, 4, 8, 15, 17, 48, 70, 99, 102–6, 108, 136–9, 142, 147, 148, 154–6, 160, 168–72, 197, 219, 230
power 33, 42, 45, 54, 56, 61–3, 70, 73, 85, 86, 90, 107, 108, 122, 159, 179, 181, 209, 219, 236
prejudice 9, 27, 40, 41, 90, 119, 138

prophecy 69, 159, 160, 199, 200, 207, 214, 215, 218
Protestant 41–3, 45, 65, 80, 119, 122, 137, 159
psychoanalysis 63–6
psychology 25, 47, 64, 90, 91, 97, 99, 106, 107, 232, 237
public discourse 10, 29, 34, 35, 131, 136

QAnon 4, 8, 17, 136, 139–44, 154–73, 233–5
qualitative 5, 7, 22, 155, 190
quantitative 4, 5, 7

race 60, 183, 188
recovery 33, 102, 103, 106, 107
Reddit 151, 154, 158, 182
religious studies, see study of religion
Republican 154, 164
Roman Catholicism 27, 42–5, 79, 82, 83, 108, 115, 119, 122, 126, 167, 232

sacrifice 42, 120, 131, 135, 136, 184, 232
Satanic cult 17, 131–9, 142–5, 147, 149, 233
 panic 17, 131–5, 137–9, 142, 145, 150–3, 233, 236
Scientology 11–13, 18, 19, 47, 49, 55, 57, 60, 63, 65–7, 69, 74, 75, 79, 84, 85, 88–90
scripture 40, 42, 43, 45, 46, 54, 74, 206
sect 63, 86, 102, 117, 119, 131, 180
secular, see secularization
secularization 3, 27, 34, 41, 46, 47, 51, 59–61, 63–5, 67, 71, 79, 81, 82, 102, 105, 106, 126, 134, 137, 150
Seventh-day Adventism 231
sex 107, 124, 141, 167, 171, 193, 203, 207, 232
Simmel, Georg 22
social media 7, 8, 11, 35, 86, 135, 137, 154, 155, 158, 164, 232
sociology 10, 25, 49, 62–5, 70, 80, 84, 90, 102, 119, 122, 126, 197, 236, 237
Soka Gakkai 49
spiritual abuse 9, 24, 33, 53–6, 103
spirituality 41, 47, 159, 167, 179, 208
study of religion 8–12, 15, 41, 90, 117, 178, 179, 184, 187, 196, 221, 234–6
supernatural 60–3, 71, 73, 135, 231, 236

survivors   9, 14, 16, 34, 35, 98, 99, 101–4, 106–8, 142, 144, 145, 157, 166, 171, 191, 198, 201, 204, 208, 211, 217, 218

technology   13, 67, 72, 73, 171
television   4, 86, 89, 91, 180, 187, 192, 195, 196, 205, 206, 219, 232
terrorism   96, 99, 102, 136, 170, 171
TikTok   144
trauma   14, 97, 100, 183, 230
Trump, Donald   3, 8, 73, 142, 144, 149, 154, 155, 157, 158, 160, 161, 163–6, 169–71, 173

Unification Church   25, 26, 36, 46, 51, 79, 231

vaccines   72, 123, 131, 138, 158
vernacular   3, 4, 6–9, 13, 15

victims   33, 52, 53, 88, 96, 106, 108, 115, 134, 200
violence   16, 32, 34, 51, 84, 85, 87, 99, 100, 105, 106, 116, 120, 123, 124, 126, 155, 157, 158, 161, 166–71, 190, 191, 197, 229, 232, 234

Waco   17, 28, 87, 168, 191, 193, 199, 201–14, 217–21, 234, 235
Weber, Max   22, 65
women   26, 32, 64, 67, 68, 87, 121, 161, 167, 193, 195, 203, 207, 213, 216
worldviews   22, 34, 48, 90, 91, 171, 184, 233, 235
worship   29, 40–3, 62, 81, 105, 115, 118–20, 122, 131, 190, 233

YouTube   11, 141, 154, 158, 165, 169, 181, 186, 187, 215, 218

www.ingramcontent.com/pod-product-compliance
Lightning Source LLC
Chambersburg PA
CBHW071823300426
44116CB00009B/1414